**OXFORD**
UNIVERSITY PRESS

**fourth
edition**

# English File

**Upper-intermediate Student's Book B**

Units 6–10

WITH ONLINE PRACTICE

Christina Latham-Koenig
Clive Oxenden
Kate Chomacki

Paul Seligson and Clive Oxenden
are the original co-authors of
*English File 1* and *English File 2*

OXFORD
UNIVERSITY PRESS

Great Clarendon Street, Oxford, OX2 6DP, United Kingdom

Oxford University Press is a department of the University of Oxford. It furthers the University's objective of excellence in research, scholarship, and education by publishing worldwide. Oxford is a registered trade mark of Oxford University Press in the UK and in certain other countries



First published in 2020
2024
10 9 8 7 6



ISBN: 978 0 19 403955 0

Printed in Great Britain by Bell & Bain Ltd, Glasgow

This book is printed on paper from certified and well-managed sources

ACKNOWLEDGEMENTS

*Back cover photograph*: Oxford University Press building/David Fisher

*The authors would like to thank all the teachers and students round the world whose feedback has helped us to shape English File.*

*The authors would also like to thank*: all those at Oxford University Press (both in Oxford and around the world) and the design team who have contributed their skills and ideas to producing this course.

*Finally very special thanks from Clive to Maria Angeles, Lucia, and Eric, and from Christina to Cristina, for all their support and encouragement. Christina would also like to thank her children Joaquin, Marco, and Krysia for their constant inspiration.*

**Student's Book**

*The publisher and authors would like to thank the following for their invaluable feedback on the materials*: Zahra Bilides, Paz Alonso, Vanessa Ferroni, Dagmara Lata, Sandy Millin, Sarah Giles, Jane Hudson, Yolana Calpe, Rosa María Iglesias Traviesas, Michale Jarvis, Pedro Irazabel Brian Brennan, Robert Anderson, Magdalena Muszyńska, Gyula Kiss, Juliana Stucker, Elif Barbaros, Kenny McDonnell

*The publisher and authors are very grateful to the following who have provided information, personal stories, and/or photographs*: Brennan Wenck-Reilly p.57, John Sloboda p.60, Thomas Ormerod p.73, Anya Edwards p.102, Simon Callow pp.74–75, George Tannenbaum pp.94–95, and The Conversation participants: Simon Warren, Joanne Bowlt, Syinat Tagaeva, Mark Boulle, John Bowlt, and Devika Pandit

*The authors and publisher are grateful to those who have given permission to reproduce the following extracts and adaptations of copyright material*: p.57 Adapted text and photo from 'Segmented Sleep' by Brennan Wenck-Reilly, www.brennanwenck.com. Reproduced by permission of the author.p.59 Adapted from 'The expert's rules for a great night's sleep' by Anna Maxted, The Times 21 July 2018, © News UK/News Licensing. Reproduced by permission. p.62 Adapted from 'Why you should listen to music while you work' by Mike Wright, 7th September 2017. © Telegraph Media Group Limited 2017. Reproduced by permission. p.62 Adapted from 'The surgeon's cut: what do doctors listen to in the operating theatre?' by Homa Khaleeli, www.guardian.com, 5 August 2015. Copyright Guardian News & Media Ltd 2019. Reproduced by permission. p.65 Adapted from 'The Power of Music for Sleep and Performance' by Dr Michael Breus, www.thesleepdoctor.com. Reproduced by permission. p.69 Adapted from 'How to win any argument using science' by Victoria Woollaston, MailOnline. Reproduced by permission of Solo Syndication. p.73 Adapted from 'The best way to spot a liar… or is it?' by Professor Thomas Ormerod, © Thomas Ormerod. Reproduced by permission of the author. p.76 Extract from 'Stay Safe' from www.met.police.uk. Reproduced by Courtesy of the Mayor's Office of Policing and Crime. p.78 Adapted from 'The 15 Unluckiest Dumb Criminals Ever' by Andy Simmons and Priscilla Torres, originally published in Readers Digest, www.rd.com. Copyright © 2018 by Trusted Media Brands, Inc. Used by permission. All rights reserved. p.79 Adapted from 'Man shocked to learn his identity has been stolen to con women' by Rosie Hopegood, www.themirror.co.uk, 1 April 2018. Reproduced by permission of Mirrorpix. p.83 Adapted from '10 tips on how to spot fake news' by Rob Waugh, The Telegraph, 7 May 2019. Reproduced by permission of the author. p.86 Adapted from '18 false advertising scandals that cost some brands millions' by Julien Rath. Copyrighted 2017. Business Insider. 2105571:0719p. Reproduced by permission of Wrights Media acting on behalf of Business Insider Magazine. p.88 Adapted text and cover image from Fifty Things that Made the Modern Economy by Tim Harford, Copyright © 2017 Tim Harford, Little, Brown Book Company Limited. Reproduced by permission. p.90 Adapted from 'What makes a city attractive?' by Francesca Perry, www.guardian.com, 10 February 2015. Copyright Francesca Perry/Guardian News & Media Ltd 2019. Reproduced by permission. p.92 Adapted text and photo from 'Sleepy in Songdo, Korea's smartest city' by Linda Poon, 22 June 2018, © 2018 CityLab, a division of The Atlantic Media Group LLC. All rights reserved. Distributed by Tribune Content Agency. p.96 Adapted from 'Quiz: Can you answer the simple science questions parents struggle to answer' by Mark Molloy, 3rd May 2016. © Telegraph Media Group Limited 2016. Reproduced by permission. p.98 Adapted from 'Science Fact or Fiction? The Plausibility of 10 Sci-fi Concepts' by Adam Hadhazy, www.livescience.com, 20 September 2013. Reproduced by permission. p.101 Adapted from 'From Martin Luther King to Churchill and Obama: the 10 best speeches – ever', Philip Collins, The Times, 25 September 2017, © News UK/News Licensing. Reproduced by permission. p.105 Adapted from 'The Voice of Reason' by John Shammas, www.thesun.co.uk, 14 March 2018 © The Sun/News Licensing. Reproduced by permission.

*Sources*: www.businessinsider.com

*Although every effort has been made to trace and contact copyright holders before publication, this has not been possible in some cases. We apologize for any apparent infringement of copyright and if notified, the publisher will be pleased to rectify any errors or omissions at the earliest opportunity.*

*Pronunciation chart artwork by*: Ellis Nadler

*Illustrations by*: Petros Bouloubasis/Advocate Art p.96; Sam Dedel/Lemonade Illustration p.76; DILBERT © 2000 Scott Adams. Used By permission of Andrews McMeel Syndication. All rights reserved p.102; Isla Fletcher p.66 (handwriting); John Haslam pp.142, 144; Joe McLaren pp.68–69

*Commissioned photography by*: MM Studios pp.88 (Playstation, Nespresso, HP printer, Gillette razor), 89 (razors); Oxford University Press video stills pp.63 (Isata Kanneh-Mason), 65 (headshots), 74 (Simon Callow), 75 (the Conversation), 83, 85, 94 (George Tannenbaum), 95 (the Conversation), 103, 105 (headshots)

*We would also like to thank the following for permission to reproduce the following photographs*: 123RF p.66 (Cathy Yeulet); Advertising Archives pp.86 (Red Bull), 87 (Olay); Alamy pp.70 Atonement 2007/Sportsphoto/AA Film Archive/Working Title, (Helen Mirren/Granada Film Productions/Sportsphoto), (Eddie Redmayne/Allstar Picture Library/Warner Bros/AF archive), (Frances McDormand/Focus Features/PictureLux/The Hollywood Archive), (Daniel Kaluuya/Warner Bros/Moviestore collection Ltd), 86 (Activia/David Lee), 91 (1/Matthias Scholz), (2/Pulsar Imagens), (3/Greg Balfour Evans), (5/J Marshall – Tribaleye Images), 94 (Boss/jeremy sutton-hibbert), 98 (speed of light/Quality Stock), (invisibility Harry Potter/ITAR-TASS News Agency), (invisibility cloisters/Francisco Martinez), 99 (Neptune/Irina Dmitrienko), 100 (Neil Armstrong/NASA Archive), 101 (Elizabeth I/IanDagnall Computing), (Emmeline Pankhurst/Granger Historical Picture Archive), (Winston Churchill/David Cole), (John F Kennedy/Pictorial Press Ltd), 159 (calf/Simon Balson), (knee/Fitness People by Vision); Courtesy of Steve Bustin p.79; Captainbijou.com p.94 (MOM Brands/Farina cereal); Stewart Cohen/stewartcohen.com p.73 (security officer); Courtesy of Anya Edwards p.102; 72 (upsidedowndog), 74 (rehearsal/Digital Vision), 80 (wine/Gabriele Allena/EyeEm), 82 (Chris Graythen), 86 (VW car/Ramin Talaie), 95 (Nike/Prashanth Vishwanathan/Bloomberg via Getty Images), (Apple/Gilles Mingasson/Liaison), 101 (Abraham Lincoln/Archive Photos), (Martin Luther King/Francis Miller/The LIFE Picture Collection), (Nelson Mandela/Pool Bouvet/De Keerle/Gamma-Rapho), (Barack Obama/Alfredo Estrella), 105 (Stephen Hawking/Bruno Vincent), 113 (jasmine/Vincenzo Lombardo), 119 (family at home/Hans Neleman), (cinema/PhotoAlto Agency RF Collections), 121 (Lovattpics), 159 (ankle/FilmMagic), (fist/JazzIRT), (wrist/George Pimentel/WireImage), (waist/MJ Kim); The Guardian/Eyevine pp.91 (4/Martin Creed, Work No 1059, the Scotsman Steps/Tom Finnie); iStockphoto pp.98 (intelligent machines/Abidal), 159 (hip/John Sommer); Little, Brown Book Group Limited p.88 Fifty Things that made the Modern Economy, by Tim Harford, 2017; Courtesy of Professor Thomas Ormerod p.73; Reproduced by permission of Oxford University Press p.60 cover image of Handbook of Music and Emotion, Edited by Patrik N. Juslin and John Sloboda, 2011; Oxford University Press p.113 (kitten and vinegar); Oxford University Press\ Shutterstock p.60 (guitar neck/AlexMaster), (cello bow/Yuriyfx), 61 (guitar/AlexMaster), (saxophone/AGCuesta), (cello/Yuriyfx), (flute/cowardlion); Courtesy of Lynne Parker p.102; Mahmud Sahran p.80 ('zebra'); By kind permission of San Antonio Aquarium & Austin Aquarium p.80 (shark theft); Science Photo Library p.159 (bottom/Ian Hooton), 159 (brain/heart/kidneys/liver/lungs/all Sciepro); Shutterstock Editorial 74 (Old Vic/Alisdair Macdonalds), (Amadeus/Graham Wiltshire), (Four Weddings and a Funeral/Polygram/Channel 4/Working Title/Kobal), 75 (Daniel Day Lewis/Miramax/Dimension Films/Kobal), 75 (Laurence Olivier/Romulus Films/Park Circus); Shutterstock pp.56 (Rawpixel.com), 57 (candle-stick/S-Belov), 58 (drill/Pavel K), (bed/babsy17), (mites/lantapix), (fly/Potapov Alexander), 60 (violin/AGCuesta), (keyboard/Smileus), 61 (drums/grekoff), (conductor/LifetimeStock),63 (surgeons/Gorodenkoff), (Dmitriy Samorodinov), 67 (head and speech bubble/olga kryukova), 71 (pathdoc), 78 (DenisProduction.com), 80 (fever/ArtOfPhotos), 90 (mart), 92 (Songdo/PKphotograph), 97 (Natykach Nataliia), 98 (aliens/Albert Ziganshin), (teleportation/Sergey Nivens), (invisibility cloak outline/Leo Stock Pix), (instant learning/Gorodenkoff), 99 (Pluto/Dotted Yeti), 109 (cabbage/matin), (mango/matin), (rose/satitsrihin), (ice lolly/Lucie Lang), (fur coat/lynnette), (fever/ArtOfPhotos), 113 (camembert/picturepartners), (chilli pepper/mexrix), 120 (Marie Linner), 158 (emoji/flower travelin' man), 159 (heel/ShotPrime Studio), (elbow/Steven Frame), (nails/Tamara83), (palm/alexandre zveiger), (chest/cristovao), (thigh/sozon), 160 (grmarc), 162 (Rawpixel.com); Courtesy of Dr Neil Stanley p.59; Brennan Wenck-Reilly/www.brennanwenck.com p.57 (night view of San Francisco, From Angel Island)

**Workbook**

*The publisher would like to thank the following for their permission to reproduce photographs*: 50 (knee/Fitness People by Vision), 50 (calf/Simon Balson), 53 (rehearsal/Keith Morris), 64 (Lagos/Ton Koene), 64 (Mahatma Gandhi/Dinodia Photos), 70 (Marie Curie/Lebrecht Music & Arts), 72 (Oprah Winfrey/PictureLux/The Hollywood Archive); Getty Images pp.44 (cello/Greg Dale), 44 (keyboard/Dave King), 50 (ankle/Jason LaVeris/FilmMagic), 50 (wrist/George Pimentel/WireImage), 50 (waist/MJ Kim), 50 (fist/JazzIRT), 53 (Juilliard Orchestra/Hiroyuki Ito); iStock.com p.50 (hip/John Sommer); Oxford University Press pp.44 (soprano/posztos), 44 (bass/Tetra Images), 44 (choir/posztos), 44 (flute/Triff), 44 (violin/Dario Sabljak), 44 (saxophone/horiyan), 44 (drums/misha), 44 (orchestra/Ferenc Szelepcsenyi), 49 (cat/Voraorn Ratanakorn), 59 (reporter/moshimochi), 63 (Detian Waterfall/4045), 67 (Kolkata/Radiokafka), 68 (researcher/l i g h t p o e t), 71 (Aconcagua/Johnathan Esper), 71 (baby/alice-photo), 71 (teacher/Monkey Business Images), 72 (storm/Wesley Aston), 73 (Pulteney Bridge, Bath/Digital VisionO); Science Photo Library pp.50 (brain/Sciepro), 50 (kidneys/Sciepro), 50 (liver/Sciepro), 50 (bottom/Ian Hooton), 50 (heart/Sciepro), 50 (lungs/Sciepro); Shutterstock pp.40 (tired man/Lenar Nigmatullin), 41 (library/SpeedKingz), 41 (cycling/Brian A Jackson), 41 (sandcastles/oliveromg), 41 (construction worker/Dmitry Bunin), 42 (business meeting/VGstockstudio), 43 (playing guitar/Siamionau Pavel), 43 (boy in tree/KaliAntye), 44 (orchestra/Martin Good), 45 (Swan Lake/Jack.Q), 45 (croissant/Yakobchuk Viacheslav), 46 (missed train/encierro), 47 (bike accident/B-D-S Piotr Marcinski), 47 (plane window/astarot), 48 (rainy picnic/Robert Wydro Studio), 49 (cake/Irina Kuzmina), 49 (garlic/Volodymyr Plysiuk), 49 (roquefort/grafvision), 50 (nails/Tamara83), 50 (elbow/Steven Frame), 50 (thigh/sozon), 50 (chest/cristovao), 50 (heel/ShotPrime Studio), 50 (palm/Alexandre Zveiger), 51 (two boys/sima), 55 (hacker/Gorodenkoff), 56 (motorbike/Rose Makin), 57 (Waterloo Station/4kclips), 57 (signing/Kritsana Karakate), 58 (cooking/Rawpixel.com), 58 (referee/Vlad1988), 59 (photographers/Denis Makarenko), 60 (kitchen staff/wavebreakmedia),60 (office/Monkey Business Images), 61 (woman/Stock image), 61 (field/Elenamiv), 62 (bank/Thinglass), 62 (vinyl/Rawpixel.com), 63 (traffic/Paolo Bona), 65 (dinner/Monkey Business Images), 65 (Mongolian yurt/peachananr), 69 (people with masks/2p.2play), 69 (using tablet/Yakobchuk Viacheslav); Shutterstock Editorial p.72 (Sidney Poitier/Anonymous/AP).

# Contents

# Course overview

# English File
*fourth edition*

Welcome to **English File fourth edition**. This is how to use the Student's Book, Online Practice, and the Workbook in and out of class.

## Student's Book and Workbook

The **Student's Book** contains all the language and skills you need to improve your English, with Grammar, Vocabulary, Pronunciation, and skills work in every File.

**Use your Student's Book in class with your teacher.**

The **Workbook** contains Grammar, Vocabulary, and Pronunciation practice for every lesson.

**Use your Workbook for homework or for self-study to practise language and to check your progress.**

Go to **englishfileonline.com** and use the code on your Access Card to log into the Online Practice.

**ACTIVITIES**   **AUDIO**   **VIDEO**   **RESOURCES**

ONLINE

## LOOK AGAIN

- Review the language from every lesson.
- Watch the videos and listen to all the class audio as many times as you like.

## PRACTICE

- Improve your skills with extra Reading, Writing, Listening, and Speaking practice.
- Use the interactive video to practise Colloquial English.

## CHECK YOUR PROGRESS

- Test yourself on the language from the File and get instant feedback.
- Try an extra Challenge.

## SOUND BANK

- Use the Sound Bank videos to practise and improve your pronunciation of English sounds.

### Online Practice

*Look again* at Student's Book language you want to review or that you missed in class, do extra *Practice* activities, and *Check your progress* on what you've learnt so far.

**Use the Online Practice to learn outside the classroom and get instant feedback on your progress**.

**englishfileonline.com**

G *used to, be used to, get used to*   V sleep   P /s/ and /z/

## 1 GRAMMAR *used to, be used to, get used to*

**a** Do you ever have problems sleeping? Why (not)? What kinds of things might make it difficult for people to sleep well?

**b** ◉6.1 Listen to three people, Rafa, Mike, and Steph, who all have problems sleeping at night. What are the main reasons they give? Have any of them managed to solve the problem?

**c** ◉6.2 Listen to six extracts from the listening. Complete the gaps with a few words.

**Rafa**
I can't get used to [1]_____ where there's light coming in from the streetlights outside.
I always used to [2]_____.

**Mike**
The main problem is that my body's used to [3]_____, not during the day.
It's very hard to get used to [4]_____ all night.
Before I became a policeman, I used to [5]_____ hours a night.

**Steph**
And just when I'm finally used to [6]_____, then it's time to fly back to the UK.

**d** Look the highlighted phrases. Answer the questions with a partner.
1 What do you think *used to* means after *be / get*?
   a tired of   b accustomed to   c good at
2 What's the difference between *be* + adjective, e.g. *be old, be used to*, and *get* + adjective, e.g. *get old, get used to*?
3 What form does the verb take after *used to* and *be / get used to*?

**e** Ⓖ p.142 Grammar Bank 6A

**f** Talk to a partner. Ask for and give more information.
1 When you were a young child, did you use to…?
   • share a room with a brother or sister
   • sleep with the light on
   • wake up very early in the morning
2 Do you ever have problems sleeping when you're staying somewhere new or different that you aren't used to (e.g. in a hotel)?
3 Do you think you would find it difficult to get used to…?
   • always going to bed after midnight
   • getting up at 5.30 a.m. every day
   • travelling long-haul very often

## 2 PRONUNCIATION /s/ and /z/

**a** ◉6.5 Listen to sentences 1–3. In which one is *used to* pronounced differently? What's the difference?
1 I used to get up really late, but now I get up early.
2 It often takes time to get used to sleeping in a new bed.
3 Valerian is a herb which is used to help people to sleep better.

**b** ◉6.6 Listen and repeat some pairs of words where the only difference in pronunciation is the final *s* or *z*.

| | a | b |
|---|---|---|
| 1 | loose | lose |
| 2 | bus | buzz |
| 3 | course | cause |
| 4 | ice | eyes |
| 5 | race | raise |
| 6 | peace | peas |
| 7 | price | prize |
| 8 | place | plays |

**c** ◉6.7 Listen to some sentences with words from **b**. Which word do you hear each time? In 1–4 the context will help you, but not in 5–8.

**d** Practise with a partner. Say one word from each pair in **b** to your partner. He / She must say if it's a or b.

## 3 READING

**a** Look at the title of the article below and read the first paragraph. What exactly is *segmented sleep*?

# The way we used to sleep

### The forgotten benefits of segmented sleep

Sleeping for eight hours a night without waking up is not natural human behaviour. For centuries, 'segmented sleep' was standard. People used to go to bed quite early, sleep for a few hours, wake for an hour or two around midnight, and then sleep for about another three or four hours until sunrise.

This time when people were awake was called 'the watch', and it was used for all sorts of activities. It was a chance to meditate and think about vivid dreams. More active people used the hour to visit sick family members, do housework, or even steal from the neighbours under the cover of darkness! It was an hour typically free from social demands. One 15th-century Italian woman wrote that it was a time when she was able to sew or write letters in privacy, when she was not 'surrounded by men, performing jobs for men'. Doctors also believed in the medical benefits that came from changing sleeping position, or taking medication during the watch. The practice of 'first sleep' and 'second sleep' is mentioned by many great authors, including Homer, Chaucer, Austen, Dickens, and Tolstoy.

Since we've got used to artificial light, however, segmented sleep has become both unfashionable and harder to achieve. We've now lost that hour between sleeps, a time when we can be awake and alone with our thoughts. Segmented sleep is arguably more natural than the sleep we experience nowadays. People who regularly wake in the night will no doubt be relieved to hear that there's nothing wrong with them.

*Adapted from the Quartz website*

**b** Now read the whole article and answer the questions.

1 What kinds of things would people do during 'the watch'?
2 Was segmented sleep considered a good thing?
3 Why don't we sleep like this nowadays?

**c** Read about photographer Brennan Wenck-Reilly, who is usually awake during the night. Answer the questions.

1 How long is he usually awake for?
2 What does he do with the time?

## Things people do at night

**Brennan Wenck-Reilly, 36, San Francisco, USA**

I spent two years living high up in the Andes, in Chacopampa in Bolivia. I was in the Peace Corps, a volunteer organization run through the US government. Chacopampa was a town that had no electricity 90% of the time. We ¹**u**_____ to follow the patterns of the sun, that is, I'd go to bed between 8.00 and 9.00 and get up at about 6 a.m. But at around midnight I'd wake up and then I'd be up till 3.00 a.m. or so. In those hours ²**b**_____ midnight and 3.00, I would normally read, sometimes as much as 100 pages of a book.

When I got back to San Francisco, I'd ³**g**_____ used to sleeping like this, and somehow, I carried on with it. I ⁴**w**_____ go to bed around 9.00, wake up between midnight and 1.00 a.m., and then be up until about 4.00. Then I'd sleep till 7.00 or 8.00. My wife and I lived in a one-bedroom apartment, and my wife is a fairly ⁵**l**_____ sleeper, so my best option was to get out of the house. That's when I started doing night photography.

San Francisco at that hour is quite magical. I often find ⁶**m**_____ alone on the streets, or at the beach, in the woods. Part of the adventure is finding new locations, part is the solitude, and the reward is the image I get to take home. One of my favourites is this one of Angel Island. It was quite ⁷**w**_____, as you can see from the grass in the foreground.

If I don't ⁸**l**_____ the house, I'll work on framing photos, or grading (I'm also a teacher), and sometimes I'll simply put on a movie. I also sometimes run – I used to have a running partner who lived a couple of blocks away. A couple of times a week we'd text each other around 1.00 or 2.00 a.m., and then meet at the street corner and run for about an hour. That lasted about a year, then we both ⁹**e**_____ up moving away. Now I have young kids, but I long for them to be more independent so that I can once again go back to my sleep pattern.

*Brennan is now running courses in night photography.*

**d** Read the text again and complete the gaps.

**e** In pairs, explain why Brennan mentions these things.

| | | | |
|---|---|---|---|
| the sun | 100 pages | one bedroom | the woods |
| Angel Island | grading | the street corner | young kids |

**f** If you woke up for an hour every night, what do you think you would do with the time?

## 4 VOCABULARY sleep

**a** Read some facts about sleep. Which did you find the most surprising? Were there any facts you already knew?

### FASCINATING FACTS ABOUT SLEEP

Studies have shown that male students **yawn** longer and more often than female students.

 Many people have a **nap** after lunch. The so-called 'post-lunch dip' is because we naturally feel **sleepy** at two times of day: 2.00 a.m. and 2.00 p.m.

People who **snore** can make a noise as loud as 100 decibels, equivalent to a pneumatic drill.

 Covering yourself with heavy **blankets** can help you relax and get a better night's sleep. The pressure on the body produces serotonin, a chemical that helps with sleep, mood, and digestion.

People often change their **sheets**, but up to one third of the weight of a **pillow** can be made up of dead skin and bugs. And if you don't wash a **duvet** at least every six months, it can contain up to 20,000 live dust mites.

 Scientists have produced flies which have **insomnia**. They lose their balance more often, are slower learners, and gain more fat – the same as humans who don't get enough sleep.

If you have taken **sleeping pills**,  you aren't actually asleep, you're sedated. Some researchers think that this can cause memory problems.

**b** Look at the **bold** words in **a**. In pairs, work out their meaning from the context.

**c** Now look at some words and phrases about sleeping habits. With a partner, say what you think they mean.

**be a light sleeper**   **fall asleep**
**be fast asleep**   **have nightmares**
**keep you awake**   **oversleep**
**set the alarm**   **sleep like a log**   **sleepwalk**

**d** Work in pairs. Do the *Vocabulary race*.

When your teacher says 'go', write the correct word or phrase from **a–c** in the column on the right. As soon as you finish, put your hand up.

| | | |
|---|---|---|
| 1 | Most people start feeling ▮ at around 11.00 p.m. | *sleepy* |
| 2 | When people are tired they often open their mouth and ▮. | ___ |
| 3 | When they get into bed, they put their head on the ▮. | ___ |
| 4 | In bed, many people sleep under a ▮ filled with feathers or synthetic material. | ___ |
| 5 | Other people prefer to sleep under ▮ and ▮. | ___ |
| 6 | Some people can't sleep because they suffer from ▮. | ___ |
| 7 | People sometimes have to take ▮ to help them go to sleep. | ___ |
| 8 | Some people who are asleep make a loud noise when they breathe, i.e. they ▮. | ___ |
| 9 | In hot countries, it's common to have a short ▮ in the afternoon. | ___ |
| 10 | A person who sleeps well '▮'. | ___ |
| 11 | Someone who doesn't sleep very deeply is a ▮. | ___ |
| 12 | Some children ▮ if they watch scary films before bedtime. | ___ |
| 13 | If you drink coffee in the evening, it may ▮. | ___ |
| 14 | In the middle of the night, most people are ▮. | ___ |
| 15 | As many as 15% of people ▮ during the night, getting out of bed and even getting dressed or eating. | ___ |
| 16 | When people need to get up early, they often ▮ (clock). | ___ |
| 17 | If you don't hear your alarm, you might ▮. | ___ |
| 18 | According to one study, 4.7% of Americans ▮ while driving. | ___ |

**e** ◖ 6.8 Listen and check. Did the pair who finished first also get the most correct answers?

## 5 LISTENING

**a** You're going to listen to a podcast by sleep expert Dr Neil Stanley. First, with a partner, discuss how you think he might complete sentences 1–8 below about his bedtime routine.

1 I sleep in a different _____ from my partner.
2 I sleep under natural _____.
3 I'm obsessive about _____.
4 I sleep with the _____ open.
5 I don't have _____ late.
6 I drink _____ in the evenings.
7 I need _____ hours' sleep.
8 I _____ before going to sleep.

**b** ◐6.9 Now listen to the podcast and complete the gaps with a word or number. Did you guess any of them correctly in **a**? Were you surprised by anything he does? What kind of person do you think he is?

**c** Listen again. Then with a partner, explain Dr Stanley's reasons, using the prompts below.

1 Because then you don't…
2 Because you don't sleep well if…
3 Because it's really important to…
4 Because you need…
5 Because your body…
6 Because he isn't…
7 Because that's the amount…
8 Because it's his way of…

**d** Look again at the list in **a**. Do you normally do any of these things? Are there any that you would like to be able to do?

## 6 SPEAKING

In pairs, **A** ask the green questions, and **B** ask the red questions. Ask for and give as much information as possible, and react to what your partner says.

Do you usually sleep with your bedroom completely dark, or with the curtains or blinds open? Do you have problems sleeping if there's too much or not enough light for you? What temperature do you like the bedroom to be?

Have you ever worked at night? Did you have any problems sleeping the next day? Why (not)? Do you think you would be able to work at night and sleep during the day for a long period?

Do you take, or have you ever taken, sleeping pills? Do you have any tips for people who suffer from insomnia?

Do you watch TV in bed on a tablet or other device? Do you ever fall asleep while you're watching a programme?

Did you use to have a bedtime routine when you were a child? Would someone read to you in bed? Did you have a favourite story?

Are you a light sleeper, or do you usually sleep like a log? Do you use something to help you wake up in the morning?

Do you often have nightmares or recurring dreams? Do you ever remember what your dreams were about? Do you ever try to interpret your dreams?

Do you snore? Have you ever had to share a room with someone who snores? Was this a problem?

Have you ever flown long haul? Where to? Did you get jet lag? How long did it take you to get used to the different time zone?

Do you find it difficult to sleep when you're travelling, e.g. in buses or planes? What do you do if you can't get to sleep?

Have you ever overslept and missed something important? What was it?

Have you ever stayed up all night to revise for an exam the next day? How well did you do in the exam?

Do you ever have a nap after lunch or at any other time during the day? How long do you sleep for? How do you feel when you wake up?

Have you ever fallen asleep at an embarrassing moment, e.g. during a class or in a meeting?

Go online to review the lesson

# 6B Music to my ears

**G** gerunds and infinitives  **V** music  **P** words from other languages

## 1 LISTENING & SPEAKING

**a** On a typical day, do you listen to music? When and where? How? Do you listen to different kinds of music at different times of day? What makes you choose one kind of music over another?

**b** 🔊 6.10 Listen to Part 1 of a talk by John Sloboda, a music psychologist, about why we listen to music. Complete the reasons and examples 1–3 by writing key words or phrases.

> **Why do we listen to music?**
> 1 to make us _____
>    e.g. _____
> 2 to help us to _____
>    e.g. _____
> 3 to intensify _____
>    e.g. _____

**c** Compare your notes with a partner, and try to remember more about what John said. Then listen again and add to your notes.

**d** Can you think of times when you listen to music for one of these three reasons? What kinds of music do you listen to?

**e** 🔊 6.11 Now listen to extracts from four pieces of music that John is going to mention in Part 2 of his talk. How do they make you feel?

1 the first movement of Beethoven's *Seventh Symphony*
2 *Mars*, from *The Planets*, by Holst
3 Albinoni's *Adagio for Strings*
4 the music from the Hitchcock film *Psycho*

**f** 🔊 6.12 Now listen to Part 2, where John explains why music can affect the way we feel. Complete the rest of the notes.

> **The human voice:**
> happy = people speak _____, the voice is _____
> sad = people speak _____, the voice is _____
> angry = people _____ their voices or _____
> **Music copies the human voice:**
> 1 _____, _____-_____ music
>    sounds happy.
> 2 _____ music with _____ pitches
>    sounds sad.
> 3 _____ music with _____ rhythms
>    sounds angry.
> **Emotions related to pieces of music:**
> 1 _____ = the Beethoven
> 2 _____ = the Holst
> 3 _____ = the Albinoni
> 4 _____ = the film music from *Psycho*

**g** Talk to a partner, and give reasons.

> **What music would you play…?**
> • if you were preparing to go out and feeling happy and excited about it
> • if you wanted to create a romantic atmosphere
> • if you were feeling furious about something or somebody
> • if you were feeling stressed or nervous
> • if you were feeling depressed

> *If I was feeling depressed, I'd play Someone Like You by Adele, because it makes me cry. It was my ex's favourite song…*

## 2 GRAMMAR gerunds and infinitives

**a** Look at some extracts from the listening in **1b**. Put the verbs in brackets in the infinitive (with or without *to*) or the gerund (-*ing* form).

1 Firstly, we listen to music to make us _____ important moments in the past. (**remember**)
2 When we hear a certain piece of music, we remember _____ it for the first time… (**hear**)
3 If we want _____ from one activity to another, we often use music to help us _____ the change. (**go, make**)

**b** 🔊 6.13 Listen and check.

## 3 VOCABULARY & PRONUNCIATION
music; words from other languages

a 🔊 6.16 Listen to some instruments and musicians and match them to a word in the lists.

| instruments | |
|---|---|
| a bass gui<u>tar</u> | a <u>ce</u>llo |
| drums | a flute |
| a <u>key</u>board | a <u>sa</u>xophone |
| a vio<u>lin</u> | |

| musicians | |
|---|---|
| a choir | a con<u>duc</u>tor |
| an <u>or</u>chestra | a so<u>pra</u>no |

c Look at sentences 1 and 2. Match the meaning of *remember* to A and B.

1 I **remember** meeting him for the first time.

2 Please **remember** to meet him at the station.

A ☐ to not forget to do sth; to do what you have to do

B ☐ to have or keep an image in your memory of sth you did or that happened in the past

d 🅖 p.143 Grammar Bank 6B

e Tell your partner about…

- a piece of music you'll never forget hearing for the first time.
- something you sometimes forget to do before you leave the house in the morning.
- something you remember doing before you were five years old.
- something you must remember to do today or this week.
- a job that needs doing in your house / flat (e.g. the kitchen ceiling needs repainting).
- something you need to do this evening.
- a skill you tried to learn but couldn't.
- something you've tried doing when you can't sleep at night.

b 🔊 6.17 Listen and check. Practise saying the words. Then in pairs, try to add more words to the two groups. Can you play any of the instruments?

> 🔍 **Foreign words that are used in English**
> English has 'borrowed' many words from other languages. In the field of music, many words come from Italian, Greek, and French. The English pronunciation is often similar to the pronunciation in the original language, e.g. *c* before *i* and *e* in words from Italian is /tʃ/, as in *cello* and *ciao*; and *ch* in words from Greek is /k/, as in *choir* and *orchestra*.

c In pairs, look at the 'borrowed' words below and try to say them. Under<u>line</u> the stressed syllable.

| Borrowed from… | |
|---|---|
| **Italian** | con**c**erto /kənˈtʃeətəʊ/   me**zz**o-soprano /metsəʊ səˈprɑːnəʊ/ |
| **Greek** | **ch**orus /ˈkɔːrəs/   rhy**th**m /ˈrɪðm/   sym**ph**ony /ˈsɪmfəni/ |
| **French** | ball**et** /ˈbæleɪ/   en**c**ore /ˈɒŋkɔː/   **g**enre /ˈʒɒnrə/ |

d 🔊 6.18 Listen and check. How are the pink letters pronounced?

e Which language do you think these words come from? With a partner, write **I** (Italian), **G** (Greek), or **F** (French). Do you know what they all mean?

architecture ☐   barista ☐   bouquet ☐   cappuccino ☐
chauffeur ☐   chef ☐   chic ☐   croissant ☐   fiancé ☐   graffiti ☐
hypochondriac ☐   macchiato ☐   microphone ☐   paparazzi ☐
philosophy ☐   psychic ☐   psychologist ☐   villa ☐

f 🔊 6.19 Listen and check. Practise saying the words.

g Does your mother tongue borrow words from other languages? Which languages in particular? In which fields (music, food, technology, etc.) are there a lot of 'borrowed' words?

## 4 READING

**a** Do you normally listen to music when you're working or studying? What kinds of music?

**b** Quickly read an article about some research into music and work habits. Choose the best summary of the research findings.

1 Music helps you work better.
2 Choose the right music for the right task.
3 Classical music is best for creative thinking.

# Music while you work?

Some prefer to work in silence. Others find playing their favourite tunes loudly helps them to be productive. Up till now, it has been a matter of personal preference. But recently, scientific research has uncovered that listening to music while you work ¹_____ – although, it depends on ²_____.

A study by Simone Ritter, at Radboud University in the Netherlands, and Sam Ferguson, at the University of Technology in Sydney, Australia, looked at how ³_____, compared to working in silence. In their study, Ritter and Ferguson divided 155 volunteers into five groups, which were then given tasks to complete. Four of the groups did so while ⁴_____, such as Holst's *Mars* and Vivaldi's *Spring*. The fifth group worked in silence.

Their study found that happy music improved 'divergent thinking', which is all about creativity. However, they found that it had no impact on 'convergent thinking', which is all about problem solving. So, if you need to be creative with your work, then you should ⁵_____. But if you're trying to solve a problem, you're better off ⁶_____.

Adapted from The Telegraph

**c** Read the article again. Complete the gaps with phrases A–F.

A listening to classical music aimed at stimulating different moods
B can actually be beneficial
C put on some uplifting music to help get your brain working
D listening to various types of music affected different types of thinking
E opting for quiet solitude
F what you're trying to achieve

**d** Think about what you said in **a**. Would you now do anything different, based on the research?

**e** You're going to read what four doctors say about playing music while they work. First, look at the photo and answer the questions with a partner.

1 Do you think that doing an operation is more of a creative task or more of a problem-solving task?
2 What do you think might be the advantages and disadvantages of having music in the operating theatre?

**f** Now read what the doctors say. Did they mention any of the things you discussed in **e**? In a discussion between these four doctors, what would the general consensus be – music or no music while you work?

## What doctors listen to in the operating theatre

**RAMON TAHMASSEBI,** *orthopaedic surgeon*

If I play cool music, it puts me in a better mood and I perform better. You want something that will get you in the right frame of mind, but what you pick depends on the length and the complexity of the operation – I try to have some crowd-pleasers, some easy listening, some singalong tracks. Last week, I started a big, three-hour operation at 4 p.m., and the team was supposed to finish work at 5 p.m. But I had a playlist, and afterwards everyone told me they were having fun, so they didn't mind staying late.

**SAFINA ALI,** *head and neck surgeon*

When you are operating, it is soothing and calming to have music. I listen to everything from hip-hop to classical. When I was training, I had to listen to Bruce Springsteen for ten hours at a time, because my boss loved him. My current boss likes to have classical music on, but we change it when he leaves. Most of the nurses are younger, so it's nice to have contemporary music like Taylor Swift, because you can talk about it. I prefer music to silence – it's too eerie; I feel like I am on my own.

**SAMER NASHEF,** *cardiac surgeon*

I never have music in the operating theatre. Firstly, it's almost impossible to find a genre that fits the musical tastes of the 12 or so people it takes to do a heart operation. Secondly,

**g** Read the article again. Write **RT, SA, SN,** or **GW**.

Who says that…?

1 ____ it's very difficult to choose music that everyone likes
2 ____ the choice of music depends on the type of operation
3 ____ playing a variety of music tends to motivate the team
4 ____ working in silence makes them feel alone
5 ____ he / she sometimes switches off the music in the middle of an operation
6 ____ his / her colleagues often choose the music
7 ____ music gets in the way of doing the job well
8 ____ he / she plays different music to suit different patients

**h** With a partner, create a playlist of five songs that would help you to do a creative group task.

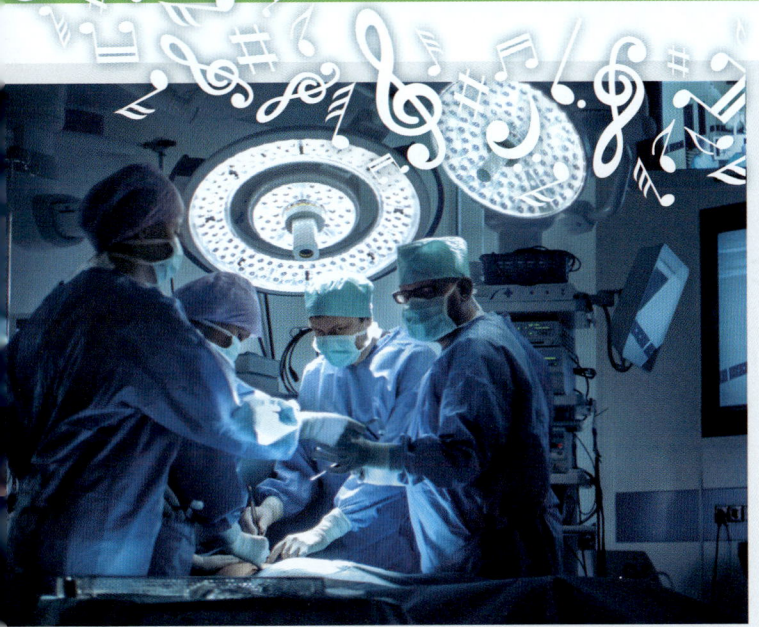

music, if it's emotionally engaging, is distracting, and if it's bland lift music, it's irritating. The real reason, however, is communication. Those 12 people need to be able to talk to each other, to provide information, ask questions, hear the answers, and act – any extraneous noise interferes with that.

**GABRIEL WESTON,** *skin cancer surgeon*

I do surgery on people's faces using local anaesthetic, and they're awake during the operation. So I use music to get them to relax. Broadly, older people prefer classical and younger people prefer pop. I think it's sensible to let them know you care about their feelings. If there is a point when things get serious, you turn the music off. But in planned operations, there are long stretches when you're doing something you've done many times, but it still requires meticulousness, and music is good for this.

*Adapted from The Guardian*

## 5 SPEAKING

Work in small groups. Discuss the statements below. Do you agree? Why (not)?

The music that means the most to you is the music you listen to as a teenager.

When music is sung, the lyrics are as important as the music.

You always enjoy music more when you listen to it live.

The best decade for pop music was the 70s.

People who listen to classical music are generally more intelligent.

People who go to music festivals don't really go to listen to the music.

Most young people nowadays are not interested in opera and classical music.

All schoolchildren should be taught to play a musical instrument.

Anyone can learn to sing.

## 6 ▶ VIDEO LISTENING

**a** Watch an interview with pianist Isata Kanneh-Mason. What is unusual about her family? Why does the interviewer say that the future looks bright for the Kanneh-Mason children?

**b** Watch the interview again and answer the questions.

1 How did she first get interested in classical music?
2 What happened to her when she was 17?
3 What is her position in the family?
4 What instrument does her brother Sheku play, and how has he been successful?
5 What kind of relationship do the siblings have?
6 What sacrifices did Isata and her siblings make when they were growing up, and how did they feel about it?
7 What is Isata's main reason for choosing a piece of music, and why?
8 What does she mean when she says 'I'm just so lucky that my escape is what I do'?

**c** Do you know any very musical people or families, or a family where they are mostly interested in or good at the same thing?

Go online to watch the video and review the lesson

## GRAMMAR

**a** Complete the second sentence so that it means the same as the first.

1  They escaped from the jungle because they found the river.
   They wouldn't have escaped from the jungle if they _____ _____ the river.

2  I can't go to dance classes because I work in the evening.
   I would be able to go to dance classes if I _____ _____ in the evening.

3  We went to that restaurant because you recommended it.
   We _____ _____ _____ to that restaurant if you hadn't recommended it.

4  Marta goes to bed late, so she's always tired in the morning.
   If Marta didn't go to bed late, she _____ _____ so tired in the morning.

5  It's a pity I can't speak French.
   I wish _____ _____ _____ French.

6  I regret not learning to play the piano when I was younger.
   I wish I _____ _____ _____ _____ the piano when I was younger.

7  I hate seeing your dirty clothes on the floor.
   I wish _____ _____ _____ your dirty clothes on the floor.

8  After living in London for a year I still find driving on the left difficult.
   After living in London for a year I still can't get _____ _____ _____ on the left.

9  My hair was very long when I was a child.
   When I was a child, I used _____ _____ very long hair.

10 I get up very early, but it's not a problem for me now.
   I'm used _____ _____ _____ very early.

**b** Complete the sentences with the correct form of the **bold** verb.

1  I don't remember _____ you before. **meet**
2  My hair needs _____. I'm going to book an appointment at the hairdresser's. **cut**
3  We managed _____ to the airport on time. **get**
4  Please try _____ late tomorrow. **not be**
5  My sister isn't used to _____ in such a big company. She was self-employed until recently. **work**

## VOCABULARY

**a** Complete the sentences with an adjective expressing a feeling.

1  Our son played brilliantly in the concert! We felt very pr_____.
2  I'm feeling a bit h_____. I really miss my family.
3  Thanks for lending me the money. I'm very gr_____.
4  I shouldn't have bought that bag – it was so expensive. Now I feel really g_____.
5  When I heard that I'd won the prize I was completely st_____. I couldn't say anything!

**b** Complete the sentences with the correct form of the **bold** word.

1  That walk was _____. I need a good rest now. **exhaust**
2  I was really _____ when I read Tim's email. **shock**
3  You really _____ me at the party last night! **embarrass**
4  It's very _____ when you think that you are going to miss your flight. **stress**
5  It _____ me when people who don't know me use my first name. **annoy**
6  Last night's concert was really _____. The orchestra didn't play well at all. **disappoint**
7  It always _____ me that people actually enjoy doing risky sports. **amaze**
8  We were _____ when we heard the news. **horrify**
9  What you said to Ruth was rather _____. I think you should apologize. **offend**
10 It was an incredibly _____ film! **scare**

**c** Complete the missing words.

1  Could I have an extra p_____ for my bed, please?
2  My husband says I sn_____ really loudly at night.
3  I didn't sleep last night, so I'm going to have a n_____ now.
4  Last night I had a horrible n_____. I dreamt that I was lost in the jungle.
5  Don't forget to s_____ the alarm for tomorrow morning.

**d** Write the words for the definitions.

1  _____ the person who directs an orchestra
2  _____ a group of people who sing together
3  _____ a stringed instrument that you hold between your knees
4  _____ a woman who sings with a very high voice
5  _____ an electronic musical instrument, like a piano

## PRONUNCIATION

**a** Circle the word with a different sound.

| | | | |
|---|---|---|---|
| 1 | 🐑 | sleepy  delighted<br>relieved  keyboard | |
| 2 | 🐕 | alarm  yawn<br>soprano  guitar | |
| 3 | 🦎 | loose  place<br>eyes  course | |
| 4 | 🦓 | raise  miserable<br>lose  homesick | |
| 5 | 🔑 | orchestra  chorus<br>psychology  chic | |

**b** Underline the main stressed syllable.

1 ab|so|lute|ly     3 in|fu|ri|a|ting     5 sleep|walk
2 de|va|sta|ted     4 in|som|ni|a

## CAN YOU understand this text?

**a** Read the article once. According to Dr Breus, what kinds of music should you listen to before going to sleep?

**b** Read the article again and choose the best words to fill the gaps.

1 a after  b while  c between
2 a effective  b affectionate  c harmful
3 a active  b relaxed  c alert
4 a adjust  b increase  c stop
5 a pride  b excitement  c boredom
6 a advise  b forbid  c order
7 a last  b first  c next
8 a possibly  b likely  c probably
9 a deeper  b comfortable  c uncomfortable
10 a as  b because  c if

## ▶ CAN YOU understand these people?

◀) 6.20 Watch or listen and choose a, b, or c.

| 1 | 2 | 3 | 4 |
|---|---|---|---|
| Christopher | Lemuel | Mary | Martina |

1 If Christopher was left alone on a desert island, he thinks ____.
   a he would survive well because he was a boy scout
   b he wouldn't worry too much about being rescued
   c he would have an idea from films about what to do

2 Lemuel finds it annoying when other people ____.
   a talk during lectures
   b don't walk fast enough in the street
   c bite their nails

3 Mary sometimes has problems sleeping when ____.
   a she's feeling depressed
   b her bedroom is too warm
   c she's been reading an exciting book

4 Martina likes listening to country music to help her to ____.
   a wake up
   b feel more energized
   c relax in the evening

# How you can use music to sleep better

## by Dr Michael Breus

Music is a regular fixture in my daily life. I listen to music to keep motivated ¹_____ I exercise or work, to relax me when I travel, and to unwind before bed. It's especially ²_____ on nights when I'm feeling tense.

**Slow beats are best.** The body and brain are highly responsive to music, including its rhythm and tempo. Use up-tempo songs to get you moving in the morning, or to keep you ³_____ on a long drive. To move your body into sleep mode, use songs that have a rhythm of about 60–80 beats per minute – you can find lots of examples on YouTube. Your heart rate will ⁴_____ to match these slower beats, and your breathing will slow down, putting you closer to a sleeping state.

**Avoid emotional triggers.** Don't listen to music that makes you feel strong emotions, whether sadness or ⁵_____. These are not the songs you want to listen to at bedtime.

**Go lyric-free.** Lyrics can be mentally stimulating. I ⁶_____ my patients to choose music without words at bedtime. Give the cognitive centres of your brain a rest, rather than lighting them up.

**Be consistent.** Research suggests that the beneficial effects of music for sleep get stronger over time. If you're stressed out in the evenings, your new music routine might not make an immediate difference in the ⁷_____ few nights. Stick with it for a few weeks, and you'll find the soothing effects become stronger.

**Don't ignore the rest of your sleep environment.** If you're playing a Bach sonata in a room blazing with lights, or looking at a computer screen, you're not ⁸_____ to benefit from the sleep-inducing effects of the background music. Make sure your nightly routine and environment is soothing, calm, and dimly lit.

**Don't fall asleep with earphones.** If you want to listen to music as you fall asleep, that's fine. But don't use earphones, which can make sleep ⁹_____ and damage your ear canal.

**Pay attention to how you feel.** We all react differently to songs and find different meaning within them. Classical music is often used in studies, and is a popular choice for bedtime listening. But ¹⁰_____ it's not your thing, that's fine. Try jazz, or new age, or folk music. Whatever makes you feel calm and puts your body and mind in a restful mode is the right choice for you.

*Adapted from a health website*

🖱 **Go online** to watch the video, review Files 5 & 6, and check your progress

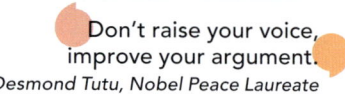

Don't raise your voice,
improve your argument.
*Desmond Tutu, Nobel Peace Laureate*

> **G** past modals: *must have*, etc., *would rather*   **V** verbs often confused   **P** weak form of *have*

## 1 GRAMMAR past modals: *must have*, etc.

*It wasn't me!*

**a** Look at the photo. With a partner, predict who the people are, where they are, and what they are arguing about. Use *could be*, *can't be*, and *must be*.

*They can't be a family, because… They must be…*

**b** 🔊 **7.1** Listen and check. Who is the 'guilty' person in the photo?

**c** 🔊 **7.2** Listen to some extracts from the conversation again and complete them with *could have*, *might have*, *must have*, *can't have*, or *should have*.

1 You _____ _____ finished it.
2 One of you _____ _____ used it.
3 It _____ _____ been me.
4 _____ you _____ drunk it last night…?
5 Someone _____ _____ given it to the cat.
6 …you _____ _____ put your name on it.

**d** Look at the gapped phrases 1–6 in **c** and think about what they mean. Then with a partner, match them to meanings A–D. Write the number in the box before each phrase.

Which phrase (or phrases) means you think…?
A ▢▢ it's very probable (or almost certain) that something happened or somebody did something
B ▢▢ it's possible that something happened or somebody did something
C ▢ it's impossible that something happened or somebody did something
D ▢ somebody didn't do the right thing

**e** 🄖 p.144 **Grammar Bank 7A**

## 2 PRONUNCIATION weak form of *have*

> have *When he got home, he realized he must of left his bag at school, so he ran back, but when he*

**a** Look at an extract from a British child's homework above. Why do you think the child made that mistake?

> 🔍 **Weak form of *have***
> When *have* is an auxiliary verb, it is usually contracted in spoken English, e.g. *I've*, *you've*. If it's not contracted, it's pronounced /əv/, e.g. after a modal verb. The pronunciation is exactly the same as the weak form of *of*.

**b** 🔊 **7.5** Now listen to six sentences with past modals and repeat.

**c** 🔊 **7.6** Listen and write six sentences with either *have* or *of*.

**d** In pairs, read the conversations and complete **B**'s responses with your own ideas (for responses 5–8 you also need to use *must have*, *might have*, *should have*, or *can't have*). Then practise the conversations.

1 **A** It was my birthday yesterday!
  **B** You should have <u>told me</u>.
2 **A** I can't find my phone anywhere.
  **B** You must have _____.
3 **A** I definitely said we were meeting them at 7.00.
  **B** They may have _____.
4 **A** I'm so tired. I can't keep my eyes open.
  **B** You shouldn't have _____.
5 **A** I failed my piano exam.
  **B** _____.
6 **A** Why do you think Fiona and Brian broke up?
  **B** _____.
7 **A** Alberto didn't come to class yesterday.
  **B** _____.
8 **A** We're going to be late. There's so much traffic.
  **B** _____.

## 3 READING & SPEAKING

**a** Imagine four young people in their 20s are sharing a flat. Which of the things in the list do you think cause the most arguments? Number them 1–5.

| | | |
|---|---|---|
| food | housework | money |
| noise | visitors | |

**b** Read an article for students about typical arguments in a shared house. What two categories are mentioned that are not in the list in **a**?

**c** Read the problems again. Then complete the article with solutions A–H.

A Don't pay in your share, either, and wait until the wi-fi gets cut off. Then suddenly, everyone will pay.

B Before you move in, get everyone to write their name on a piece of paper, and put them in a hat. The first person to be picked chooses first.

C Encourage everyone to have a go. Don't criticize other people's attempts. Try to help them improve.

D Get some ear plugs. Wax ones are the best.

E Have a rota for all jobs, including washing-up, drying, cleaning, and tidying.

F If you often need to get ready at similar times, take turns to go first.

G Make sure everyone has their own fridge shelf space and cupboard space.

H Suggest that if they are going to stay over often, then maybe they should contribute to rent / bills.

**d** Talk to a partner.

1 Look at the two solutions to each problem. Which one do you think is better? Can you suggest any other solutions?

2 Which problem would you find the most annoying? Have you ever had to deal with any of these problems yourself? What did you do?

### Glossary

**the direct debit 'bounced'** a bill that was supposed to be paid automatically through the bank wasn't paid because there wasn't enough money in the account

# Classic student house arguments— and how to avoid them

**Living in a shared student house can be one of university's greatest pleasures, but arguments will happen. What are the solutions?**

**Who gets the biggest room when moving in?** There's always one housemate who is convinced they have the right to the biggest room.
Solutions:
• Adjust the rent, so that the person with the biggest room pays more.
• 1 ▢

**The mess in the kitchen** You come home from a long day at uni and can't get to the sink because of the enormous pile of pots and pans.
Solutions:
• Establish the 30-minute rule – nothing stays unwashed for over 30 minutes.
• 2 ▢

**The housemate whose boyfriend / girlfriend spends more time in your house than their own** They definitely do not live at your house, but you see them more than some of your housemates. And they use the electricity, the water, the wi-fi...
Solutions:
• Explain why it's annoying. It isn't personal, but with them there, there's less space for the rest of you.
• 3 ▢

**How to pay and split the bills** The joint account seemed like a good idea until some people's money stopped going in, and the direct debit 'bounced' (incurring a charge), and the electricity bill, which was enormous, was forgotten about (another charge), and someone has gone to South America for three months.
Solutions:
• Get everyone to put in more money than will be needed in the account – then later pay the excess back (this is a good way of keeping a little extra cash in reserve, too).
• 4 ▢

**Taking too long in the bathroom** What are they doing in there?
Solutions:
• Have a kind word about the fact that there's only one bathroom.
• 5 ▢

**When they come in at 3 a.m.,** waking everybody up the night before an exam.
Solutions:
• Make sure your housemates know if you have to be up early for something. Likewise, let them know if you intend to be back late.
• 6 ▢

**Food stealing, 'borrowing' clothes, etc.** 'It was just there, so I took it.'
Solutions:
• Label your stuff, so that it's obvious what's yours.
• 7 ▢

**Who can't cook, who won't cook?** Why is it always you who's left alone to make dinner in the evening? How come as soon as you've finished, everyone suddenly appears?
Solutions:
• Draw up a cooking rota, so you know whose turn it is.
• 8 ▢

Adapted from The Independent

## 4 LISTENING & SPEAKING

**a** **C** Read the situation below. Then go to **Communication** Argument! **A** p.109  **B** p.113 Role-play an argument.

> You share a flat with someone you didn't know before. At first, you got on really well, but recently there have been several things that have been annoying you, which you've both avoided talking about. Now you think the time has come to have a talk about them.

**b** 🔊7.7 Listen to a psychologist giving some tips about how to argue better. Which two general points does she make?

1. ☐ Never avoid an argument by refusing to talk.
2. ☐ Try to avoid having an argument in the first place.
3. ☐ It isn't a bad thing to argue from time to time.
4. ☐ Always involve another person to mediate.

**c** Listen again. Tick (✓) the ones you should say and cross (✗) the ones you shouldn't. Why are they right or wrong?

1. ☐ 'Look, you're not doing your share of the housework.'
2. ☐ 'I think we should have another look at how we divide up the housework.'
3. ☐ 'Sorry, it was my fault.'
4. ☐ 'You always forget our wedding anniversary.'
5. ☐ 'I didn't mean to shout. I'd rather we didn't argue, but this is very important to me.'
6. ☐ 'And another thing: I was really disappointed with my birthday present.'
7. ☐ 'I'd rather talk about this tomorrow, when we've both calmed down.'

**d** Look at the things in **c** that the psychologist recommends you <u>should</u> say in an argument. Then do the **Communication** activity in **a** again, with a new partner. Try to follow the psychologist's advice.

## e  Grammar in context *would rather*

> 1. *Listen, <mark>I'd rather talk</mark> about this tomorrow, when we've both calmed down.*
> 2. *<mark>I'd rather we didn't argue</mark>, but this is very important to me.*

> 1. We use *would rather* with the infinitive without *to* to talk about present / future preferences, as an alternative to *would prefer to*.
>
>    *I'd rather go on holiday in July than August.*
>    *Would you rather stay in or go out tonight?*
>    *I'd rather not go out tonight. I'm really tired.*
>    **NOT** *I'd not rather.*
>
> 2. We can also use *would rather* + person + past tense to talk about what we would like another person to do, as an alternative to *I would prefer it if…*, e.g. *I'd rather you came on Saturday; I'm a bit busy on Friday. I'd rather you didn't smoke in here, if you don't mind.*

Rewrite the <mark>highlighted</mark> phrases using *would rather*.

1. <mark>I'd prefer to go to the cinema</mark> than to a club.
2. <mark>I'd prefer not to go to the party</mark> if my ex is going to be there.
3. <mark>Would you prefer to meet</mark> on Thursday morning or afternoon?
4. <mark>I'd prefer it if you didn't</mark> take photos.
5. <mark>I'd prefer it if your parents stayed</mark> in a hotel and not with us.

**f** Work in pairs. Look at the options and take turns to ask and answer. Say why.

Would you rather…?
1. live on your own or share a flat with friends
2. do an English course in London or New York
3. have a summer holiday or a winter holiday
4. stay up very late or get up very early
5. go to a concert or a sporting event

## 5 VOCABULARY verbs often confused

**a** 🔊7.8 Listen to six short extracts. What's happening? Use a verb from the list.

| advise | argue | deny | discuss | refuse | warn |
|--------|-------|------|---------|--------|------|

1. *He's denying something.*

**b** **V** p.158 **Vocabulary Bank** Verbs often confused

**c** Complete the questions with the correct verb from each pair, in the right form. Then ask and answer with a partner.

1 Do you _____ if people are a bit late when you have arranged to meet them, or do you think it doesn't _____? **matter / mind**

2 Can you usually _____ family birthdays, or do you need somebody to _____ you? **remember / remind**

3 Have you ever been _____ when you were on holiday? What was _____? **rob / steal**

4 What would you _____ people to do if they want to come to your country in the summer? What might you _____ them to be careful about? **advise / warn**

5 Do you think taking vitamin C helps to _____ colds? What other things can people do to _____ catching colds? **avoid / prevent**

6 Do you ever _____ clothes from friends or family? Have you ever _____ clothes to someone which they then ruined? **borrow / lend**

7 Have you ever _____ a cup or medal for anything? Are there any games or sports where you absolutely hate being _____? **beat / win**

## 6 READING & WRITING

**a** Read the article once. Which of the tips do you think could also apply to a face-to-face argument? Which do you think are the most important?

**b** Look at some examples of posts on ChangeMyView. Which advice in the article could you use to improve the highlighted phrases? What could you change them to?

1 **You must be crazy!** Everybody knows that it will never be possible to completely eradicate plastic.

2 **According to my mother**, children who grow up bilingual find it easier to learn a third language.

3 **You're completely wrong to say that** all young people are addicted to technology.

**c** Work in groups of four. Each take one of the arguments below, and write a response arguing either for or against the statement.

1 Private schools and hospitals should be abolished.
2 The best way to save the planet is to become a vegan.
3 It's impossible to like the works of an artist or musician if you think they were bad people.
4 People should not be allowed to inherit money or property from their parents.

**d** Pass your paper to the next person in the group, and continue the thread. When you have all responded to each statement, read all the comments on each one. Who do you think argued most effectively, and why?

**Glossary**
**thread** a series of connected messages on a message board on the internet which have been sent by different people, e.g. *a Twitter ~*

# How to win an online argument

When it comes to arguing face-to-face, many people use persuasive intonation or facial expressions to help win the argument. However, these are no use when you want to argue your case online. A recent study of comment threads on online forums has found that some words are more effective than others and that using numbers makes you more persuasive. Lillian Lee and her PhD students at Cornell University analysed almost two years of posts made on the forum site ChangeMyView, a website where users invite others to challenge their views and present alternative opinions.

## The best ways to win an argument

**Get your timing right** Typically, the first person to reply to the thread has a greater chance of changing the view of the original poster (OP) than someone who joins the debate later on.

**Use alternative terminology** Use words that are different from those used in the post. For example, if discussing climate change, describing it as *global warming* in a reply makes more of an impact than using the same terminology as the OP.

**Be polite** The study suggests that swearing or using aggressive terms instantly makes your argument less effective.

**Think about length** Longer replies in general tend to be seen as more persuasive.

**Use evidence** Using numbers, statistics, and examples to back up opinions makes people sound more convincing. The same is true of links to examples and outside sources.

**Show consideration for other's opinions** Phrases like 'It could be the case that…' or 'It may be true that…' show that you are open to other points of view. Although this sounds like it might signal a weaker argument, the researchers said it may make your argument easier to accept, by softening its tone.

**Check the language in the original post** Personal pronouns, such as *I*, suggest that a person is more open-minded to persuasion, whereas *we* and *us* suggest they are more stubborn. Stubborn people also use more emotive language and use decisive words such as *certain*, *nothing*, and *best*.

**Know when to give up** Finally, the researchers found that after four or five 'back-and-forth' posts have been made, the chances of changing someone's opinion significantly drops.

G verbs of the senses  V the body  P silent consonants

> Botox should be banned for actors…Acting is all about expression; why would you want to iron out a frown?
> *Rachel Weisz, UK actress*

## 1 GRAMMAR verbs of the senses

**a** Look at the adjectives for feelings in the list. In pairs, take turns to mime one of them for your partner to guess. You can only use your face and hands.

astonished  embarrassed  disappointed
shocked  miserable  scared stiff

**b** Look at the film still of Keira Knightley. What kind of film do you think it is? In pairs, focus on her expression and body language and choose a, b, or c to complete sentences 1–3 below.

1 She **looks like**…
   a the daughter of a rich family.
   b a servant who has dressed up in her mistress's clothes.
   c a singer who is about to perform.

2 She **looks**…
   a nervous.
   b embarrassed.
   c miserable.

3 She **looks as if**…
   a she's just broken off a relationship.
   b she's running away from someone she dislikes.
   c she's unsure about what to do.

**c** 🔊 7.10 Now listen to a film critic describing what's happening in the scene. Check your ideas in **b**.

**d** Look again at the sentences in **b**. What kinds of words or phrases do you use after *looks*, *looks like*, and *looks as if*?

**e** G p.145 **Grammar Bank 7B**

**f** Look at four more film stills. With a partner, decide which of the film types they belong to. Do you know anything about any of the films?

comedy  fantasy  historical drama
horror

Keira Knightley, in *Atonement*

Helen Mirren

Eddie Redmayne

Frances McDormand

Daniel Kaluuya

**g** Now look carefully at their expressions and body language, and describe:

1 who you think the character is (using *look like* + noun).
2 how you think he / she is feeling (using *looks* + adjective).
3 what you think is happening (using *look as if* + clause).

**h** 🔊 **7.12** Listen to the film critics and check your answers to **f** and **g**. Did you guess correctly?

**i** 🔊 **7.13** Listen to these sounds. What do you think is happening? Use *It sounds as if…* or *It sounds like…*

( *I think it sounds as if they've…*

**j** 🌐 **Communication** Guess what it is **A p.109 B p.113** Describe objects for your partner to identify using *looks, feels, smells,* or *tastes* + adjective, or *like* + noun.

## 2 READING & LISTENING

**a** Have you ever acted in a play or film / video? Where and when? What was your role? Did you enjoy it?

**b** Read the first paragraph, the introduction to an article. What is the best way to do the exercises?

# How to improve your acting skills

Being an actor means having a lot of 'waiting time', for example, when you're off set during a film, not on stage in a play, or between jobs. One way to carry on practising and improving is to do some exercises and games which will develop your acting skills. Some of these can be done by yourself, but many are more fun in groups. Most of these techniques, acting games, and exercises were created by drama teachers, and are used in drama schools. They can also benefit you in everyday life, especially with communication skills.

### Exercise 1 Developing your imagination

This exercise is aimed at developing your imagination, which is one of the most important components of an actor's success. In order for the audience to believe your acting, it's you who has to believe first that the life of your character is real. And to do that, you need to be able to build a small world of your character's life in your mind. Even just for one scene, you have to come up with answers for why you are doing what you are doing, why it is that way, etc.

The exercise is best done in a group. Look at an image of a person showing an emotion, e.g. smiling. Then between you, try to think of all the possible reasons why the person might be smiling, for example, he looks as if he might be remembering a funny film, or he might have just booked a holiday abroad.

*Adapted from the Acting in London website*

**c** Now read the instructions for the first exercise, **Developing your imagination**. Then do it in groups of 4–5, using the photograph below.

**d** 🔊 **7.14** Look at the names of three more exercises. Listen to a drama teacher explaining the exercises to his students. Which exercise is to help with…?

▢ paying attention to details
▢ showing emotions
▢ using body language

### Exercise 2 Stroking an animal

Think of ¹_____.
Then ²_____.
Now ³_____.

### Exercise 3 What were they wearing?

One person ⁴_____.
Sit ⁵_____ and focus on
⁶_____.
After three minutes, ⁷_____
unless ⁸_____.
Then the host ⁹_____.

### Exercise 4 The 'magic' image

Choose ¹⁰_____,
e.g. ¹¹_____,
and write down ¹²_____.
Show ¹³_____ to other people in the group. Choose no more than ¹⁴_____.
When you have ¹⁵_____, think of
¹⁶_____.
Then create ¹⁷_____ that
combines ¹⁸_____.

**e** Listen again and complete the instructions. Then compare with a partner and add anything you missed.

**f** Now, in your same groups, do the three exercises.

## 3 VOCABULARY & SPEAKING the body

a Look at the photos. Where do you think they were taken? What emotion do you think he is showing?

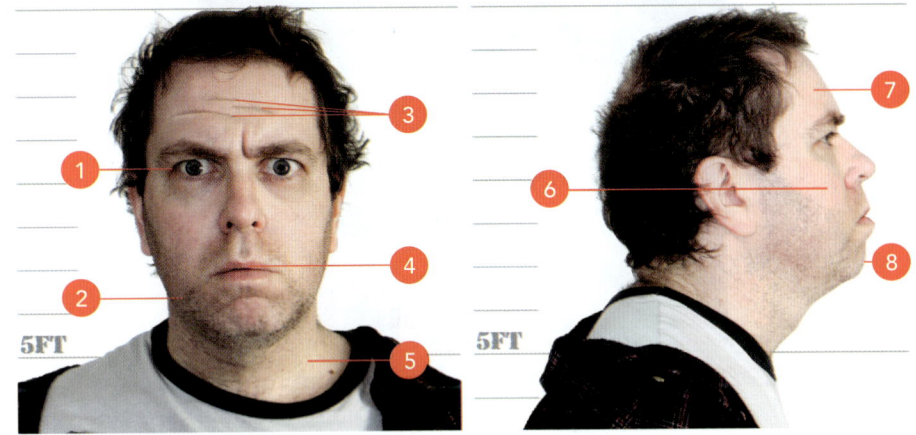

b Look at the photos and match the words in the list with 1–8.

| | cheek | 8 | chin | | eye | | forehead |
|---|---|---|---|---|---|---|---|
| | lips | | neck | | stubble | | wrinkles |

c Which word in **b** goes with these? Can you find them in the photo?

_____ brow     _____ lash     _____ lid

d 🔊 7.15 Listen and check your answers to **b** and **c**.

e Ⓥ p.159 **Vocabulary Bank** The body

## 4 PRONUNCIATION silent consonants

a Cross out the 'silent' consonant in these words.

calf   comb   kneel   palm   thumb   wrinkles   wrist

b 🔊 7.19 Listen and check. What can you deduce about the pronunciation of…?
- *kn* and *wr* at the beginning of a word
- *mb* at the end of a word

c Look at the phonetics for some more words with silent consonants. In pairs, try to say them.

| 1 | /ˈɒnɪst/ | 4 | /ˈwɪsl/ | 7 | /dɪˈzaɪn/ | 10 | /kɑːm/ |
|---|---|---|---|---|---|---|---|
| 2 | /ˈfɑːsn/ | 5 | /aɪl/ | 8 | /hɑːf/ | 11 | /klaɪm/ |
| 3 | /ˈmʌsl/ | 6 | /daʊt/ | 9 | /həʊl/ | 12 | /nɒk/ |

d 🔊 7.20 Match words A–L to the phonetics in **c**. Then listen and check. What is the silent consonant in each one?

| | | | | | | | |
|---|---|---|---|---|---|---|---|
| A | aisle | D | design | G | half | J | muscle |
| B | calm | E | doubt | H | honest | K | whistle |
| C | climb | F | fasten | I | knock | L | whole |

e Practise saying the phrases below.

half an hour    I doubt it    calm down, dear    an aisle seat, please    designer clothes    anti-wrinkle cream    kneel down

## 5 READING & SPEAKING

a Look at the title of an article by Professor Thomas Ormerod about his research and read the first paragraph. What is the accepted 'best way to spot a liar'? What was the purpose of Ormerod's experiment?

b Now read the rest of the article and match Ormerod's five key principles A–E to gaps 1–5.

A **Ask open questions**
B **Build rapport**
C **Look for changes in style**
D **Try to find contradictions**
E **Use surprise questions**

c Read the article again and mark the statements **T** (true) or **F** (false). Correct the **F** statements.

1 Body language as a way of identifying a liar can be helpful if you know someone well.
2 The 'fake' passengers in Ormerod's experiment were given a false cover story.
3 All passengers passing through airport security during the experiment were interviewed by the trained security officers.
4 The more information passengers were asked for, the more difficult it was for them to lie successfully.
5 Officers were told to be suspicious of passengers who always gave short answers.
6 The experiment proved that verbal clues are as effective as body language in helping to identify a liar.

d In pairs, play *Truth or lie*. Swap roles for question 2, etc.

A Ask **B** question 1 below. Ask follow-up questions, using techniques from the article, and decide if **B** is telling the truth.
B **A** will ask you question 1 below. You must answer, *Yes, I have*. If you have had the experience, tell the truth. If you haven't, invent answers to **A**'s follow-up questions.

1 Have you ever walked out in the middle of a play, film or concert?
2 Have you ever sprained your wrist or ankle?
3 Have you ever been caught cheating in an exam?
4 Have you ever been stopped by the police?

e Did any of Thomas Ormerod's techniques help you to tell if your partner was telling the truth or not?

# The best way to spot a liar...or is it?

**H**ow easy is it to know whether someone is telling the truth or lying? Some people aren't very good at pretending, whilst others are far more expert. Most of us are familiar with the kind of body language which tends to indicate deception, such as avoiding eye contact, blushing, fidgeting, or laughing nervously; and identifying whether somebody is telling the truth can be fairly straightforward with people we know well, our children, family, or friends. However, research shows that relying only on body language to spot a liar is in fact very unreliable, especially when you are not familiar with how a person usually behaves. In fact, according to one study, just one in 400 people manage to make a correct judgement based on non-verbal indicators with more than 80% accuracy. Just because someone looks nervous does not mean they are guilty, and in more formal contexts, such as interviewing crime suspects or in security screening at airports, the consequences of getting it wrong can be very serious. So, my research team and I devised an experiment to develop a more reliable method of lie detection, which relies not on how people behave, but on what they say.

We tested out our method on passengers at airport security. Firstly, we recruited a selection of 'fake' passengers of different nationalities, such as American, German, Swiss, and Canadian, and offered them an extra fee if they managed to pass through a security interview without being spotted. Each person prepared a convincing cover story about their life and work history and the purpose of their plane journey. They were all given valid tickets and passports, and were asked to dress appropriately and carry suitable luggage. A team of trained officers then made a random selection of passengers passing through security, and carried out specially constructed interviews in order to try to spot the 'fakes'.

**So, what kinds of things did the officers ask in these interviews?** These are the key principles we used to increase the chance of finding out if someone was lying:

**1** _____ Officers were asked to give the impression that this was a fairly casual conversation, and to put passengers at their ease with general, friendly questions such as 'How are you today?' and 'Did you have a good trip to the airport?'.

**2** _____ We told officers to use questions such as 'Can you tell me about…?', 'Can you explain to me who…?' and so on, that required passengers to give more information, rather than just answering 'yes' or 'no'.

**3** _____ Passengers were asked, for example, for extra information about a family member or about the company that they worked for; handling unexpected questions is more difficult for a liar than for a truthful person.

**4** _____ Officers were encouraged to ask follow-up questions to test passengers' statements. For example, if the passenger claimed to work in Oxford, the officer might ask them about their journey to work, to check if they could report that accurately, and to try to spot any gaps in expected knowledge.

**5** _____ Liars are often more confident when they feel in control of a conversation, but if they start to feel undermined or challenged, they begin to limit their responses. We told officers to watch out for people who started to reply with much shorter answers, or who showed a tendency to become evasive in their answers, not replying directly to the questions.

The aim was to put all passengers under gentle pressure, which would increase the chance that something a 'fake' passenger might reveal during a conversation would give them away. The officers were also told not to pick up a lie immediately – rather, to encourage the liar to continue to talk, and then to challenge them when they were sure they were lying. And the results were striking. The security officers using our interview technique were over 20 times more likely to detect the lying passengers than officers using traditional behaviour observation methods.

Professor Thomas Ormerod

---

**6 WRITING**

Ⓦ **p.119 Writing** Describing a photo  Write a description of a picture, speculating about what the people are doing, feeling, etc.

Ⓡ **Go online** to review the lesson

## 1 ▶ THE INTERVIEW Part 1

a Read the biographical information about Simon Callow. Have you seen any of his films?

**Simon Callow** is an English actor, writer, and theatre director. He was born in London in 1949 and studied at Queen's University, Belfast, and the Drama Centre in London.

As a young actor he made his name when he played the part of Mozart in Peter Shaffer's production of *Amadeus* at the Royal National Theatre in London in 1979 and he later appeared in the film version. As well as acting in the theatre he has also appeared in TV dramas and comedies and in many films including *Four Weddings and a Funeral* and *Shakespeare in Love*. He has directed both plays and musicals and was awarded the Laurence Olivier award for Best Musical for *Carmen Jones* in 1992. He has written biographies of the Irish writer Oscar Wilde and Orson Welles, the American actor and film director. He was awarded the CBE in 1999 for his services to drama.

b Watch Part 1 of an interview with him. Mark the sentences **T** (true) or **F** (false).

1 His first job was as an actor at The Old Vic theatre.
2 When he watched rehearsals he was fascinated by how the actors and the directors worked together.
3 Acting attracted him because it involved problem solving.
4 Playing the part of Mozart in *Amadeus* was a challenge because he wasn't a fictional character.
5 Mozart was the most exciting role he has had because it was his first.

c Now watch again and say why the **F** sentences are false.

**Glossary**
**The Old Vic** one of the oldest and most famous of the London theatres
*Amadeus* is a play by Peter Shaffer about the life of the composer Wolfgang Amadeus Mozart. It was also made into a film of the same name. In the play, Mozart is portrayed as having a very childish personality, which contrasts with the genius and sophistication of his music.
*The Marriage of Figaro* one of Mozart's best-known operas
**box office** the place at a theatre or cinema where tickets are sold
**rehearsals** /rɪˈhɜːslz/ time that is spent practising a play or a piece of music
**auditorium** /ˌɔːdɪˈtɔːriəm/ the part of a theatre where the audience sits

d Have you seen any films or plays based on the life of real people? Did you agree with the way they were portrayed?

## ▶ Part 2

a Now watch Part 2. Answer the questions.

1 Which does he prefer, acting in the theatre or in films?
2 Complete the two crucial differences he mentions about acting in the theatre:
There's an _____.
Every single performance is utterly _____.
3 Who does he say are the most important people in the making of a film, the director, the editor, or the actors? Why?
4 Does he think acting in film is more natural and realistic than theatre acting? Why (not)?

b Watch again. What is he referring to when he says…?

1 'It's important because you have to reach out to them, make sure that everybody can hear and see what you're doing.'
2 '…I mean you never do, you never can.'
3 'So, in that sense, the actor is rather powerless.'
4 '…there are some, you know, little metal objects right in front of you, sort of, staring at you as you're doing your love scene…'

**Glossary**
**(film) editor** the person whose job it is to decide what to include and what to cut in a film
**editing suite** /ˈedɪtɪŋ swiːt/ a room containing electronic equipment for editing video material

c Do you ever go to the theatre? Do you prefer it to the cinema? Why (not)? What plays have you seen?

# performances

## ▶ Part 3

**a** Now watch Part 3. What does he say about…?

1 watching other actors acting
2 the first great actors he saw
3 Daniel Day-Lewis
4 wearing make-up
5 the first night of a play

Daniel Day-Lewis

> ### Glossary
> **John Gielgud** a famous stage and film actor (1904–2000)
> **Ralph Richardson** a famous stage and film actor (1902–1983)
> **Laurence Olivier** a famous stage and film actor (1907–1989)
> **Edith Evans** a famous stage and film actor (1888–1976)
> **Peggy Ashcroft** a famous stage and film actor (1907–1991)
> **Daniel Day-Lewis** a famous film actor (1957– )
> **stage fright** nervous feelings felt by actors before they appear in front of an audience

Laurence Olivier

**b** Are there any actors you particularly enjoy watching? Why do you like them? Which of their characters do you like best?

## 2 ▶ LOOKING AT LANGUAGE

> 🔍 **Modifiers**
> Simon Callow uses a wide variety of modifiers (*really*, *incredibly*, etc.) to make his language more expressive.

Watch some extracts from the interview and complete the missing adjective or modifier.

1 '…I thought what a wonderful job, what a _____ **interesting** job…'
2 'My job was to reconcile that with the fact that he wrote *The Marriage of Figaro*, and that was **tremendously** _____.'
3 '…its fame, almost from the moment it was announced, was **overwhelmingly** _____ than anything I had ever done…'
4 'They're _____ **different** media, they require different things from you as an actor…'
5 '…you bring _____ **different** things to them.'
6 'The beauty of the theatre is that every single performance is **utterly** _____ from every other one.'
7 'As a young man, and a boy, I was _____ **lucky** to see that fabled generation of actors, of, of Gielgud and Richardson, Olivier,…'

## 3 ▶ THE CONVERSATION

Mark    John    Devika

**a** Watch the conversation. Tick (✓) the correct option to sum up their conclusion.

They agree that…
1 ☐ a live performance is always better because of the atmosphere.
2 ☐ a recorded performance is usually better because there are no distractions.
3 ☐ it's impossible to generalize because it depends on the event.

**b** Watch again. What do Devika and Mark say about the following things? Are they positive or negative?

1 **Devika** a big flashy superhero film
2 **Devika** some Shakespeare or any modern plays
3 **Mark** factors that could sway your enjoyment
4 **Mark** a major rugby match recently
5 **Devika** a crowd of other people enjoying the music

**c** Do you agree with the participants about the live performances being better than recorded ones?

**d** Watch some extracts and complete the missing phrases.

1 That's a _____ _____ _____. I love going to the cinema.
2 I think _____ _____ _____ _____ it's better or worse…
3 But if you go to a live one though, then you participate, _____ _____, because you're part of it…
4 If you're sitting, _____ _____, high up or with a slightly obstructed view…
5 I've been to plenty of live music events – concerts and festivals and things, _____ _____, around the country, and I love them.
6 That's intriguing _____ _____, the difference between the two.

**e** Which of the phrases in **d** do they use to…?

☐☐☐☐ give themselves time to think
☐☐ check the others agree

**f** Now have a conversation in groups of three.

1 Do you think it's essential nowadays for an actor to be good looking?
2 Which is more important in a film, the actors or the special effects?

🔄 **Go online** to watch the video, review the lesson, and check your progress

A society gets the criminals it deserves.
*Val McDermid, Scottish crime writer*

**G** the passive (all forms); *have something done; it is said that..., he is thought to...,* etc. **V** crime and punishment **P** the letter *u*

## 1 LISTENING

**a** Imagine you are alone in the street at night in an area that you don't know well. Would you feel nervous? What might you do to feel safer?

**b** Read the introduction to a page from a police crime prevention website and look at the pictures. With a partner, decide what advice you think is shown in each picture, and what the missing word in the headings might be.

**c** 🔊 8.1 Now listen to a Metropolitan Police podcast. Complete the headings. What advice did you predict correctly in **b**?

**d** Listen again and answer the questions.
1 What should you plan in advance?
2 Why is it important to look confident?
3 What three things shouldn't you do in the street on a mobile phone?
4 What kinds of things should you keep out of sight?
5 Why should you walk facing oncoming traffic?
6 What three things make places safer to walk at night?
7 What should you do during an evening when you're out with friends?
8 Why shouldn't you let your drink out of your sight?

**e** Was any of the advice about street crime new to you? Which tip do you think is the most useful? How safe / unsafe is your town, or the area where you live?

# Stay safe

Street crime is often unplanned, so making yourself less of a target, moving with purpose, and being aware of your surroundings will go a long way to keeping you safe when you're out and about. Here are eight important pieces of advice.

**1 Be _____**

**2 Be _____**

**3 Be _____**

**4 _____ it**

**5 Go _____ the flow**

**6 Trust your _____**

**7 Make a _____**

**8 Look out for _____**

*Adapted from the Metropolitan Police website*

## 2 VOCABULARY crime and punishment

a How much do you think you know about keeping your home safe? Can you 'beat the burglar'? Do the quiz to find out.

### Beat the burglar

1 **What's the most common time of day to be burgled?**
   a between 10.00 and 12.00 a.m.
   b between 2.00 and 5.00 p.m.
   c between 10.00 and 12.00 p.m.

2 **How long do you think a burglar normally takes to search someone's house?**
   a 10 minutes   b 20 minutes   c 30 minutes

3 **What two things influence a burglar to choose a house to break into?**
   a it's in an expensive area
   b there's no one at home
   c there are trees and bushes around the house

4 **Which are the most common things that burglars steal, apart from money?**
   a laptops and tablets
   b paintings and antiques
   c jewellery

5 **What is the best place in the house to hide your valuables?**
   a the living room          d the kitchen
   b the main bedroom         e the study
   c a child's bedroom

6 **What is most likely to prevent a burglary?**
   a a dog   b a burglar alarm

b **C Communication** Beat the burglar **A p.112 B p.113** Find out the answers, according to an ex-burglar.

c Now **A** tell **B** the answers to questions 1–3, and **B** tell **A** the answers to questions 4–6.

d Match the highlighted words in the quiz to definitions 1–5.

1 _____ (noun) a person who breaks in and steals from a private house
2 _____ (verb, passive) to have sb enter your house and take things that belong to you
3 _____ (noun) the crime of entering a house illegally and stealing things from it
4 _____ (phr. verb) to enter a place by force
5 _____ (verb) to take sth without intending to return it or pay for it

e 🔊 8.2 Listen and check.

f **V p.160 Vocabulary Bank** Crime and punishment

## 3 PRONUNCIATION & SPEAKING
### the letter u

a Look at the words in the list. Which sound does the letter u make? Put them in the correct row.

| | |
|---|---|
| acc**u**se  dr**u**gs  j**u**dge  j**u**ry m**u**gger  p**u**nishment  sm**u**ggling | |
| Λ | |
| ʊ | |
| /juː/ | |

b Now look at the pink letters in some more words which include the letter u. Put them in the correct row, according to how the vowel sound is pronounced.

| | |
|---|---|
| b**ur**glar  c**au**ght  c**ou**rt  fr**au**d  g**ui**lty  m**ur**derer | |
| (fish) | |
| (bird) | |
| (horse) | |

c 🔊 8.5 Listen and check your answers to **a** and **b**. Then answer the questions.

1 Is the vowel sound before a double consonant short or long?
2 Which two words are pronounced exactly the same?
3 How do we pronounce *gu* before the letters *a*, *e*, and *i*, as in *guard*, *guess*, *guilty*?

d 🔊 8.6 Listen and write five sentences. Then practise saying them.

e Talk in small groups. Ask for more details.

What do you think are the most common crimes in your town or city?

Have you ever witnessed a crime? What was it? Where? What happened?

Do you know anyone...?
- whose phone or bicycle has been stolen
- whose car has been vandalized
- who has been stopped by the police while driving
- who has been mugged
- who has been burgled
- who has been offered a bribe

## 4 GRAMMAR the passive (all forms); *have something done*; *it is said that…*, *he is thought to…*, etc.

**a** Read three true crime stories. In which story was someone…?

A caught because of what they stole
B caught because of what they were wearing
C caught because of what they said

---

**(1) The telltale trousers**

When an attempted robbery at a DIY store went wrong, Milton J. Hodges fled across the street and jumped over a fence to avoid ¹*catching / being caught*. Unfortunately, he ²*landed / was landed* in the grounds of the Cypress Cove Nudist Resort & Spa. Hodges ³*spotted / was spotted* by police easily, as he was the only person wearing clothes.

---

**(2) The Apple iDiot**

Last week in San Francisco, a woman had her iPhone stolen. A thief cycled up to her on the pavement, ⁴*snatched / was snatched* the iPhone out of her hands, and rode away. However, unknown to him, the woman worked for Apple and ⁵*was demonstrating / was being demonstrated* the iPhone's new GPS tracking device to some customers. The tracker worked, and the thief ⁶*caught / was caught* a few minutes later.

---

**(3) Parlez-vous français?**

The victim was hysterical when the Calgary police arrived at her house. A window ⁷*had broken / had been broken* and her jewellery had gone. While the police officer was there, her French-speaking father ⁸*called / was called*. She explained to him, in French, that it was all a plan to get the insurance money. What she didn't know was that Officer Meharu speaks six languages, including French. She ⁹*has been charged / has charged* with fraud.

---

**b** Read the stories again. Circle the correct form of verbs 1–9, active or passive.

**c** Look at the extract from story 2.

> A woman **had her iPhone stolen**.

Does it describe…?
1 something the person arranged for someone to do for her
2 something bad that happened to her

**d** 🔊 8.7 Now look at another headline and listen to the news story. In what way was the robber polite?

> **Britain's most polite robber**

**e** Listen again and complete extracts 1–4. How is the structure different between 1 and 4, and 2 and 3?

1 Police in Stockport are looking for a man who is said _____ _____ Britain's most polite armed robber.
2 It is believed _____ _____ _____ a tall man in his early 40s…
3 It is thought _____ _____ _____ _____ at least four shops in Stockport in recent weeks.
4 He is reported _____ _____ _____ to his victims…

**f** 🌀 p.146 Grammar Bank 8A

---

## 5 READING

**a** Work in pairs. Discuss the questions.

1 Do you post photos on social media sites like Facebook or Instagram? How often? What kinds of photos do you post?
2 Who do you allow to see your posted photos? Why?
3 How do you feel when other people post photos of you without your permission?

**b** You're going to read an article about Steve Bustin, who had problems with some photos he posted on Facebook. First, look at the four photos. Then read the article once and answer the questions.

1 Who are the people in photo A? Who did 'Martin' say they were?
2 Why did photos B and C make Constance suspicious?
3 What had happened in photo D? How did the scammer use it?

**c** Read the article again. Choose a, b, or c.

1 When Steve received Constance's email he felt _____.
   a surprised   b pleased   c sorry
2 Constance was attracted to Martin because _____.
   a she liked his profile photo
   b he paid her a lot of attention
   c he reminded her of her husband
3 Thanks to a website about dating scams, Constance was able to find out who _____.
   a 'Martin' really was
   b the photo was really of
   c had originally posted the photo
4 In a typical dating scam, men like Martin start by _____.
   a being very nice to women
   b asking women for money
   c trying to get women's sympathy
5 As a result of the scam, Steve has decided to be more careful about _____ on social media.
   a posting holiday photos
   b who can see what he posts
   c contacting friends and family

**d** Look at the highlighted words in the article related to scams and try to work out what they mean. Then match them to a synonym in the list.

| | | | |
|---|---|---|---|
| ▢ careful | ▢ chosen | ▢ fraud | ▢ give |
| ▢ make use of (in a dishonest way) | | | |
| ▢ said that (even though it wasn't true) | | | |
| ▢ thought that | ▢ trick *(verb)* | | |

# A case of identity theft

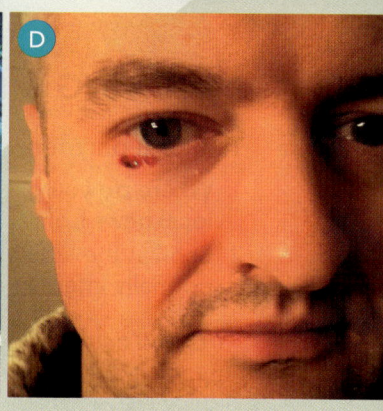

*Adapted from the Mirror website*

**I sighed when I glanced at the email on my phone.** It was from a woman called Constance, a complete stranger to me, who [1] was under the impression that we'd been in a relationship for several months. It has become an all-too-familiar story. Over the past two years, my photos have been used to [2] con 11 women on dating websites. These are just the ones I know about; the real number could be much higher.

I rang Constance and listened as she explained she'd met a man called Martin Peterson on Elite Singles. He said he was Danish and a widower. Constance had joined the website hoping to find love, after losing her husband three years earlier, and Martin had seemed kind and understanding. He was interested in everything about her, texting her every morning and ringing her for cosy chats in the evening. But on his dating profile were several photos, which were in fact, of me! She forwarded me the pictures, and I shuddered when I saw one of me and my sister, who Martin had said was his dead wife.

Constance had begun to be suspicious of Martin when she noticed his hair colour and style change within the space of a few hours. He [3] claimed he was on a business trip, and sent her a photo of me sitting in a hotel garden having breakfast, with my curly grey hair in need of a trim. Later in the day, he sent a second photo of me by a swimming pool, in which my hair was shorter and darker. In fact, these photos had been taken several years apart and had been 'harvested' from my Facebook account. Constance began to look carefully at all the pictures he had sent. She researched dating [4] scams online, and found a way to find out where a picture had originated. By dragging a picture of Martin into a 'reverse image search' on Google, she discovered that the pictures of the man she'd believed to be a Danish widower were actually of me, a public speaker from Brighton.

People like 'Martin' are known to [5] prey on older women. First, they gain their trust and bombard them with attention, then they say they are travelling abroad for work, where they are involved in an accident. Finally, they ask the woman to transfer money for medical treatment or flights home. A few years ago, I scratched my face, and posted a photo online of me with blood on my face. This picture has now been used by the scammer several times – he sends it alongside a picture of a smashed-up car, and says he's been involved in a serious accident. Fortunately, Constance didn't [6] hand over any money. But other women have, including one woman who lost thousands of pounds.

These days, I'm a lot more conscious of what I post online. I always used to share pictures of everything: holidays by the pool, work speeches, me and my dog, fancy dress parties... Now I've changed my privacy settings on social media. I suppose my account was [7] targeted because I had a range of photos and the scammer could build a whole life from them. An expert told me that my pictures had probably been sold on as a bundle on the black market. I now encourage all my friends and family to be [8] wary about what they post – once they're out there, there's nothing you can do about it. Unfortunately for me, my identity is no longer my own.

## 6 SPEAKING

a How common do you think identify theft is nowadays? What can people do to avoid it happening?

b Look at the questions on the right. For each one...
- decide what you think.
- think of reasons for your opinions.
- decide how you think the 'crime' should be punished.

c Now discuss the questions in groups.

**Do you think it should be illegal to...?**
- post a photo or video of someone online without their permission
- post aggressive or threatening 'tweets' or messages
- download music, books, and films without paying for them
- own an aggressive breed of dog
- squat in an unoccupied house (live there without paying rent)
- paint graffiti on a wall or fence
- smoke outdoors, e.g. in parks or in the street
- kill another person in self-defence

**If yes, how do you think they should be punished? If no, say why not.**

## 7 WRITING

 **p.120 Writing** Expressing your opinion  Write an article for an online forum, saying what you think about some aspects of crime.

Go online to review the lesson

For most people no news is good news, but for journalists good news is not news.
*Gloria Borger, US political commentator*

## 1 LISTENING & SPEAKING

**a** Talk to a partner.

1 Where do you get your international, national, and local news from?

2 Look at the list below. What kinds of news are you normally interested in?

arts and culture   business   celebrity gossip
crime   the environment   food & drink   health
local / national news   politics   sport   technology
TV and entertainment   the weather   world news

3 What kinds of news headlines, e.g. a death, news about a celebrity, a sports result, might make you want to read the whole article?

4 What stories are in the news at the moment in your country?

**b** Look at the headlines and photos for two news stories that were reported in the same week. What do you think they are about?

**Wine goes blue**

**Egyptian zoo denies their zebra is a donkey**

**c** 🔊 8.11 Listen to the stories and check. Were you correct?

**d** Listen again and complete the information.

1 Vindigo wine gets its colour from…

2 The wine is being produced in…because…

3 A bottle of Vindigo costs…

4 Monsieur Le Bail says the wine is ideal for…

5 Mahmoud Sarhan was visiting the zoo when he saw…

6 He was sure it was a donkey because…

7 A vet who looked at the photo said that…

8 The zoo's owner wouldn't accept that…

**e** Look at two more headlines and photos from the same week's news. With a partner, guess what they are about.

**Football fan gets World Cup fever**

**Shark baby drama**

**f** 🅒 **Communication** Strange, but true **A** p.109 **B** p.113 Read the stories and check, then tell each other what happened.

**g** Three of the four stories are true and one is fake news. Which one do you think is the fake?

## 2 GRAMMAR reporting verbs

**a** Look at some extracts from the four news stories. Match them to the direct speech A–F.

1 He **persuaded a company** in Almeria in Spain, **to produce** the wine.
2 **He…recommends drinking** it on the beach, or around the swimming pool.
3 A zoo in Egypt **has denied painting** a donkey with black stripes…
4 …a local vet…**agreed to examine** the photo.
5 He **advised me not to take** football so seriously.
6 He **threatened to steal** another shark if he felt it was necessary.

A ☐ 'OK, I'll have a look at it.'
B ☐ 'That's the best place to have it.'
C ☐ 'I'll do it again if I have to.'
D ☐ 'Don't do it – it's not very important.'
E ☐ 'Please make it for me.'
F ☐ 'We definitely didn't do it.'

**b** **ⓖ p.147 Grammar Bank 8B**

## 3 PRONUNCIATION word stress

**a** Look at the two-syllable reporting verbs in the list. All of them except four are stressed on the second syllable. ⟨Circle⟩ the four exceptions.

| | | | |
|---|---|---|---|
| a\|ccuse | ad\|mit | ad\|vise | a\|gree |
| con\|vince | de\|ny | in\|sist | in\|vite | o\|ffer |
| or\|der | per\|suade | pro\|mise | re\|fuse |
| re\|gret | re\|mind | su\|ggest | threa\|ten |

**b** ◀) 8.13 Listen and check.

> 🔍 **Spelling of two-syllable verbs**
> If a two-syllable verb ends in consonant–vowel–consonant and is stressed on the second syllable, the final consonant is doubled before an -ed ending, e.g. re*gret* > regretted, ad*mit* > admitted. However, when the stress is on the first syllable, the final consonant is not doubled, e.g. *offer* > offered, *threaten* > threatened.

**c** Complete the sentences below with the correct reporting verb in the past tense.

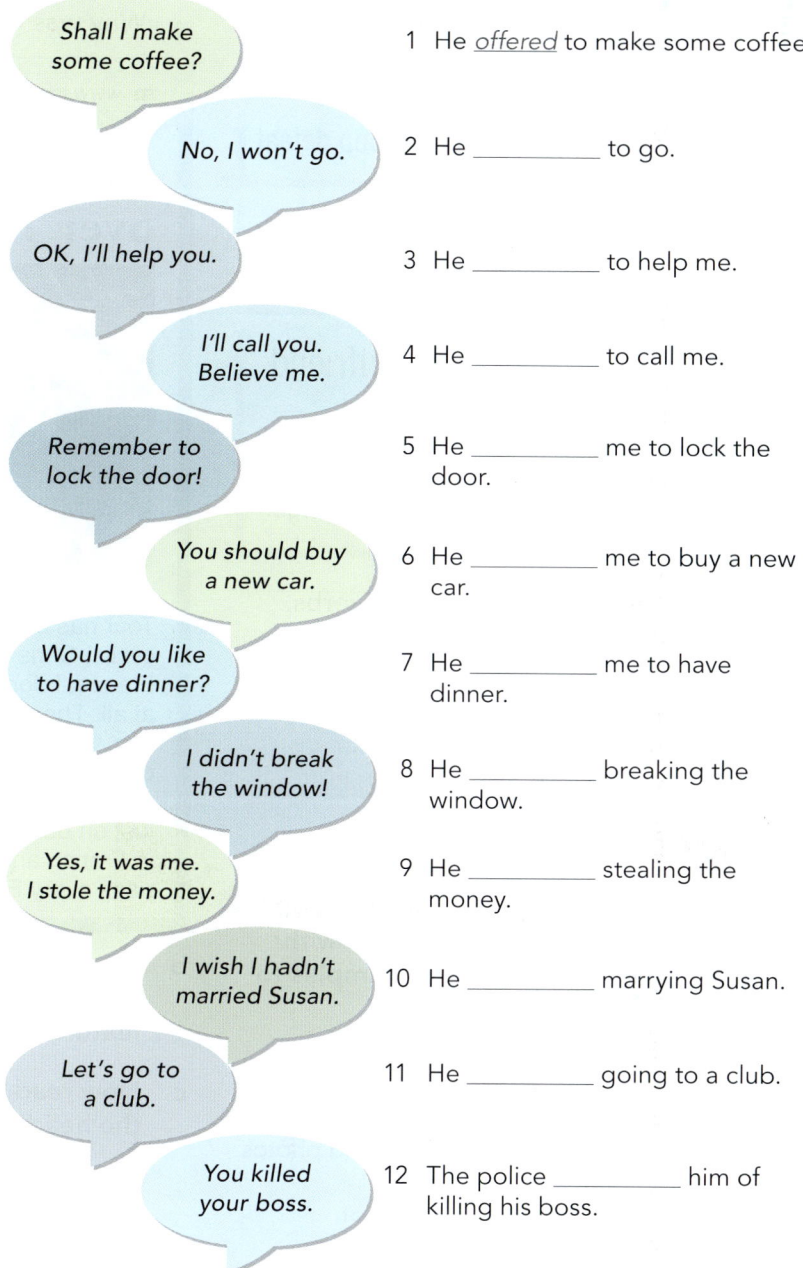

1 He *offered* to make some coffee.
2 He _____ to go.
3 He _____ to help me.
4 He _____ to call me.
5 He _____ me to lock the door.
6 He _____ me to buy a new car.
7 He _____ me to have dinner.
8 He _____ breaking the window.
9 He _____ stealing the money.
10 He _____ marrying Susan.
11 He _____ going to a club.
12 The police _____ him of killing his boss.

**d** ◀) 8.14 Listen and check.

**e** Cover the right-hand column in **c**. Look at the direct speech and say the reported sentence, linking the verbs and *to* where appropriate.

> 🔍 **Linking**
> Remember that if a word ends in a /t/ or /d/ sound, e.g. regular past tense verbs, and the next word begins with a /d/ or /t/ sound, the two words are linked, e.g. offered‿to.

**f** ◀) 8.15 Listen to some more sentences in direct speech. Then report them using the verb you hear.

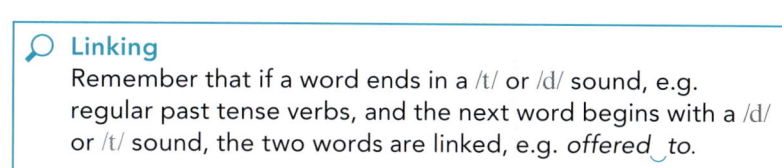

1 ◀)) *I didn't steal the wallet!* **deny** ( *He denied stealing the wallet.*

## 4 VOCABULARY & SPEAKING
the media

**a** Look at the four headlines. What four categories of news are they?

1. Manager **quits** following shock Cup defeat

2. 21-year-old **tipped** to become party leader

3. Reality TV star **to wed** girlfriend after one-week engagement

4. Companies **split** after unsuccessful merger

**b** Guess the meaning of the **bold** verbs. Then match them to a word or phrase from the list.

| | |
|---|---|
| is going to marry ☐ | is predicted ☐ |
| leaves ☐ | separate ☐ |

**c** **ⓥ p.161 Vocabulary Bank** The media

**d** Look at the questions below. Decide if you personally agree or disagree with them. Think of reasons and examples to support your opinion.

**Is it ever OK...?**
- for journalists to access other people's phones or email accounts
- for the media to publish stories and photos about celebrities' private lives
- for the paparazzi to take photos of well-known people when they are at home or on holiday
- to censor the news
- to publish news articles that aren't completely true

*I think it's perfectly OK for / to...*

*I think it can be OK for / to..., depending on the circumstances.*

*I don't think it's ever OK for / to...because...*

**e** Work in small groups. Take turns to ask one question. Give your opinion and explain why. Then discuss with the group. What is the majority opinion on each topic?

## 5 READING

**a** Read a news report about the Tour de France cycle race. Why was Chris Froome said to be disappointed?

www.thedailymash.co.uk/sport

### Competitors' disappointment over Tour de France route

CYCLISTS have begun to complain that their enjoyment of the Tour has been spoiled by periods of intense uphill cycling. British cyclist Chris Froome said, 'Even though it's called the Tour de France, I don't feel like I'm getting to experience the real France at all. The organizers have planned a route that goes right through some of the hilliest parts of the country, when there are much quicker flat roads we could use. I was hoping we could stop off at a vineyard, or have lunch at an authentic local brasserie, but we're just on our bikes all day. I spent six months doing night courses in French and have barely been able to speak a word, because I pass every French person I meet at 30 mph.'

**b** Read the article again. At what point did you realize that this is not a serious piece of news? Are there any other features of the article that made you suspicious?

**c** Now read an article about how to spot fake news. Complete the headings with a word from the list.

addresses   date   fake   images   name   sense   spellings   trust

**d** Read the article again and answer the questions about each section.

Introduction  Why do many online sites publish fake news?
1  Why don't you need to worry about a Category Six hurricane?
2  What was suspicious about the story in the *Denver Guardian*?
3  What was the problem with the URL *ABC.com.co*?
4  What was wrong with the photos of a news report about a terror attack in Brussels?
5  Why does a lot of spelling mistakes in a news article mean that it might be fake?
6  How would you know that the Twitter handle @WarrenBuffet was fake?
7  Why might an emotionally disturbing image with a news story be a telltale sign?
8  What should you do before making an important decision based on online information?

# 8 tips on how to spot fake news

Fake content has become a daily reality of life online, with hundreds of sites creating false or exaggerated stories for political or personal gain. In spite of the efforts of big tech companies to limit the spread of fake news, some stories fall through the cracks. The expert advice is that it's always useful to have a critical eye and to be on the lookout for misleading stories. There are several telltale signs to look for. Fake news experts Will Moy, director of British fact-checking charity Full Fact, and Cambridge University researcher Sander van der Linden offer their tips.

### 1 Beware of stories that don't make _____

One of the key signs of fake news is that the stories are highly improbable. During last year's Hurricane Irma, a hugely popular viral story claimed that it was a Category Six hurricane that would 'wipe cities off the map'. Category Six hurricanes do not exist. Moy says, 'Extraordinary claims need extraordinary evidence. If somebody says Elvis is alive, ask for a song before you believe it.'

### 2 Check the _____ of the news site that published it

Unfamiliar sites built to sound like news organizations are behind many fake news stories, but the names of the sites are often a hint that stories may be fake. When the *Denver Guardian* made claims about Hillary Clinton's emails, there was one small problem – there is no such paper as the *Denver Guardian*. It sounds real, but it is completely fake. 'Be careful of websites that you haven't heard of before,' says Moy.

### 3 Beware faked website _____

Some sites may try to impersonate real news outlets with URLs which seem similar but have slight differences. For instance, one fake news site impersonated ABC news using a URL which read *ABC.com.co*, rather than *abcnews.go.com*.

### 4 Check the _____

False news stories often include timelines which make no sense, or contain the wrong dates. For instance, images purporting to be of a 2016 terror attack in Brussels were actually from a 2011 attack on Moscow's Domodedovo Airport.

### 5 Look for unusual _____ and mistakes

Often, the sign that news is fake is that it is of low quality, with spelling errors and an over-use of capital letters. Real news sources will employ editors to remove these errors and ensure accuracy.

### 6 Look out for _____ celebrity accounts

'Sometimes stories can spread online after being shared by a social media account designed to impersonate a real person,' says Sander van der Linden. 'Think about the fake tweets that were supposedly sent out by billionaire Warren Buffett. Someone was impersonating him, and millions of people did not notice that the Twitter handle read 'WarrenBuffet', while his real name is Warren Buffett.'

### 7 Google-search the _____

Fake news sites will often use unrelated or doctored photos. Google-search them to see where they came from and check how accurate they are against other legitimate news sites. Other hoaxers will use deliberately disturbing imagery in an attempt to hook in readers, van der Linden says. 'Emotional content is more likely to go viral, for example, imagine the effect of a fake story containing disturbing images about the effects of a fake disease.'

### 8 If you're unsure, double check with a source you _____

Fake news stories will often appear on just one site, so if you're unsure, check against a reliable news source. 'When it matters, double check,' says Moy, 'particularly when it comes to health or other life decisions. Always use a trustworthy source.'

Adapted from The Telegraph

---

**e** Can you remember these adjectives from the text for…?

1 something you shouldn't believe:
exa_____, mis_____, impr_____, doc_____

2 something you should believe:
leg_____, rel_____, tru_____

**f** Which news websites do you think are a) reputable, b) untrustworthy? Can you think of any examples of exaggerated or fake news?

## 6 ▶ VIDEO LISTENING

**a** Watch the documentary *The speed of news* once. Number the ways of delivering news in the order they are mentioned.

- [ ] cable TV
- [ ] Facebook
- [ ] live Twitter feeds
- [ ] radio and television
- [ ] the Boston newsletter
- [ ] the telegraph line

**b** Watch the documentary again and answer the questions.

1 Where is the Newseum? How many different newspapers are there?
2 Who was Edward Teach? When was he killed?
3 How were early newspapers distributed? Why was this a problem?
4 How was news communicated during the American Civil War?
5 Why were Civil War news reports not very accurate?
6 Which inventions created the age of mass media?
7 What event appeared on Twitter seconds after it occurred?

**c** Are there any newspapers or magazines in your country that have existed for a long time? What reputation do they have nowadays? Do you ever read them?

---

🔍 **Go online** to watch the video and review the lesson

## GRAMMAR

Complete the second sentence so that it means the same as the first.

1 I'm almost sure you left your phone in the restaurant.
You _____ _____ _____ your phone in the restaurant.

2 It was wrong of you not to tell me you'd borrowed my car.
You _____ _____ _____ me you'd borrowed my car.

3 It's possible that the backpackers got lost.
The backpackers _____ _____ _____ lost.

4 I'm sure it wasn't Jake's fault. He wasn't there last night.
It _____ _____ _____ Jake's fault. He wasn't there last night.

5 I think somebody has tried to break in.
It looks _____ _____ somebody has tried to break in.

6 This meat has a very similar taste to beef.
This meat _____ _____ beef.

7 I don't like cooking fish because then there's an awful smell in the kitchen.
I don't like cooking fish because then the kitchen _____ _____.

8 The accident happened when they were repairing the road.
The accident happened when the road _____ _____ _____.

9 They'll probably never find the murderer.
The murderer will probably _____ _____ _____.

10 People think the burglar is a teenager.
The burglar is thought _____ _____ a teenager.

11 People say that crime doesn't pay.
It _____ _____ that crime doesn't pay.

12 We want someone to fix the shower.
We need to have _____ _____ _____.

13 'I think you should talk to a lawyer,' I said to Sarah.
I advised Sarah _____ _____ to a lawyer.

14 'I didn't kill my husband,' Margaret said.
Margaret denied _____ _____ _____.

15 'I'm sorry I'm late,' James said.
James _____ _____ _____ late.

## VOCABULARY

a Circle the correct verb.

1 Please *remind / remember* the children to do their homework.
2 A I'm terribly sorry.
   B Don't worry. It doesn't *mind / matter*.
3 The robbers *stole / robbed* €50,000 from the bank.
4 If you know the answer, *raise / rise* your hand, don't shout.
5 Don't *discuss / argue* about it! You know that I'm right.
6 My brother *refuses / denies* to admit that he has a problem.

b Circle the word that is different.

1 palm    calf    wrist    thumb
2 kidney    lung    hip    liver
3 wink    wave    hold    touch
4 robber    vandal    burglar    pickpocket
5 fraud    smuggler    theft    terrorism
6 evidence    judge    jury    witness

c Write the verbs for the definitions.

1 _____ to bite food into small pieces in your mouth
2 _____ to rub your skin with your nails
3 _____ to look at sth or sb for a long time
4 _____ to make a serious, angry, or worried expression
5 _____ to find a way of entering sb's computer
6 _____ to demand money from sb by threatening to tell a secret about them
7 _____ to give sb money so that they help you (especially if it's dishonest)
8 _____ to leave your job (especially in newspaper headlines)

d Complete the missing words.

1 The *Sunday Times* TV cr_____ wrote a very negative review of the programme.
2 This paper always supports the government. It's very b_____.
3 The journalist's report was c_____ by the newspaper. They cut some of the things he had wanted to say because of government rules.
4 My favourite n_____ is the woman on the six o'clock news on BBC1.
5 The article in the newspaper wasn't very acc_____ – a lot of the facts were completely wrong.

## PRONUNCIATION

**a** Circle the word with a different sound.

| | | | | | |
|---|---|---|---|---|---|
| 1 | aʊ | elb**ow** | fr**ow**n | eyebr**ow**s | v**ow** |
| 2 | h | **h**onest | **h**eart | **h**ip | **h**ack |
| 3 | ɔː | fr**au**d | c**au**ght | w**ar**n | j**ou**rnalist |
| 4 | ʌ | l**u**ngs | t**ou**ch | sh**ou**lder | sm**u**ggle |
| 5 | /juː/ | arg**ue** | ref**u**se | n**ew**s | j**u**ry |

**b** Underline the main stressed syllable.

1 re|a|lize     3 van|da|lism     5 ob|jec|tive
2 black|mail     4 co|mmen|ta|tor

## CAN YOU understand this text?

**a** Read the article once. What is a *web sleuth*?

**b** Read the article again and complete it with phrases A–F.

A any information is obviously welcome
B are fascinated with crime and missing persons
C there's still a debate about whether amateur sleuthing is good or bad
D the police have come to the site for help
E these instances aren't very common
F she never looked back

## ▶ CAN YOU understand these people?

🔊 **8.19** Watch or listen and choose a, b, or c.

| 1 | 2 | 3 | 4 |
|---|---|---|---|
| Melanie | Erica | Hugo | Diarmuid |

1 Melanie ____.
 a argues with her sister about housework
 b always wins arguments with her sister
 c hates arguing with her sister
2 When Erica acted in the play *A Woman's Worth* she ____.
 a felt nervous because her family were in the audience
 b played a woman who was afraid of marriage
 c played a woman who had problems with her boyfriend
3 Hugo witnessed a crime where the criminal ____.
 a was arrested
 b escaped
 c was injured
4 Diarmuid ____.
 a is sceptical about what he reads in the news
 b gets his news mainly from newspaper apps
 c is only really interested in sports news

## Solving crimes from the bedroom

**It seems that people are starting to take the law into their own hands. Is it time for the police to take web sleuths seriously?**

Ella Hamilton, a 23-year-old from Scotland, is part of a not-so-small community of citizen-detectives who ¹____. They look through all the clues, police reports and online tips to uncover what the police may have missed. Ella discovered the world of sleuthing after watching a documentary about unsolved mysteries. She was keen to discuss it with other people, and after finding an online forum, ²____. Ella says that most citizen detectives are valuable assets, providing the police with ideas they might not have thought of. 'I've watched hundreds of videos, trying to spot people in the background. It feels good to help.'

Tricia Arrington-Griffith owns the website WebSleuths. She can recall many times that ³____. 'In 2014, a detective came to us with a piece of evidence, a particular T-shirt, from an unsolved murder. Within 36 hours, one of our members had found out exactly where the T-shirt was made, how much it cost, and where it was sold.' Tricia says that the police were incredibly grateful on this occasion, but she admits that ⁴____. She believes that the police mainly view citizen-detectives as troublemakers. 'And we have had other problems,' she admits. 'WebSleuths was my first introduction to unpleasant behaviour online.'

So what do the police really think? Stewart Smith, an ex-Crime Prevention Officer, says, 'I personally feel that the work many of these sleuths do is fantastic. Police resources are limited, so ⁵____.' But sleuths must be 'careful and considerate in their investigations, especially towards family members'. Family members just like Karen Downes. Her daughter, Charlene, disappeared over 14 years ago in Blackpool, and there's been no trace of her since, but hundreds of people are still trying to solve the mystery online. Karen is delighted with the helpful and respectful amateur sleuths, but her husband Bob disagrees. Claims that he killed his own daughter were posted all over the internet by citizen-detectives; he was even physically attacked on the street, and this is not unusual behaviour. So ⁶____. It's clearly a fascinating hobby, but all citizen-detectives need to make sure they are familiar with the law and behave appropriately.

*Adapted from a university website*

🔍 **Go online** to watch the video, review Files 7 & 8, and check your progress

> Many a small thing has been made large by the right kind of advertising.
> *Mark Twain, US author*

## 1 VOCABULARY & SPEAKING

**a** Look at the advert for Red Bull. Do you think it's a clever advert? Why do you think it might have got Red Bull into trouble?

## Advertising scandals that cost some brands millions

In advertising, there's a big difference between exaggerating the truth and making false **claims**.

Many companies have been caught using **misleading** claims like 'scientifically proven' with 'guaranteed results' in their **advertisements**. For such companies, it can cost millions, and lead to a damaged reputation.

Several examples of false advertising scandals have affected big **brands** – some are still ongoing, and not all companies have had to pay up, but each suffered a certain amount of negative **publicity**.

### Red Bull

Energy drinks company Red Bull **was sued** in 2014 for its **slogan** 'Red Bull gives you wings'. The slogan, which the company has used in **advertising campaigns** for nearly two decades, went alongside marketing claims that the caffeinated drink could improve a consumer's concentration and reaction speed.

Benjamin Careathers was one of several **consumers** who brought the case against the Austrian drinks company. He said he had been a regular consumer of Red Bull for 10 years, but that he had not developed wings – or shown any signs of improved intellectual or physical abilities.

The company settled the case by agreeing to pay out a maximum of $13 million – including $10 to every US consumer who had bought the drink since 2002.

*Adapted from Business Insider*

**b** Read the article and check your answers to **a**. Why do you think Benjamin Careathers did what he did?

**c** Look at the **highlighted** words and phrases related to advertising. With a partner, try to work out what they mean. Then match them to their meanings 1–9.

1 *advertisements* (also *ads*, *adverts*) notices, pictures, or films telling people about a product

2 _____ (*noun*) statements that sth is true, although it has not been proved and other people may not agree with or believe it

3 _____ (*noun*) types of product made by a particular company

4 _____ (*verb*) was taken to court to ask for money because of sth they said or did that harmed you

5 _____ (*adj.*) giving the wrong idea or impression, making you believe sth that is not true

6 _____ (*noun*) people who buy goods or use services

7 _____ (*noun*) series of advertising messages with the same theme

8 _____ (*noun*) the attention that is given to sb / sth by newspapers, television, etc.

9 _____ (*noun*) a word or phrase used in advertising that is easy to remember, to attract people's attention or to suggest an idea quickly

**d** Work in threes, **A**, **B**, and **C**. Look at three products whose adverts cost their brands money. What problems do you think there were with the adverts?

e **C Communication** Misleading ads **A** p.110 **B** p.112 **C** p.113
Read about the advertisements and tell each other what the problem was.

f Talk in groups of three. Give examples.

1 Have you bought something recently which wasn't as good as the advertisement made you think it would be? How was the advert misleading?
2 What are viral adverts? Have you ever forwarded one to other people? Do you have a favourite one?
3 Is there a brand which you think has a really good logo or slogan? Does it make you want to buy the product?
4 Can you think of a recent advert which made you <u>not</u> want to ever buy the product? Why did the advert have this effect on you?
5 Do you find pop-up adverts annoying when you are doing something online? Do you think they are necessary? Why is it that they often seem directed at you personally?
6 Do you think it's immoral of advertisers to try to persuade people without much money to buy products they can't afford?

## 2 LISTENING

a **9.1** Listen to a marketing expert talking about six marketing techniques used by advertisers. Complete the messages they use with two or three words.

1 'Get a _____ when you subscribe to our magazine for six months.'
2 'There are _____ left! Buy now while stocks last!'
3 '_____ it.'
4 '_____ can look like this.'
5 'A recent _____ found that our toothpaste cleans your teeth better than any other brand.'
6 '_____, I'm a doctor (or a celebrity).'

b Listen again. Answer the questions for each message in **a**.

1 Why does it attract us?
2 Why is it misleading?

c Which of the six techniques might influence you to buy the product? Are there any that would actively discourage you? Why do you think we keep falling for these techniques, even though we know what's going on?

OLAY DEFINITY

Because younger-looking eyes never go out of fashion

"Olay is my secret to brighter-looking eyes"

Olay Definity eye illuminator.
Reduces the look of wrinkles and dark circles for brighter, younger-looking eyes.

## 3 GRAMMAR clauses of contrast and purpose

a Look at some extracts from the listening in **2**, and complete them with phrases A–G.

1 In spite of _____, its price was really included in the magazine subscription.
2 Even though _____, and maybe don't even like them, we immediately want to be among the lucky few who have them.
3 So as to _____, they use expressions like, 'It's a must-have'…
4 …and they combine this with a photograph of a large group of people, so that _____.
5 The photo has been airbrushed in order to _____, with perfect skin, and even more attractive than they are in real life.
6 It was probably produced for _____, and paid for by them, too.
7 Although _____, do you really think she colours her hair with it at home?

A the company itself
B the actress is holding the product in the photo
C we can't fail to get the message
D make us believe it
E we don't really need the products
F what the advert said
G make the model look even slimmer

b **9.2** Listen and check. Then look at the highlighted word(s) in 1–7 and the phrases A–G that follow them. Which ones express a purpose?

c **G** p.148 **Grammar Bank 9A**

d **Sentence race** Try to complete as many sentences as you can in two minutes.

1 I think the advertising of junk food should be banned, so that…
2 In spite of a huge marketing campaign,…
3 Although they have banned cigarette advertising,…
4 She applied for a job with a company in London, so as to…
5 He's decided to carry on working, despite…
6 Even though the advert said I would notice the effects after a week,…
7 I took my laptop to the shop to…
8 We went to our head office in New York for…

87

## 4 READING

**a** Look at the products in the photos. Can you think of anything they have in common?

A

B

C

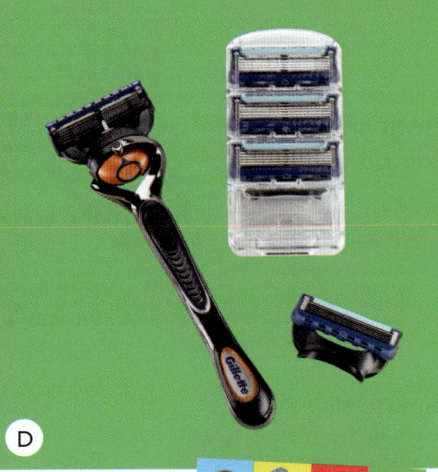
D

**b** Read the first part of 'Razors and Blades', an unadapted chapter from a book by economist Tim Harford. As you read, in order to quickly check any words or phrases that you can't guess, first, try to guess meaning from context, then use the glossary, and finally, if necessary, use a dictionary. Check your answer to **a**.

FIFTY THINGS THAT MADE THE MODERN ECONOMY
'Every Tim Harford book is cause for celebration' MALCOLM GLADWELL
**Tim Harford**
AUTHOR OF THE UNDERCOVER ECONOMIST

**c** Read it again and mark the sentences **T** (true) or **F** (false). Underline the information in the text which tells you this.

1 King Camp Gillette's idea behind the United Company was that it would provide basic products cheaply.
2 This vision of the United Company had a great influence on the modern economy.
3 It is more expensive to produce a printer than to produce the ink.
4 Two-part pricing involves selling one thing cheaply, but making another essential component very expensive.
5 King Camp Gillette's first blades were relatively inexpensive.
6 Sony only makes a very small profit on each PlayStation 4 it sells.

# RAZORS & BLADES
## Part 1

In 1894, a book was written by a man who had a vision. The book argues that 'our present system of competition' breeds 'extravagance, poverty, and crime'. It advocates a new system of 'equality, virtue, and happiness', in which just one corporation – the United Company – will make all of life's necessities as cost-effectively as possible. These, by the way, are 'food, clothing, and habitation'. Industries which 'do not contribute' to life's necessities will be destroyed. The book's author had a vision that has ended up shaping the economy. But, as you may have guessed, it wasn't this particular vision. No, it was another idea, which he had a year later. His name was King Camp Gillette, and he invented the disposable razor blade.

If you've ever bought replacement cartridges for an inkjet printer, you are likely to have been annoyed to discover that they cost almost as much as you paid for the printer itself. That seems to make no sense. The printer's a reasonably large and complicated piece of technology. But how can it possibly cost almost as much to supply a bit of ink in tiny plastic pots? The answer, of course, is that it doesn't. But for a manufacturer, selling the printer cheaply and the ink expensively is a business model that makes sense, and is known as two-part pricing. It's also known as the razor-and-blades model, because that's where it first drew attention – suck people in with an attractively priced razor, then repeatedly fleece them for extortionately priced replacement blades.

King Camp Gillette invented the blades that made it possible. Before this, razors were bigger, and when the blade got dull, you'd sharpen it, not throw it away and buy another. He didn't immediately hit upon the two-part pricing model, though: initially, he made both parts expensive. The model of cheap razors and expensive blades evolved only later. Nowadays, two-part pricing is everywhere. Consider the PlayStation 4. Whenever Sony sells one, it loses money: the retail price is less than it costs to manufacture and distribute. But that's okay, because Sony coins it in whenever a PlayStation 4 owner buys a game. Or how about Nespresso? Nestle makes its money not from the machine, but the coffee pods.

### Glossary

**suck sb in** (*phr. verb*) to involve somebody in an activity or a situation, especially one they do not want to be involved in

**fleece** (*verb, informal*) to take a lot of money from somebody by charging them too much

**hit upon** (*phr. verb*) think of a good idea suddenly or by chance

**coin it (in)** (*idiom*) make a lot of money

*From Fifty Things that Made the Modern Economy*

**d** Now read the rest of the chapter. Answer the questions with a partner.

1 How are companies which have been successful with two-part pricing products trying to stop other companies selling the disposable parts cheaper?

2 Why might customers stay with a more expensive original brand?

3 What does the author suggest that King Camp Gillette might have thought of the razor-and-blades sales model?

## Part 2

Obviously, for this model to work you need some way to ¹_____ customers putting cheap, generic blades in your razor. One solution is legal: patent-protect your blades. But patents don't last forever. Patents on coffee pods have started expiring, so brands like Nespresso now face competitors selling ²_____, compatible alternatives. Some are looking for another kind of solution: technological. Just as other people's games don't work on the PlayStation, some coffee companies have put chip readers in their machines to stop you trying to brew a generic cup of coffee.

Two-part pricing models work by imposing what economists call 'switching costs'. They're especially prevalent with digital goods. If you have a huge library of games for your PlayStation, or books for your Kindle, it's a big thing to switch to another platform. Switching costs don't have to be ³_____. They can come in the form of time, or hassle. Say I'm already familiar with Photoshop; I might prefer to pay for an expensive upgrade ⁴_____ buy a cheaper alternative, which I'd then have to learn how to use. Switching costs can be psychological, too – a result of brand loyalty. If the Gillette company's marketing department persuades me that generic blades give ⁵_____ shave, then I'll happily keep paying extra for Gillette-branded blades.

Economists have puzzled over why consumers ⁶_____ the two-part pricing model. The most plausible explanation is that they get confused by the two-part pricing. Either they don't realize that they'll be exploited later, or they do realize, but find it hard to pick the best deal out of a ⁷_____ menu of options. The irony is that the cynical razors-and-blades model – charging customers a premium for basics like ink and coffee – is about as far as you can get from King Camp Gillette's vision of a single United Company producing life's necessities as cheaply as possible.

### Glossary

**patent** (*noun*) an official right to be the only person to make, use, or sell a product or invention

**chip reader** (*noun*) a device to get information from a microchip

**switching costs** (*noun phrase, idiom*) how much it will cost you to change from one brand to another

**hassle** (*noun, informal*) a situation that is annoying because it involves doing something difficult or complicated that needs a lot of effort

**puzzle over** (*phr. verb*) to think hard about something in order to understand or explain it

**e** Read it again and choose the correct word or phrase for each gap.

1 a avoid    b encourage    c prevent
2 a cheaper    b pricier    c more expensive
3 a economical    b inevitable    c financial
4 a as well as    b rather than    c in order to
5 a an inferior    b a superior    c a similar
6 a tolerate    b reject    c like
7 a simple    b straightforward    c confusing

**f** Do you own any products which use a two-part pricing system? Do you buy generic ink, coffee, etc. or do you buy the branded ones? Why?

## 5 VOCABULARY business

**a** Look at two extracts from 'Razors and Blades'. Which two verbs mean 'to make things in large quantities'? Which one is specifically 'using machinery'?

> Consider the PlayStation 4. Whenever Sony sells one, it loses money: the retail price is less than it costs to manufacture and distribute.

> … King Camp Gillette's vision of a single United Company producing life's necessities as cheaply as possible.

**b** 🅥 p.162 **Vocabulary Bank** Business

## 6 PRONUNCIATION & SPEAKING changing stress on nouns and verbs

**a** 🔊 9.8 Listen and underline the stress on the **bold** words. Which syllable is stressed when the word is a) a verb, b) a noun?

1 We **ex|port** to customers all over the world.
2 Our main **ex|port** is wine.
3 Sales have **in|creased** by 10% this month.
4 There has been a large **in|crease** in profits this year.
5 The new building is **pro|gre|ssing** well.
6 We're making good **pro|gress** with the report.
7 Most toys nowadays are **pro|duced** in China.
8 The demand for organic **pro|duce** has grown enormously.

**b** Look at some more words which can also be verbs and nouns, and have the same pronunciation rule. Practise saying them first all as verbs and then as nouns.

| decrease | import | permit | record | refund | transport |
|---|---|---|---|---|---|

**c** Say if the following are true of your country / region, or of you. Give examples.

We export more food than we import.
Not many shops sell organic produce.
Unemployment has decreased over the last five years.
Smoking is not permitted in public places.

Go online to review the lesson

> The city is not a concrete jungle, it is a human zoo.
> *Desmond Morris, UK zoologist*

## WHAT MAKES A CITY ATTRACTIVE?

Is there an 'art of making attractive cities'? Alain de Botton, writer and founder of alternative education group *The School of Life*, seems to think so, and has made a video that he claims explains just how to do it. 'It's not a mystery why we like some cities so much better than others,' he says. 'There are six fundamental things a city needs to get right.'

**Order and variety**
A love of order is one of the reasons people love Paris and New York, but we must avoid too much of it. The key is to create an 'organized complexity'. De Botton gives the example of the square in Telč, Czech Republic, where the individual houses are different in colour and detail, but all the buildings are the same height and width.

**Visible life**
Streets need to be full of people and activity in order to be beautiful instead of bleak. Sadly, modern cities often contain too many characterless office blocks and industrial zones where there is no street life.

**Compactness**
Good cities are compact, not sprawling. Think Barcelona as opposed to a spread-out city like Phoenix, Arizona. De Botton says that attractive cities have beautiful squares which are ideal meeting places. The best designed are those which are not too large, so that people can recognize a face on the other side of the square.

**Orientation and mystery**
The best cities offer a mixture of big and small streets. But too many cities prioritize vehicles over humans. A city should be easy to navigate for both humans and vehicles, with big boulevards for orientation and small streets to allow us to wander and create a sense of mystery and exploration.

**Scale**
Our urban skylines have become dominated by tall buildings dedicated to banking and commerce. Instead, we should be building at an ideal height of five stories, resulting in dense and medium-rise cities, like Berlin and Amsterdam.

**Local colour**
The sameness of cities is a problem. Cities need to demonstrate their local culture and history. They should be built from locally sourced materials in a way which suits their individual climate and traditions.

*Adapted from The Guardian*

## 1 READING

a Look at the title of the article. How attractive do you think the city where you live (or your nearest city) is? What score would you give it out of 10?

b Read the article once. With a partner, explain what the six criteria mean. Do you agree with any of them? Does your city meet any of them?

c Can you think of any things that Alain de Botton hasn't mentioned? Make a note of them. Then talk in small groups, and make a group list.

> *For me, one thing that's missing is water. I think the most beautiful cities always have a river running through them, or are near the sea.*

## 2 LISTENING & SPEAKING

a 🔊 9.9 You're going to listen to five well-travelled people talking about the most beautiful city they've been to. Look at the countries. Which city do you think they're going to say? Listen to their first sentences and check.

1 _____, Italy     4 _____, Scotland
2 _____, Brazil    5 _____, Japan
3 _____, Belgium

b 🔊 9.10 Listen and try to write the names of some places in these cities that they're going to mention. Compare in pairs and agree the spelling.

Piazza _____ _____
the _____ Bridge
the _____ Canal
the _____ Opera House
the Bosque _____
the _____ Steps
the River _____
the _____ Temple

c 🔊 9.11 Now look at photos 1–5 and listen to what the speakers say about each city. What is the place in the photo? Is it something to see or something to do? What information do they give about it?

d Listen again. What other thing(s) does each speaker recommend? Did they mention any of Alain de Botton's six criteria?

**e** Did they mention anything from your group's list in **1c**?

**f** Talk in small groups.

1 Have you been to any of the cities the speakers mention? Do you agree with what they say? Of those you haven't visited, which one would you most like to go to? Why?

2 What's the most beautiful city you've ever been to? What's one thing you would recommend to see and do there?

3 Are there any cities you haven't really liked? Why?

**3 GRAMMAR** uncountable and plural nouns

**a** Circle the correct form.

1 A good city guidebook will give you *advice / advices* about what to see.

2 You may have *some bad weather / a bad weather* if you go to London in March.

3 In Rome and Paris, *accommodation is / accommodations are* extremely expensive.

4 It's best not to take *too much luggage / too many luggages* if you go on a city break.

5 The old town centre is amazing, but *the outskirts is / the outskirts are* a bit depressing.

6 I really liked the hotel. The rooms were beautiful and *the staff was / the staff were* incredibly friendly.

**b** Ⓖ p.149 Grammar Bank 9B

**c** Play **Just a minute** in small groups.

# JUST A MINUTE

> **RULES**
>
> One person starts. He / She has to try to talk for a minute about the first subject below.
>
> If he or she hesitates for more than five seconds, he / she loses his / her turn and the next student continues.
>
> The person who is talking when one minute is up gets a point.

the most beautiful scenery I've seen

the traffic in my town / city

tourist accommodation in my country

the weather I like most

good advice I've been given

what's in the news at the moment

clothes I love wearing

modern furniture

chocolate

## 4 READING & SPEAKING

**a** Look at this photo of Songdo, a new city in South Korea. What do you think might be the advantages or disadvantages of living there?

**b** Now read an article about Songdo. Answer the questions with a partner.

1  What are the three main advantages of living in Songdo?
2  Which two things that were promised haven't happened yet?
3  What other disadvantages are mentioned?

**c** Read the article again. For each of the highlighted words and phrases, choose the best meaning, a or b.

1  a  advantages    b  disadvantages
2  a  break its promise    b  keep its promise
3  a  leaving home    b  going home
4  a  not enough    b  too much
5  a  very advanced    b  very simple
6  a  be different from    b  be similar to
7  a  overpopulated    b  underpopulated
8  a  close together    b  spread out

**d** Talk to a partner.

1  If you went to live in Songdo, what would you like best and what would you miss the most?
2  What's the most modern city you've ever been to? Why did you go there? What did you think of it?
3  If you had to choose between an ultra-modern megacity and a classically beautiful old city, which would you prefer?
4  What is the approximate population of your city or nearest big city? Do you think it will grow? What effect might the change in population have on the city and its services?

# Is this the future

Three years ago, 35-year-old English teacher Lee Mi-Jung moved with her husband from the small coastal city of Pohang across the South Korean peninsula to Songdo. Described as the world's 'smartest city', it was planned as a showpiece of 21st-century urban design, promising an efficient rubbish system, an abundance of parks, and a vibrant international community – all the [1] perks of megacity Seoul without the capital city's crowded pavements, choking traffic, and air pollution. The city claimed to do 'nothing less than banish the problems created by modern urban life.' And for foreign corporations looking for access to Asian economies, Songdo would be a glitzy business capital to rival Hong Kong and Shanghai. 'I'd imagined this would be a well-designed city, that it would be new, modernized, and simple –unlike other cities,' says Lee. 'So my expectations were high.'

As far as hi-tech conveniences go, Songdo does [2] deliver. Pneumatic tubes send rubbish straight from Lee's home to an underground waste facility, where it's sorted, recycled, or burned for energy generation. Everything, from the lights, to the temperature in her apartment, can be adjusted via a central control panel, or from her phone. During the winter, she can warm up the apartment before [3] heading home. But the one thing she hasn't been able to find is a vibrant community.

'When I first came here during the winter,' Lee says, 'I felt something cold.' She wasn't just talking about the coldness of the weather, or the chilly modernism of the concrete high rises all over town. She felt [4] a lack of human warmth from neighbourhood interaction. 'There's an online forum where we share our complaints,' she said, 'But only on the internet – not face to face.'

Songdo was built on reclaimed land from the Yellow Sea. The 1,500-acre development sits an hour outside of Seoul. It was planned as an eco-city. Its buildings and streets have sensors that monitor energy use and traffic flow. There's a [5] state-of-the-art water-recycling facility and plenty of green spaces, including a 100-acre seaside park modelled on, and named after, New York City's Central Park.

# of cities?

For a place that is striving to become car-free, however, the roads of Songdo are crazily wide, with as many as ten lanes. These are partly intended to ⁶echo the wide, tree-lined boulevards of Paris, and also wide enough for city planners to, say, put in a light rail or streetcar network, which may bring Songdo one step closer to fulfilling its car-free promise. But for now, cars are still common, and, for residents like 32-year-old Lindy Wenselaers from Belgium, they're an essential tool. Lindy ended up buying a car after only five months in Songdo – she could no longer face a 20-minute walk to the nearest supermarket in the wintry weather. She misses the lack of direct connections from one part of town to another; at weekends, she often drives an hour to Seoul.

Songdo's biggest problem is that it only has a third of the people it was designed for. Parts of it feel more like a ⁷sparsely populated American 1970s suburb. The wide roads and ⁸sprawling scale means that human activities are located far apart from one another. Occasionally, you see small touches, like an artificial *hanok* village (a traditional village where houses with old-school architecture remain intact) to remind you that, yes, you are still in Korea. It's not exactly a ghost town, as some reports have claimed, but as you drive past cluster after cluster of identical concrete residential high-rises, it feels empty, and there's a curious urban silence. 'There's a ton of people living here, but you don't really see them,' says Wenselaers. 'The city is alive, but it's invisible.'

*Adapted from the CityLab website*

## 5 VOCABULARY word building: prefixes and suffixes

> **🔍 Prefixes and suffixes**
>
> A **prefix** is something that you add to the beginning of a word, usually to change its meaning, e.g. *pre* = before (**pre**-*war*), or a negative prefix like *un-* or *dis-* (**un**healthy, **dis**honest). A **suffix** is something you add to the end of a word, usually to change its grammatical form, e.g. -*ment* and -*ness* are typical noun suffixes (enjoy**ment**, happi**ness**). However, some suffixes also add meaning to a word, e.g. -*ful* = full of (stress**ful**, beauti**ful**).

a  Answer the questions. Check your answers in the article in **4**.

  1  What prefix can you put before *city* to add the meaning a) *enormous*, b) *environmentally friendly*?
  2  Add suffixes to the words in the list to make nouns.

  abundant   cold   connect   convenient   develop
  expect   modern   neighbour   pollute   silent

b  **Ⓥ p.163 Vocabulary Bank** Word building

## 6 PRONUNCIATION & SPEAKING word stress with prefixes and suffixes

> **🔍 Word stress on words with prefixes and suffixes**
>
> Multi-syllable words always have a main stressed syllable. This usually remains the main stress even when we add a prefix or suffix – the exception is -*ation*. However, there is usually secondary stress on prefixes, e.g. *un-* in un**em**ployment.

a  Under<u>line</u> the main stressed syllable in these words.

  a|cco|mmo|da|tion   an|ti|so|cial   bi|ling|ual   en|ter|tain|ment
  go|vern|ment   home|less   lone|li|ness   mul|ti|cul|tu|ral
  neigh|bour|hood   o|ver|crow|ded   po|ver|ty   un|der|de|ve|loped
  un|em|ploy|ment   van|da|li|sm

b  **◀) 9.18** Listen and check. Practise saying the words.

c  Talk in small groups. Give reasons and examples.

  **Which city (or region) in your country or abroad do you think…?**

  - is very multicultural
  - offers great entertainment
  - has low levels of poverty and unemployment
  - has a bilingual or trilingual population
  - is very eco-friendly

  - is very overcrowded
  - has very serious pollution problems
  - has a lot of homeless people
  - has some very dangerous neighbourhoods
  - suffers from vandalism and antisocial behavior

## 7 WRITING

**Ⓦ p.121 Writing** A report  Write about the features of a city you know.

## 1 ▶ THE INTERVIEW Part 1

**a** Read the biographical information about George Tannenbaum. Have you seen any adverts for the companies he has worked with?

**George Tannenbaum** was born in 1957 in Yonkers, New York and was educated at Columbia University in New York. He has worked on advertising campaigns for many well-known companies such as IBM, Mercedes-Benz, Gillette, Citibank, and FedEx.

Today, he is Executive Creative Director and Copy Chief at Ogilvy and Mather Advertising in New York.

**b** Watch Part 1 of an interview with him and answer the questions.
1 Which other members of his family have worked in advertising?
2 When did George start working in advertising?
3 What wasn't he allowed to do when the family were watching TV?
4 Why does he think jingles are so memorable?
5 What kind of adverts were the H.O. Farina TV commercials?
6 What happens in the story of Wilhelmina and Willie?

### Glossary
**jingle** a short song or tune that is easy to remember and is used in advertising on radio or television
**H.O. Farina** a company which has been making cereals since the 1940s. They ran an advertising campaign in the 50s based on a cartoon character called Wilhelmina.

**c** Are there any jingles or slogans that you remember from your childhood? Why do you think they were so memorable? Are there any others that have got into your head since then?

## ▶ Part 2

Tommy Lee Jones in a BOSS advertising campaign

**a** Watch Part 2. Complete the notes with one or two words.
1 George says that a commercial is made up of three elements:
   1 _____
   2 _____
   3 _____
2 The acronym AIDA stands for:
   A _____
   I _____
   D _____
   A _____
3 According to George, using a celebrity in advertising is a way of _____, but he isn't a _____ of it.
4 George thinks that humour in advertising is _____.

### Glossary
**a depilatory** /ə dɪˈpɪlətri/ a product used for removing unwanted hair
**Tommy Lee Jones** a US actor born in 1946, winner of an Oscar for the 1993 film *The Fugitive*
**Mad Men** a well-known US TV series about advertising executives in the 1960s who worked in offices in Madison Avenue in New York

**b** How important do you think celebrities are in advertising? What about humour?

# advertising

## ▶ Part 3

**a** Watch Part 3 and (circle) the correct phrase.

1 He thinks that billboard and TV advertising will *remain important / slowly decline.*

2 He tends to notice *only bad adverts / only well-made adverts.*

3 He thinks Nike adverts are very successful *because of their logo and slogan / because they make people feel good about themselves.*

4 He thinks Apple's approach to advertising was very *innovative / repetitive.*

5 Their advertising message was *honest and clear / modern and informative.*

> **Glossary**
> **billboard** /ˈbɪlbɔːd/ a large board on the outside of a building or at the side of the road, used for putting advertisements on

**b** Are there many billboards in your town or city? Do you think they make the streets uglier or more attractive?

## 2 ▶ LOOKING AT LANGUAGE

> 🔍 **Metaphors and idiomatic expressions**
> George Tannenbaum uses a lot of metaphors and idiomatic expressions to make his language more colourful, e.g. *took the baton* = carry on in the family tradition, (from relay races in athletics).

**a** Watch some extracts from the interview and complete the missing words.

1 'You know they, what do they call them, _____ **worms**?'

2 'They **get into your** _____ and you can't get them out sometimes…'

3 'And I bet you I'm getting this _____ **for word** if you could find it.'

4 '…we do live in a celebrity culture and people, you know, **their ears** _____ **up** when they see a celebrity.'

5 'Have billboards and TV commercials **had their** _____?'

6 '…because you've got a **captive** _____.'

7 'they became kind of the gold standard and they rarely **hit a** _____ **note**.'

**b** Look at the **bold** expressions in **a** with a partner. What do you think they mean?

**a** Watch the conversation. What do they all conclude by the end?

**b** Watch again. Mark the sentences **T** (true) or **F** (false).

1 Syinat thinks we recognize certain brands because we are surrounded by advertising.

2 Joanne says her children don't see advertising at home because they don't have a TV.

3 Simon sometimes buys things without realizing that he's been influenced by advertising.

4 Joanne says her children don't understand the power of advertising.

5 Simon thinks it's a good idea to restrict advertising to children, like in Sweden.

6 Syinat thinks advertising doesn't really affect children.

**c** Do you agree with the participants that everybody is influenced by advertising?

**d** Watch the extracts and complete the highlighted phrases. In which extracts does the speaker a) give themselves time to think, b) make something clearer?

1 …and you're being influenced, so, for example we, _____ _____ _____ certain brands just because they're everywhere around us.

2 You know, we barely, we _____ _____ _____ watch TV and we have a TV, we just don't watch very much…

3 …but you see pictures in magazines and they're starting to be – my eleven-year-old, is _____ _____ _____ a little bit more cynical about what he sees…

4 Yeah, especially for children, I mean I, I, _____ _____, _____ _____ younger siblings and it's kind of like 'Ooh, all of my friends have this toy, so I must have it as well'

5 So, I think, um, _____ _____ definitely I think that the answer to the question is yes…

**e** Now have a conversation in groups of three.

1 Are there any products you think shouldn't be advertised, or shouldn't be advertised to young children?

2 Do you think adverts reinforce stereotypes?

In science, we must be interested in things, not in persons.
*Marie Curie Sklodowska, Polish scientist*

**G** quantifiers: *all, every, both,* etc. **V** science **P** stress in word families

## 1 SPEAKING & LISTENING

**a** Look at the cartoon. Do you think the father gives a good answer? Why (not)?

**b** Read the article. With a partner, try to explain the meaning of the highlighted science words. Use the context to help you.

**c** Now answer questions 1–8. Choose the correct option.

**d** 🔊 10.1 Listen to a scientist explaining each fact. Did you get the answers right?

**e** Listen again. What did the scientist say about…?
1 the reason we can see more blue light than violet light
2 the effect of the Sun's heat on sea water
3 the number of daylight hours that the moon is visible
4 six hours per year
5 what happens in your brain when you blink
6 the function of the cornea
7 the effect of cooler air on water vapour
8 what happens when something with a high mass is compressed

**f** Which questions do you think you could now answer if you were asked them by a child?

# Daddy, why…?

**'Why is the sky blue?' 'Why is the sea salty?' Children are always asking difficult questions like these about the world around us, but in a recent survey, nearly 25% of parents said they didn't know the answers, and 21% admitted that they made the answers up!**

**Can you answer eight simple science questions that parents struggle to answer?**

**1 Why is the sky blue?**
**A** Because the light from the Sun reflects off the blue water of the ocean.
**B** Because the Earth's atmosphere scatters more blue light than red light from the Sun.

**2 Why is the sea salty?**
**A** Because salt dissolves into the water from seaweed and other plants.
**B** Because salt dissolves into the water from the land around it.

**3 Why can we sometimes see the moon during the day?**
**A** Because as it rotates around the Earth, it reflects the Sun's rays during daytime as well as night time.
**B** Because sometimes during the day, the Sun doesn't shine as brightly.

**4 Why do we have a leap year?**
**A** Because every four years, the Earth goes round the Sun slightly faster.
**B** Because the Earth takes slightly more than 365 days to go round the Sun.

Daddy, where does rain come from?

Well, rain is liquid water in the form of droplets that have condensed from atmospheric water vapour and then become heavy enough to fall under gravity. The major cause of rain production is moisture moving along three-dimensional zones of temperature…

**5 Why do we blink?**
**A** To keep our eyes moist and clean.
**B** To help us stay awake.

**6 Why does cutting onions make us cry?**
**A** Because they produce a gas which irritates our eyes.
**B** Because they give off dry particles which irritate our eyes.

**7 What is a cloud?**
**A** A mixture of warm gases rising from the Earth.
**B** A mixture of water vapour, ice, and dust floating in the sky.

**8 What is a black hole?**
**A** A place in space where gravity pulls so hard that even light cannot get out.
**B** A 'vacuum cleaner' in space that swallows up everything around it.

Adapted from The Telegraph

## 2 VOCABULARY & PRONUNCIATION science; stress in word families

**a** Look at the questions and complete the subject column in the chart.

What is the name for the study of….?
1 the natural and physical world
2 forces, heat, light, sound, and electricity
3 how solids, liquids, and gases react with each other
4 people, animals, and plants
5 the moon and the planets
6 how characteristics are passed through generations
7 plants and their structure
8 animals and their behaviour

| subject | person | adjective |
|---|---|---|
| 1 *science* | *scientist* | *scientific* |
| 2 | | |
| 3 | | |
| 4 | | |
| 5 | | |
| 6 | | |
| 7 | | |
| 8 | | |

**b** ◗ 10.2 Listen and check. Then try to complete the other two columns.

> 🔍 **Stress in word families**
> In some word groups, the stressed syllable changes in the different parts of speech, e.g. *science*, *scientist*, *scientific*.

**c** ◗ 10.3 Listen and check. Underline the stressed syllables in the words. In which groups does the stress change on the adjective?

**d** Practise saying the word groups.

**e** ◗ 10.4 Listen and write six phrases using words from the chart in **a**.

**f** Complete the sentences with a word from the list.

clone   discovery   drugs   ~~experiments~~   guinea pigs
laboratory   research   side effects   tests   theory

1 Scientists **carry out** *experiments* in a _____.
2 Archimedes **made** an important _____ in his bath.
3 Isaac Newton's experiments **proved** his _____ that gravity existed.
4 Before a **pharmaceutical company** can sell new _____, they have to do _____ to make sure they are safe.
5 Scientists have to **do** a lot of _____ into the possible _____ of new drugs.
6 People can **volunteer** to be _____ in **clinical trials**.
7 In 1996, scientists were able for the first time to _____ a sheep, which they named Dolly.

**g** ◗ 10.5 Listen and check, and mark the stress on the multi-syllable words in **bold**. Practise saying the sentences.

## 3 SPEAKING

Work with a partner. **A** interview **B** with the questions in the green circles. Then **B** interview **A** with the blue circles.

Which scientific subjects do / did you study at school? What do / did you enjoy the most / the least?

Which scientific subjects from school are / have been most useful to you?

Do you think it's more important to study science than arts at school / university?

Which scientist (living or dead) do you most admire? Why?

Are you happy to eat genetically-modified food? Why (not)?

If you were ill, would you agree to be a guinea pig for a new kind of treatment?

Do you think it is acceptable for animals to be used for cosmetics testing? Is any animal testing acceptable?

Is it worth spending millions of pounds sending expeditions to distant planets, e.g. Mars? Why (not)?

Would you clone your pet? Do you think it will ever be acceptable to clone a person?

What would you most like scientists to discover in the near future?

## 4 READING

**a** Talk to a partner. Have you seen any films or TV programmes, or read any books, where…?

- people discover aliens that look a bit like humans on another planet
- spaceships travel faster than the speed of light
- people can teleport themselves long distances
- people can make themselves invisible
- machines look and behave like humans
- people can learn something very quickly by plugging themselves into a computer

**b** Read an article about the sci-fi concepts in **a**. Score each one from 1–5, according to what the writer says about how likely it is to happen (1 = very unlikely, 5 = very likely). Then compare with a partner. Did you agree on the scores?

# The reality of sci-fi

Just how **plausible** are the ideas we hear about in science-fiction? *LiveScience* examines some popular concepts.

### Aliens that look like us

Many fictional aliens have a human-type body. But how likely is it that intelligent alien life would develop a body shape similar to ours? It seems unlikely that organisms evolving for millions of years on another world would fit comfortably into our clothes. But the evolutionary circumstances on alien planets may have been similar to those that led humans to develop arms and legs, and fingers to manipulate tools. Some scientists say that our two-legged, symmetrical body shape could be the 'optimal design for an intelligent being'. Perhaps there is no other choice than for intelligent aliens to look like humans.

### Travelling faster than light

Einstein's general theory of relativity says that nothing can travel faster than light. However, this theory doesn't place limits on the speed at which space expands or contracts. Some physicists believe that faster-than-light travel is **a real possibility**. A type of energy bubble around a

spaceship, for instance, **could in theory** make space-time contract in front of the ship and expand behind it. Gerald Cleaver, a physicist at Baylor University, says that the objects inside the bubble would move faster than the speed of light in relation to the space around.

*Adapted from the LiveScience website*

### Teleportation

Digital information can be transmitted via computers, and in a similar way, some physicists have transmitted another type of information (called quantum information) nearly 10 miles (16 kms). However, this is **a long way from** teleporting

actual material, or indeed, a person. Scientifically speaking, teleportation **faces extreme obstacles**. There are ideas for how to do it, but these are **only speculative** at the moment.

### Invisibility cloaks

In the Star Trek universe, enemies hide, or 'cloak', their spaceships. Scientists say that anti-detection technologies **might be possible**, but invisibility cloaks like those in science-fiction and fantasy are **quite a way off**. 'What you

see in Harry Potter is **far-fetched**,' says David Smith, professor of electrical and computer engineering at Duke University. 'However, in the last few years, researchers have made a lot of progress on making objects invisible. Partial cloaks that work like sophisticated camouflage – rather like the alien in the 1987 movie *Predator* – **might be achievable**', says Smith.

### Intelligent machines

Robots and computers are already far better than humans at factory work or calculations. However, machines still cannot manage many basic activities, such as tying a shoelace while having a conversation. 'From 50 to 60 years of Artificial

Intelligence research, we know that teaching machines to do a specific task, for example, playing a game, is a lot easier than creating a machine that has the common sense of a three-year-old child,' said Shlomo Zilberstein, a professor of computer science. Many scientists believe that highly intelligent machines will be available in the coming decades. But it is questionable whether computers will achieve the human-like ability to feel or understand free will – an idea at the heart of many sci-fi stories.

### Instant learning

In the film *The Matrix*, knowledge can be uploaded into the brain in seconds, via a computer plugged into the skull. Some emerging research suggests that the speed at which we learn a skill can be technologically boosted. For
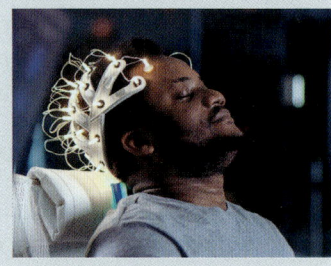
instance, scientists have managed to stimulate the brain to improve performance of visual tasks. Perhaps someday, the acquisition of knowledge and skills could happen at broadband-like speeds via surgically implanted and plug-in hardware. 'The concept is **not totally implausible**,' says neuroscientist Bruce McNaughton. 'But it might take a couple of hundred years.'

c With a partner, look at the highlighted words and phrases in the article on p.98. Check what ideas they refer to. Then decide whether they mean a) quite likely, b) not very likely, but possible, or c) extremely unlikely.

d Which thing in the article do you think…?
- might happen in the next 50 years
- you would really like to happen
- will never happen

> 🔍 **Talking about future possibilities**
> *I'm pretty sure…will*
> *I'd really like…to happen / exist / be invented*
> *I don't think…will ever…*

e In small groups, discuss the possibility of the following things happening, and whether or not they would be a good thing.

a colony on Mars
bringing extinct animals back to life
flying cars   space tourism
controlling the weather

5 **GRAMMAR** quantifiers: *all, every, both,* etc.

a With a partner, circle the correct word or phrase.

1 Some scientists think that *all / every* intelligent aliens would have a human-like body shape.

2 *All the / All* evidence suggests that scientists could invent a way to make things invisible.

3 Einstein's theory of relativity doesn't explain *all / everything* about the universe.

4 *No / None* machines can currently tie a shoelace and hold a conversation at the same time.

5 *Both / Both of* David Smith and Shlomo Zilberstein are computer scientists.

6 *Either / Neither* teleportation nor instant learning are going to be easy to achieve.

b 🇬 **p.150 Grammar Bank 10A**

c Do the Science quiz with a partner.

d 🔊 10.9 Listen and check.

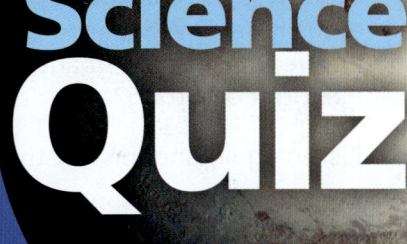

# Science Quiz

**1 In 'direct current', the electrons…**
a move in only one direction.
b move in both directions.
c don't move at all.

**2 Helium gas can be found…**
a only in liquid form.
b in neither liquid nor solid form.
c in both liquid and solid form.

**3 Adult giraffes remain standing…**
a some of the day.
b all day.
c most of the day.

**4 Of all the water on our planet,… is found underground.**
a hardly any of it
b about half of it
c most of it

**5 Snakes eat…**
a only other animals.
b either other animals or eggs.
c either other animals or fruit.

**6 A diamond can be destroyed…**
a by either intense heat or acid.
b by both intense heat and acid.
c only by intense heat.

**7 The human brain can continue to live without oxygen for…**
a nearly two minutes.
b nearly six minutes.
c a few hours.

**8 In our solar system,…**
a neither Pluto nor Neptune are now considered to be planets.
b both Pluto and Neptune are considered to be planets.
c Pluto is no longer considered to be a planet.

**9 When we breathe out,…**
a most of that air is oxygen.
b none of that air is oxygen.
c some of that air is oxygen.

**10 An individual blood cell makes a whole circuit of the body in…**
a nearly 60 seconds.
b nearly 45 seconds.
c a few minutes.

**G** articles   **V** collocation: word pairs   **P** pausing and sentence stress

## 1 GRAMMAR articles

a Who was the first man to walk on the moon? In what year?

b ◖) **10.10** Listen to the original recording of the first words spoken from the moon. With a partner, try to complete the sentence and answer the questions.

THAT'S ONE _____ STEP FOR _____,
ONE GIANT LEAP FOR _____.

1 What do you think the difference is between *a step* and *a leap*?
2 What do you think *mankind* means?

c ◖) **10.11** Listen to an interview about the moon landing. What was the controversy about the words Armstrong actually said? What's the difference in meaning between *a man* and *man*? Did new technology prove him right or wrong?

d Listen again and answer the questions.

1 When did Armstrong write the words he was planning to say when he first stepped on the moon?
2 Does Armstrong say he wrote, '*That's one small step for man…*' or '*That's one small step for a man…*'?
3 Why doesn't the sentence everybody heard make sense?
4 What did Armstrong think he said?
5 Who is Peter Shann Ford? What did he discover?
6 How did Armstrong feel when he heard about this?

e Read some more facts about Armstrong. Are the highlighted phrases grammatically right or wrong? Correct the mistakes.

1 Neil Armstrong was born in the USA.
2 He was a shy boy, who loved the books and the music.
3 He studied aeronautical engineering at the university.
4 He was the first man who set foot on moon.
5 His famous words were heard by people all over the world.
6 Before becoming a astronaut, he worked for the US navy.
7 After 1994, he refused to give the autographs.
8 In 2005, he was involved in a lawsuit with an ex-barber, who tried to sell some of the Armstrong's hair.

f **G** p.151 **Grammar Bank 10B**

g **C Communication** True or false **A** p.110 **B** p.112 Complete quiz sentences with articles.

## 2 READING

a Read the introduction to the article. What do the highlighted words and phrases mean?

b Look at the eight people in the photos on p.101. What do you know about them? Match sound bites A–H to the people in the photos.

A 'I have the heart and stomach of a king.'
B 'Government of the people, by the people, for the people.'
C 'The laws that men have made.'
D 'We shall never surrender.'
E 'Ask not what your country can do for you; ask what you can do for your country.'
F 'I have a dream.'
G 'It is an ideal for which I am prepared to die.'
H 'Yes, we can.'

c ◖) **10.15** Listen and check.

d Now read about the circumstances in which four of the speeches in **b** were made. Complete them with the person and the sound bite. Do you know in what context the other four people made their speeches?

e Read about the speeches again and answer the questions with **QE**, **AL**, **EP** or **NM**.

Who…?

1 ____ conveyed his / her message without mentioning a key word
2 ____ gave part of his / her speech without notes
3 ____ gave the speech before a famous sea battle
4 ____ summed up his / her message in ten words
5 ____ wanted to convince his / her critics at home that they were wrong
6 ____ was applauded for a long time after the speech
7 ____ was helped in the delivery of the speech by his / her former occupation
8 ____ did not live to see his / her cause made law

f Talk to a partner.

1 Whose speech would you most like to have heard? Why?
2 Do you know anyone today who you consider to be a great speaker?
3 Which past or present politicians or public figures in your country do you think are or were a) very good speakers, b) very poor speakers?

# The best speeches of all time

**Using [1]sound bites and having [2]the gift of the gab – the secrets of some of the world's greatest orators.**

The perfect speaker, says Cicero, the Roman statesman considered the greatest [3]orator of all time, must be well read in the history of his country and the politics of the day. He (it was always 'he' in those days) must command the language with humour, [4]wit and psychological insight. The main point, though, says Cicero, is that you need to know the main point. If you cannot describe your main point, you probably haven't got one. By this standard, who is or was a great speaker? Who gave the finest speeches?

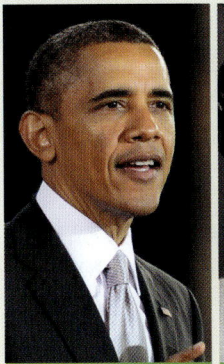

■ Barack Obama

■ Emmeline Pankhurst

■ Nelson Mandela

■ Abraham Lincoln

■ Elizabeth I

■ Winston Churchill

■ John F Kennedy

■ Martin Luther King

**1** _____ to her troops before the invasion of the Spanish Armada Tilbury (port on the River Thames), August 9, 1588

### THE SOUND BITE

**WHY IS IT SO GOOD?** This is a speech all about character, and it is a defiant speech about gender. With the Spanish Armada gathering in the North Sea, about to attack, Elizabeth knew the nation was in peril and that she faced her sternest test. She would have known, as she spoke at Tilbury, that at court, people were saying that a woman could not command the armed forces. A failure by a king would be attributed to one of many factors. A failure by a queen would be put down to her gender. Rather than ignore the question, Elizabeth chooses, brilliantly, to confront it.

**2** _____ to soldiers during the American Civil War Gettysburg, Pennsylvania, November 19, 1863

### THE SOUND BITE

**WHY IS IT SO GOOD?** Lincoln describes the ideal of democratic government in a single sentence. He gets so much into those ten words that it is surprising he needs all 272 for the whole speech. Lincoln is saying that the Civil War has to be waged for the principles of the founding fathers, who drafted the Declaration of Independence, particularly the principle of all people being equal, and at this moment, they are being betrayed. What he means, in a word he never actually uses, is slavery. Almost every American president since Lincoln has gone to Gettysburg, usually on Memorial Day, to pay homage to Lincoln and to the American constitution. One who did not was John F Kennedy, who, in 1963, had to ask ex-president Eisenhower to stand in for him. Kennedy had to go down to Dallas on urgent political business. He never came back.

**3** _____, campaigning for votes for women Portman Rooms, London, March 24, 1908

### THE SOUND BITE

**WHY IS IT SO GOOD?** Some of the finest speakers in the history of rhetoric got into trouble because of their speeches. Pankhurst was in prison several times, and gave this speech after being released from one of them. The audience was not expecting her to appear, and the ovation when she did was prolonged. Over and above the injustice of women being excluded from the vote, she is making the practical case that the law would be improved and democracy would be enriched if it opened the door to women. Tragically, Pankhurst died three weeks before her case was accepted by the British government in 1928.

**4** _____ at his trial Supreme Court of South Africa, Pretoria, April 20, 1964

### THE SOUND BITE

**WHY IS IT SO GOOD?** The greatest speeches are the words said at the most momentous occasions, as here, where a political prisoner pleads for his life against an unjust apartheid state. Mandela speaks for more than three hours. Throughout, he is extremely reasonable, like the lawyer he once was, taking pains to reassure the white population he means them no harm. He had learned the last words by heart, and delivered them from memory, looking directly at Judge De Wet. When he finished, there was a 30-second pause – an eternity. In the gallery, a woman burst into tears.

Adapted from The Times

# 3 LISTENING & SPEAKING

**a** Have you ever had to make a speech or give a talk or presentation in front of a lot of people? When and where? How did you feel? Was it a success?

**b** Look at the cartoon. What point is it making about public speaking?

**c** 🔊 10.16 Now listen to Part 1 of a radio programme where expert Lynne Parker gives tips for public speaking. Complete her six tips using between one and four words. Were any of your ideas mentioned?

1 Be _____.
2 If you're using PowerPoint, don't just _____.
3 Maintain _____ with your audience.
4 _____, _____, _____.
5 Include a couple of good _____.
6 Listen to _____.

**d** Listen again and add more information about each tip.

|       | Dos | Don'ts |
|-------|-----|--------|
| Tip 1 |     |        |
| Tip 2 |     | —      |
| Tip 3 |     |        |
| Tip 4 |     | —      |
| Tip 5 |     |        |
| Tip 6 |     | —      |

**e** 🔊 10.17 Now listen to Part 2, an interview with Anya Edwards from Chile, who was a finalist in an International Public Speaking competition. Does she agree with any of Lynne's points?

**f** Listen again. Choose a, b, or c.

1 Participants in the competition have to first compete ____.
   a in London  b in their own country  c in their own language
2 In the impromptu speech in the finals, you have to speak for ____ minutes.
   a three  b five  c fifteen
3 Anya thinks that being nervous is ____.
   a unavoidable  b an advantage  c a disadvantage
4 She thinks public speaking is more difficult than acting because ____.
   a you have to know your subject  b you have to be more convincing
   c you have less support
5 She thinks learning to speak in public ____.
   a was useful for her, but may not be useful for everybody
   b is useful for everybody  c wasn't a particularly useful experience
6 Her tip for creating the content of a speech is to start by ____.
   a recording ideas  b drawing a mind map
   c organizing your thoughts

**g** Which one tip did you think was the most useful? Were there any that you don't really agree with?

# 4 VOCABULARY collocation: word pairs

> 🔍 **Word pairs**
> *Try not to continually walk **up and down**...*
> Some pairs of words in English which go together always come in a certain order, for example, we always say *black and white*, not *white and black*. This order may sometimes be different in your language. Some word pairs are idioms, e.g. *do's and dont's* means things you should or shouldn't do.

**a** How do you say *up and down* and *black and white* in your language? Are the words in the same order?

**b** Take one word from **box A** and match it to another from **box B**. Then decide which word comes first, and join them with *and*.

> **A** backwards, effect, forget, health, learn, lightning, pros, quiet, supply, sweet

> **B** cause, cons, demand, forgive, forwards, live, peace, safety, short, thunder

**c** Look at some common word pairs joined with *or*. What is the second word?

right or _____     sooner or _____     dead or _____
now or _____       all or _____         rain or _____
more or _____      once or _____

**d** 🔊 10.18 Listen and check your answers to **b** and **c**.

**e** Match the word pair idioms to their meanings.

1 ___ I'm sick and tired of hearing you complain.
2 ___ I didn't buy much, just a few bits and pieces.
3 ___ I get headaches now and again.
4 **A** What's for lunch? **B** ___ Wait and see.
5 ___ By and large, I enjoyed my time at school.
6 ___ The army were called in to restore law and order.
7 ___ Despite the storm, we arrived safe and sound.
8 ___ It was touch and go whether we'd get to the airport in time, but luckily we just made it.

A in general
B a situation in which the law is obeyed
C fed up
D without problem or injury
E sometimes
F uncertain, with the possibility that something may go wrong
G small things
H wait patiently

**f** Complete the sentences with a word pair from **e**.

1 I haven't got much work to finish, just a few _____.
2 I don't see my uncle very often, just _____.
3 Let's _____ if the weather improves before we decide to go out or not.
4 After lots of adventures, she arrived home _____.
5 A few things went wrong on the first night of the play, but _____, it was a success.
6 After the riots, the government sent soldiers in to try to establish _____.
7 I'm _____ of my boss! I'm going to look for a new job.
8 The operation was successful, but for a few hours it was _____.

## 5 PRONUNCIATION & SPEAKING
pausing and sentence stress

**a** 🔊 **10.19** When people give a talk, they speak more slowly than usual, and they divide what they say into small chunks, with a brief pause between each. Listen to the beginning of a talk and mark the pauses.

> Good afternoon everyone/and thank you for coming. I'm going to talk to you today about one of my hobbies, baking. I've loved baking since I was a child. My grandmother taught me to make simple biscuits and cakes, and later, when I was a teenager, I watched a lot of TV programmes and online videos to learn how to make more complicated ones. What I like about baking is that it's very creative and it makes other people happy…

**b** Now practise giving the beginning of the talk, pausing and trying to get the correct rhythm.

**c** You are going to give a three-minute presentation to other students. You can choose what to talk about, for example:

- a hobby you have or a sport you play
- an interesting person in your family
- a famous person you admire
- the good and bad side of your job or course

Decide what you are going to talk about and make a plan of what you want to say.

**d** In groups, take turns to give your presentation. Then have a short question and answer session.

## 6 ▶ VIDEO LISTENING

**a** Watch a short film called *Giving presentations: a voice coach*. What did Sandie criticise Louise for in her first presentation? What suggestions did she make? How did she think Louise had improved at the end of the session?

**b** Watch it again and complete the sentences with two or three words.

1 The one thing Louise hates about her job is _____.
2 Nowadays, in most jobs you need to be able to deliver a message _____ and _____.
3 RADA opened in the Haymarket in _____ in the year _____.
4 Actors and public speakers use a lot of the _____ to engage an audience.
5 The RADA approach can be summarized as '_____, _____, _____'.
6 After Louise's first presentation, the instructor gives her some _____ _____.
7 Louise learns that getting your _____ _____ right will help your breathing.
8 In public speaking, it's important to _____ an _____ from the beginning.
9 It's equally important to end on a _____ _____.
10 The RADA technique gives you the skills to _____ in _____.

**c** What did you learn that might help you next time you have to speak in public?

🟢 **Go online** to review the lesson

## GRAMMAR

Choose a, b, or c.

1 He got a good job, _____ not having the right degree.
   a although   b despite   c in spite

2 My uncle still works, _____ he won the lottery last year.
   a in spite of   b despite   c even though

3 I called my sister to remind her _____ the flowers.
   a to buy   b for buy   c for buying

4 Jane opened the door quietly _____ her parents up.
   a to not wake   b so that she not wake
   c so as not to wake

5 Adrian is looking for _____ in London.
   a some cheap accommodations
   b some cheap accommodation
   c a cheap accommodation

6 Let me give you _____ – don't marry him!
   a a piece of advice   b an advice   c some advices

7 I need to buy a new _____.
   a trouser   b trousers   c pair of trousers

8 There's _____ milk. I'll have to get some from the shop.
   a no   b any   c none

9 _____ in that shop is incredibly expensive.
   a All   b All of them   c Everything

10 They shouldn't go sailing because _____ of them can swim.
   a both   b either   c neither

11 Let's take them _____ flowers or chocolates when we go for dinner.
   a both   b either   c neither

12 I was in _____ hospital for two weeks with a broken leg.
   a the   b –   c a

13 I now live next door to _____ school where I used to go.
   a the   b –   c a

14 _____ Lake Constance is the biggest lake in Switzerland.
   a The   b –   c A

15 _____ British Museum is in central London.
   a The   b –   c A

## VOCABULARY

a Complete with the correct form of the **bold** word.

1 Many people think that behaviour is _____ rather than learnt. **gene**

2 Many important _____ discoveries were made in the 19th century. **science**

3 We live in a very safe _____. **neighbour**

4 Many people in big cities suffer from _____. **lonely**

5 His _____ came as a terrible shock. **die**

b Add a prefix to the **bold** word.

1 New Delhi in India is a very **populated** city.

2 I asked for an aspirin, but the receptionist didn't understand me because I had **pronounced** it.

3 A **national** company is a large company that operates in several different countries.

4 Gandhi wrote most of his **biography** in 1929.

5 Anne is unhappy with her job, because she's **paid**.

c Complete the missing words.

1 Will the company make a l_____ this year?

2 He borrowed £10,000 to s_____ _____ his own business.

3 Ikea is the market l_____ in cheap furniture.

4 The company are planning to l_____ their new product in the spring.

5 The bank has br_____ all over the country.

6 It's a bad idea to mix b_____ with pleasure.

7 In a property boom, house prices r_____.

8 The drug has some very unpleasant s_____ effects.

9 We need to c_____ out some more experiments.

10 Would you ever be a g_____ pig in a clinical trial?

d Complete the two-word phrases.

1 I'm going to the mountains for some peace and _____.

2 He arrived back from his adventure safe and _____.

3 Sooner or _____, we'll have to make a decision.

4 It's a very dangerous city. There's no law and _____.

5 It's our last chance to do this. It's now or _____.

## PRONUNCIATION

a Circle the word with a different sound.

1 æ   br**a**nch   exp**a**nd   **a**ntidote   gr**a**vity

2 ɒ   pr**o**duct   g**o**vernment   p**o**verty   m**o**dernism

3 ɪə   volunt**eer**   th**eo**ry   res**ear**ch   id**ea**

4 ʃ   rece**ssi**on   expecta**ti**on   deci**si**on   antiso**ci**al

5 θ   dea**th**   **th**ough   wid**th**   **th**ought

b Underline the main stressed syllable.

1 bi|o|lo|gi|cal   3 mul|ti|cul|tu|ral   5 man|u|fac|ture
2 phy|si|cist   4 in|crease (*verb*)

# ▶ CAN YOU understand this text?

**a** Read the article once. Why did Stephen Hawking never change his computer voice?

**b** Read the article again and choose a, b, or c.

1 Stephen Hawking used a computer voice synthesizer to communicate for over...
   a 30 years.
   b 40 years.
   c 55 years.

2 He started using the voice when...
   a he was diagnosed with motor neurone disease.
   b he lost the power of speech after an operation.
   c pneumonia caused him to lose his voice.

3 His accent surprised people because...
   a the synthesizer was made in Britain.
   b they expected his voice to sound British.
   c American accents were not popular in Britain.

4 Stephen Hawking...
   a thought that his accent sounded very American.
   b told the Queen that his accent wasn't American.
   c said his accent sounded different to different people.

# ▶ CAN YOU understand these people?

🔊 10.20 Watch or listen and choose a, b, or c.

| 1 | 2 | 3 | 4 |
| Thomas | Devika | Noel | Sophie |

1 Thomas admires Nike because of its ____.
   a slogan and customer service
   b logo and marketing
   c name and the quality of its product

2 Devika thinks that ____ cities will change a lot in the next 20 years.
   a some European
   b modern, wealthy cities
   c developing industrial

3 Noel thinks that science ____.
   a is just as creative as the arts
   b is more useful than maths
   c should focus on climate change

4 Sophie passed her exam although ____.
   a she didn't do her PowerPoint presentation
   b she didn't enjoy doing her PowerPoint presentation
   c her PowerPoint presentation was a disaster

# THE VOICE OF REASON

## Why Stephen Hawking's voice computer spoke with an American accent

Stephen Hawking, the legendary English cosmologist, author of *A Brief History of Time*, was regarded as a brilliant theoretical physicist, and for the British people, a national treasure. However, his famous computer-generated voice left many people puzzled.

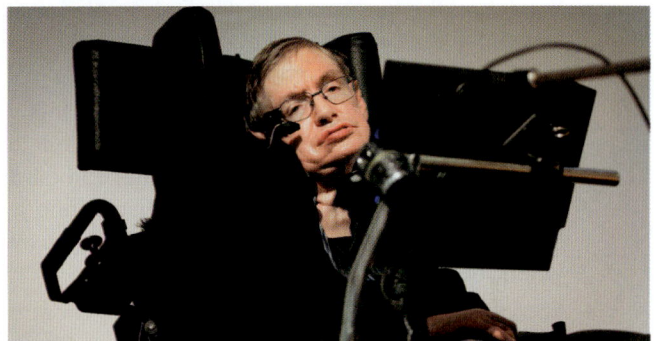

Hawking died in 2018 at the age of 76. In 1963, while studying at Oxford, he was diagnosed with amyotrophic lateral sclerosis (ALS), a rare form of motor neurone disease. Incredibly, despite a poor prognosis, he lived with the disease for 55 years until his death. After catching pneumonia in 1985, Hawking had to have a tracheotomy to allow him to breathe. This left him unable to speak. After that, the professor's primary means of communication was a computer voice synthesizer which he controlled first with a hand-held clicker, and later with a sensor attached to his cheek. This computer-generated voice, known by its US developers as 'Perfect Paul', became Hawking's iconic voice, recognized around the world.

One thing that puzzled many people, however, was why his computer spoke with an apparent American accent, in spite of the fact that he was born in Oxford, in the UK. The Queen even quizzed him on the matter, asking him, 'Have you still got that American voice?' when meeting him at an event at St James' Palace. He joked back, 'Yes, it is copyrighted actually.'

Hawking had previously answered the question on his own website. Explaining how his speech worked, he wrote: 'When I have built up a sentence, I can send it to my speech synthesizer. I use a separate hardware synthesizer, made by Speech Plus. It is the best I have heard, although it gives me an accent that has been described variously as Scandinavian, American, or Scottish.'

He also explained that he would have been able to change the accent of his computer when the technology advanced, but had decided against it. Hawking added: 'My old system worked well and I wrote five books with it, including *A Brief History of Time*. It has become my trademark and I wouldn't change it for a more natural voice with a British accent. I am told that children who need a computer voice want one like mine.'

*Adapted from Mashable*

# Communication

## 7A ARGUMENT! Student A

a Read the instructions carefully for the role-play and think about what you are going to say.

> You share a flat with **B**. The problems are the following:
>
> - You found the flat, and moved in first, so obviously, you chose the best room. Recently **B** has been making some sarcastic comments about this.
> - **B** has two friends who are always round at the flat. You don't have a problem with them, but they are often in the kitchen or sitting room and you don't have much privacy. They also spend a lot of time online and you think the wi-fi is slower when they're around.
> - You often eat at home in the evening; it's cheaper, and anyway you like cooking, especially spicy dishes like curries. You sometimes offer food to **B** if you've just made something, which he / she frequently accepts. However, **B** never ever cooks. You think that at the very least, **B** should pay for a takeaway from time to time, for you to share.
>
> This is your chance to tell **B** how you feel but try not to lose your temper. Try to find a good solution to each problem.

b Have the argument with **B**. Try to agree on a course of action.

> You start the conversation: *OK, I think now is a good moment to talk about a few problems that have come up recently…*

## 7B GUESS WHAT IT IS Student A

a Look at the pictures below. You are going to describe them to **B**. Say what kind of thing each one is, and then use *looks*, *smells*, *feels*, or *tastes*.

cabbage   mango   rose   ice-lolly   fur coat

b Describe your first thing to **B** in as much detail as possible. **B** can then ask you questions to identify what the thing is.

> *It's a kind of vegetable. It looks a bit like a green ball. It tastes quite strong and I think it smells awful when it's being cooked. You can use it to make…*

c Now listen to **B** describe his / her first thing. Don't interrupt until he / she has finished describing. You can ask **B** questions to identify what the thing is.

d Continue taking turns to describe all your things. Who guessed the most right?

## 8B STRANGE, BUT TRUE Student A

a Read the article once. Then write down ten key words on a piece of paper to help you remember the story.

b Tell **B** your story in your own words, using your key words to help you.

> *There was this man called Tom Booker, and just before the World Cup, he started to feel ill…*

c Now listen to **B**'s story, and ask **B** to clarify or rephrase if there's anything you don't understand.

> **Glossary**
> **hallucinate** (*verb*) see or hear things that aren't really there (e.g. because of a high temperature)

### Football fan gets World Cup fever

*A man who thought he had 'World Cup fever' had actually got malaria, doctors have confirmed.*

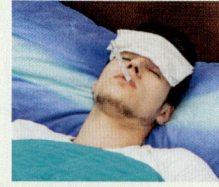

Tom Booker, from Swindon, had been telling friends that he was so excited about the start of the World Cup that he had started to feel quite ill. 'I was shaking all the time,' he told our reporter. 'When I started feeling awful, I thought it must be the football. It seemed obvious that the prospect of non-stop football on the TV featuring the best players in the world was making me hallucinate.'

Booker, who had just returned from a holiday in Goa, continued to suffer from headaches and stomach pains, and eventually fainted during the semi-final. He was rushed to hospital, where he was diagnosed with malaria. 'My doctor advised me not to take football so seriously.' Booker is now recovering well. 'I do feel a bit stupid,' he admitted. 'But football is my life.'

## 9A  MISLEADING ADS  Student A

a  Read about the **Volkswagen** ad. Find out…

   1  what the advertising campaign claimed.
   2  why it was misleading.
   3  what happened in the end.

b  Take turns to tell each other the information about your ad.

c  Which of the three ads do you think was the most seriously misleading? Why?

> **Volkswagen**
>
> On March 29 2016, the Federal Trade Commission (FTC) filed a lawsuit against Volkswagen about the advertising campaign it used to promote its supposedly 'Clean Diesel' vehicles.
>
> The FTC alleged that 'Volkswagen deceived consumers by selling or leasing more than 550,000 diesel cars based on false claims that the cars were low-emission, and environmentally friendly'. In 2015, it had also been discovered that VW had been cheating in emissions tests on its diesel cars in the US for the past seven years.
>
> In the end, the company agreed to pay a fine of over $4 billion for false advertising, and may have to pay much more for violating the Clean Air Act.

## 10B TRUE OR FALSE  Student A

a  Complete the gaps in your sentences with *the* where necessary.

   1  ____ Andes is ____ longest mountain range in ____ world. (**T**)
   2  ____ Loch Ness is ____ largest lake in Scotland. (**F** – It's the second largest. Loch Lomond is the largest.)
   3  ____ capital of ____ United States is ____ New York City. (**F** – It's Washington DC.)
   4  ____ Mallorca is an island in ____ Mediterranean sea. (**T**)
   5  ____ Uffizi gallery is ____ most famous art museum in ____ Rome. (**F** – It's in Florence.)
   6  ____ South America is larger than ____ North America. (**F**)
   7  ____ Mount Vesuvius is a volcano in ____ north-west Italy. (**F** – It's in south-west Italy.)
   8  ____ Brooklyn Bridge connects ____ Brooklyn and ____ Manhattan. (**T**)

b  Now read your sentence 1 to **B**. He / She must say if the information is true or false. Correct his / her answer if necessary.

c  Now listen to **B**'s sentence 1 and say if you think it's true or false. If you think it's false, say what you think the right answer is.

d  Continue taking turns to say your sentences. Who got the most right answers?

## 7A  ARGUMENT!  Student B

a  Read the instructions carefully for the role-play and think about what you are going to say.

> You share a flat with **A**. The problems are the following:
>
> - When you started sharing the flat with **A**, he / she was already living in the house and he / she had taken the best and biggest room. Your room is much smaller and there's only really enough room in it for your bed!  But you're both paying the same rent. This isn't fair!
>
> - You have two good friends who often come to see you at the flat. Recently, **A** has been quite unfriendly to your friends, sometimes not even saying hello when they come in. And **A** has also started complaining that the wi-fi is slow because your friends are using it. How ridiculous! That can't be true.
>
> - **A** seems to spend all his / her time in the kitchen cooking. He / She makes a lot of spicy food, which means that the whole flat smells of curry. You don't dislike curry, and have even occasionally accepted some of **A**'s cooking, just to be polite, but you hate the smell in the flat. You can't see the point of cooking and prefer getting your own takeaways or ready meals.
>
> This is your chance to tell **A** how you feel, but try not to lose your temper. Try to find a good solution to each problem.

b  Have the argument with **A**. Try to agree on a course of action. **A** will start.

## 9A MISLEADING ADS Student B

a Read about the **Danone** ad. Find out…

    1 what the advertising campaign claimed.
    2 why it was misleading.
    3 what happened in the end.

b Take turns to tell each other the information about your ad.

c Which of the three ads do you think was the most seriously misleading? Why?

### Danone

Ads for Danone's popular Activia brand yogurt landed the company with a bill of $45 million in 2010. The yogurts were marketed as being 'clinically' and 'scientifically' proven to boost your immune system and able to help to regulate digestion.

The Activia ad campaign, endorsed by actress Jamie Lee Curtis, claimed that the yogurt had special bacterial ingredients. As a result, the yogurt was sold at 30% higher prices than other similar products.

The lawsuit against Danone began in 2008, when US consumer Trish Wiener made a complaint. The judge overseeing the case said that the claims were not proven. As well as being given a fine of $45 million, Danone was ordered to remove the words 'clinically' and 'scientifically proven' from its labels.

## 8A BEAT THE BURGLAR Student A

Read the answers to questions 1–3.

1 **a** Most burglaries take place between 10 a.m. and lunchtime. The average burglar will wait for adults to go to work and children to school, to be sure the house is empty.

2 **b** An experienced burglar would spend a maximum of 20 minutes in a house.

3 **a and c** A burglar will normally go for a house that looks quite expensive, in a good area. They'll often choose a house where there are trees or bushes outside which are good places to hide before or after. That way, there's less chance of neighbours seeing them. Most burglars wait for a house to be empty before they break in, but there are others who prefer it if the owners are at home in bed, so they know where they are and won't get surprised by them suddenly coming home.

## 10B TRUE OR FALSE Student B

a Complete the gaps in your sentences with *the* where necessary.

    1 ____ capital of ____ Netherlands is ____ Amsterdam. (**F** – It's The Hague.)

    2 ____ Amazon is ____ longest river in ____ world. (**F** – It's the Nile.)

    3 ____ Panama Canal connects ____ Atlantic Ocean to ____ Pacific Ocean. (**T**)

    4 ____ Atacama desert is in ____ north of ____ Chile. (**T**)

    5 ____ Black Sea is in ____ south-west Europe. (**F** – It's in south-east Europe.)

    6 ____ biggest lake in ____ world is ____ Lake Victoria in ____ Africa. (**F** – It's Lake Superior in Canada / the USA.)

    7 ____ Mont Blanc is ____ highest mountain in ____ Alps. (**T**)

    8 ____ Hyde Park is in ____ central London. (**T**)

b Now listen to **A**'s sentence 1 and say if you think it's true or false. If you think it's false, say what you think the right answer is.

c Now read your sentence 1 to **A**. Correct his / her answer if necessary.

d Continue taking turns to say your sentences. Who got the most right answers?

## 7B  GUESS WHAT IT IS  Student B

**a**  Look at the pictures below. You are going to describe them to **A**. Say what kinds of thing each one is, and then use *looks, smells, feels,* or *tastes*.

 camembert  jasmine  kitten  vinegar  chilli pepper

**b**  Now listen to **A** describe his / her first thing. Don't interrupt until he / she has finished describing. You can ask **A** questions.

**c**  Now describe your first thing in as much detail as possible. **A** can then ask you questions to identify what the thing is.

> It's a kind of French cheese. It's round and usually comes in a wooden box…

**d**  Continue taking turns to describe all your things. Who guessed the most right?

## 9A  MISLEADING ADS  Student C

**a**  Read about the **Olay** ad. Find out…
1  what the advertising campaign claimed.
2  why it was misleading.
3  what happened in the end.

**b**  Take turns to tell each other the information about your ad.

**c**  Which of the three ads do you think was the most seriously misleading? Why?

> **Olay**
>
> In 2009, an Olay ad for its Definity eye cream showed former model Twiggy looking wrinkle-free – and a whole lot younger than her then 60 years. It turned out that the ads were retouched.
>
> The British Advertising Regulator (ASA) banned the ad, after more than 700 complaints were made against it. It was concluded that the digitally-altered ads gave a 'misleading impression of the effect the product could achieve'.
>
> Olay's parent company Procter & Gamble responded that it was 'routine practice to use post-production techniques to correct for lighting and other minor photographic deficiencies before publishing the final shots as part of an advertising campaign'.

## 8A  BEAT THE BURGLAR  Student B

Read the answers to questions 4–6.

> 4  a  These days burglars are usually looking for things like laptops and tablets, which are easy to sell, and not so easy for the owner to identify if the burglar later gets caught.
>
> 5  c  There's a typical order burglars use when they search a house for valuables. They start with the main bedroom, and then the living room. After that, the dining room, the study, and then the kitchen. The last place would be a child's bedroom. You wouldn't normally expect to find anything worth taking there.
>
> 6  a  Burglars don't like dogs, especially noisy ones, because they're unpredictable.

## 8B  STRANGE, BUT TRUE  Student B

**a**  Read the article once. Then write down ten key words on a piece of paper to help you remember the story.

### Shark baby drama

*A man who was accused of stealing a shark from a Texas aquarium has said he did so in an attempt to rescue it.*

On a visit to the San Antonio Aquarium, 38-year-old Anthony Shannon was caught on CCTV trying to steal a shark. He lifted the 40cm long shark, named Miss Helen, from a tank, wrapped her in a blanket, and took her away in a pushchair. Shannon has now been charged with stealing the fish and taking her to his home. Miss Helen was reported to be one of around 25 sharks being kept at Mr Shannon's home, along with an unknown number of crabs.

Shannon claimed he was afraid that Miss Helen's life was in danger. In an interview with local news, Shannon said that he was sorry for the theft, but that he could justify his behaviour because it was an 'emergency'. He threatened to steal another shark if he felt it was necessary. Miss Helen was returned to the aquarium. Staff denied keeping the animals in bad conditions and said the water was tested every day.

> **Glossary**
> **pushchair** (*noun*) a folding chair on wheels in which a small child can be pushed along

**b**  Listen to **A**'s story, and ask **A** to clarify or rephrase if there's anything you don't understand.

**c**  Tell **A** your story in your own words, using your key words to help you.

> There was this man called Anthony Shannon, and when he visited the San Antonio Aquarium in Texas, he…

# Writing

## 5 DESCRIBING A PHOTO

**a** Look at photo 1 and read the description. Do you agree with what the writer says about the people?

**b** Complete the description with a word or phrase from the list.

> behind   in front of   in the background
> in the centre   ~~in the foreground~~
> on the left   opposite   outside

**c** You are going to write a description of photo 2. **Plan** the content. With a partner, look at the photo carefully and decide what you think the people are thinking or feeling. Decide how to organize what you want to say into paragraphs.

**d** **Write** 140–190 words. Use the phrases in **Useful language** to help you.

> 🔍 **Useful language: describing a photo or picture**
> *In the foreground / centre / background of the photo…*
> *The (man) looks as if / looks as though…*
> *It looks as if / as though…*
> *The (woman) may / might be… / Perhaps the woman is…*
> *The photo reminds me of…*

**e** **Check** your description for mistakes (grammar, punctuation, and spelling).

↩ p.73

I think this is a photo of a family in their house. However, they are not posing. None of the people are looking at the camera.

[1] *In the foreground*, we can see the inside of a room with glass doors leading into a garden. [2]_____ of the photo, there is a girl sitting at the table, resting her head on one hand, with an open book [3]_____ her. There are two other empty chairs around the table. The girl is smiling; she looks as if she's daydreaming, maybe about something she's read in the book. [4]_____ of the photo, there is a woman, who looks older than the girl, perhaps her mother. She's standing with her arms folded, looking out of the glass doors into the garden. She seems to be watching what's happening [5]_____, and she looks a bit worried.

[6]_____, we can see a terrace, and [7]_____ that, a beautiful garden. Outside the glass doors on the right, we can see a boy and a man, who may be father and son. The boy is standing, facing the man, who is crouching down [8]_____ him. It looks as though they're having a serious conversation. Maybe the boy has been naughty, because it seems as if he's looking at the ground.

This photo reminds me of a David Hockney or Edward Hopper painting – it makes you speculate about who the people are and what they are thinking.

## 6 EXPRESSING YOUR OPINION

### CRIME FORUM

## Do punishments usually fit the crime?
What do you think? Write a short article and post it here.

**Rob87**
Nottingham
16:29  23 July

**Community service is the best punishment for young people who commit a minor offence.**

[1]*Nowadays* in the UK, when a young person commits a minor offence, he or she is normally given community service, given a fine, or sometimes, sentenced to a few months in prison. [2]_____ I believe that community service is the best option.

[3]_____, community service often persuades a young person not to re-offend. [4]_____ working with sick children or old people makes young offenders realize that there are people who have more difficult lives than they do. So community service can be an educational experience, [5]_____ other punishments are not.

[6]_____, I do not think that a fine is a suitable punishment for young people. They do not usually have much money themselves, [7]_____ it is often their parents who pay the fine for them.

[8]_____, spending time in prison results in young people meeting other criminals and learning more about the criminal world, which may tempt them into committing more crimes. [9]_____, in prisons many of the inmates take drugs, and this is a terrible example for young offenders.

[10]_____, I believe that community service has important advantages both for minor offenders and for the community.

---

a  Read the title of the post. Do you agree or disagree? Then quickly read the article and see if the writer's opinion is the same as yours.

b  Complete the article with a word or phrase from the list below.

finally   firstly   for instance   in addition   in conclusion
in most cases   ~~nowadays~~   secondly   so   whereas

c  You are going to write an article to post on the forum. With a partner, choose one of the titles below.

> **Downloading music or films without paying is as much of a crime as stealing from a shop.**

> **Squatters who live in an unoccupied property should not be forced to leave it.**

d  **Plan** the content. The article should have four or five paragraphs.
   1  **The introduction:** Think about what the current situation is and what your opinion is.
   2  **The main paragraphs:** Try to think of at least two clear reasons to support your opinion. You could also include examples to back up your reasons.
   3  **The conclusion:** Think of how to express your conclusion (a summary of your opinion).

e  **Write** 140–190 words, organized in four or five paragraphs (introduction, opinions and reasons, conclusion). Use a formal style (no contractions or colloquial expressions). Use the phrases in **b** and in **Useful language**.

> 🔍 Useful language: ways of giving your opinion
> (Personally) I think… / I believe…
> In my opinion,…
> In addition,… / Also,…
> In conclusion,… / To sum up,…
>
> Ways of giving examples
> There are several things we can do,
> for example / for instance / such as…
> Another thing we can do is…
> We can also…
>
> Sequencing words
> Firstly, / Secondly, / Thirdly, / Finally,…

f  **Check** your article for mistakes (grammar, punctuation, and spelling).

 p.79

# Living in Milton Keynes

**Introduction**

This report describes the town of Milton Keynes. It gives some information about the history of the town and some of its features and facilities, and includes a personal view of what it is like to live there.

**1** _____

In the 1960s, town planners wanted to encourage people to move out of London. Their idea was to create a modern, efficient town with good facilities that would be easy to travel around and healthy to live in. So, the 'new town' of Milton Keynes was built in the south-east of England.

**2** _____

The town now has a population of around 250,000. Wide, straight roads join the different living districts, with many lakes and green spaces between them. The centre is a business and shopping district. In terms of transport, Milton Keynes is particularly well-connected; it is near the M1 motorway and is mid-way between London, Birmingham, Oxford, and Cambridge.

**3** _____

In general, it is a town that is easy to walk or cycle around. For those who enjoy more challenging sports, there are some superb facilities. These include Treetop Extreme, the biggest 'high rope' adventure course in the UK, and Snozone, an indoor real snow slope where you can learn to ski and snowboard.

**4** _____

Milton Keynes was the first place in the UK to have a multiscreen cinema, and there is also a large concert venue called The Bowl. It has an international orchestra and over 200 works of public art – it is particularly famous for the sculpture of concrete cows.

**Conclusion**

To sum up, it seems that _____. Some people feel that new towns lack atmosphere and a sense of community, but the majority of residents here are proud of their town. 'Things tend to be more modern and spectacular in Milton Keynes than anywhere else,' says Simon Clawson, who has lived there since he was four years old. On balance, the planners of the 1960s have achieved their aims.

---

**a** Read the introduction to the report. What is it going to cover?

**b** Read the rest of the report. With a partner, match the headings to paragraphs 1–4.

   **Activities   Culture   History   Present day**

**c** Tick (✓) the kinds of information that are mentioned in the main paragraphs of the report.

   - [ ] what the town planners wanted to achieve
   - [ ] the size of the town
   - [ ] the layout of the town
   - [ ] where people work
   - [ ] transport connections
   - [ ] the cost of accommodation
   - [ ] things to see
   - [ ] things to do

**d** Choose the best option to complete the conclusion of the report.

   some people aren't happy living in Milton Keynes

   the new town of Milton Keynes has been a success

   Milton Keynes has the best facilities in the UK

**e** You have been asked to write a report for an English language magazine on life in a modern city. **Plan** the content. With a partner, decide…

   1 which city you are going to write about.
   2 what headings you can use to divide up your report.
   3 what information to include under each heading.
   4 the aim and content of the introduction.

**f** **Write** 140–190 words, including an introduction, and three or four paragraphs with headings. Summarize the main point(s) in your conclusion. Use a neutral / formal style, and use expressions from **Useful language**.

> 🔍 **Useful language: Signposting**
>
> **Introductions and conclusions:**
> *This report describes… / The purpose of this report is to…*
> *To sum up / To conclude / In conclusion*
>
> **To introduce a topic:**
> *In terms of (transport)…*
>
> **To emphasize sth:**
> *(Milton Keynes) is particularly / especially (well positioned)*
>
> **To generalize:**
> *In general / Generally speaking, (it's a town that's easy to walk around)*
> *On balance,… / On the whole,…*
> *The majority of / Most (residents)…*
> *Things tend to be / are usually…*

**g** **Check** your report for mistakes (grammar, punctuation, and spelling).

⬅ **p.93**

# Listening

**1 Rafa**

**Interviewer** Why do you have problems sleeping?

**Rafa** Well I'm Spanish, but I moved to London a few years ago when I married a British woman. I've been living here for three years now. I have a lot of problems getting to sleep at night because our bedroom just isn't dark enough. I can't get used to sleeping in a bedroom where there's light coming in from the streetlights outside. In Spain, I always used to sleep in complete darkness because my bedroom window had blinds and when I went to bed I used to close the blinds completely. But here in England, our bedroom window just has curtains and curtains don't block out the light properly. It takes me a long time to get to sleep at night and I always wake up more often than I used to do in Spain.

**Interviewer** So why don't you just get thicker curtains?

**Rafa** Because my wife doesn't like sleeping in a completely dark room. She says that she feels claustrophobic if the room is too dark.

**Interviewer** Ah, yes, some people do feel like that.

**2 Mike**

**Interviewer** Why do you have problems sleeping?

**Mike** Well, I'm a policeman so I have to do shift work, which means I work at night every other week, so I start work at 10 o'clock at night and finish at 6.00 in the morning the following day. The main problem is that my body's used to sleeping at night, not during the day. So it's very hard to get used to being awake all night and trying to work and concentrate when your body is just telling you to go to bed.

**Interviewer** But isn't it something you eventually get used to?

**Mike** Actually no, because I work during the day for one week and then the next week I work at night, which means that just when my body has got used to being awake at night then I go back to working in the day, and then of course I can't get to sleep at night because my body thinks it's going to have to work all night.

The other problem is that when I get home after working a night shift, everyone else is just starting to wake up, so that means that it can be really noisy. The neighbours put on the radio, and bang doors and shout to wake their children up. So even though I'm really tired, it's just very hard to get to sleep.

**Interviewer** How many hours do you usually sleep?

**Mike** Before I became a policeman, I used to sleep about eight or nine hours a night, but I think now I probably don't sleep more than six hours.

**3 Steph**

**Interviewer** Why do you have problems sleeping?

**Steph** I have a lot of problems sleeping because of jet lag. I have to travel a lot in my job and I take a lot of long-haul flights. I fly to New York quite often and I arrive maybe at 6.00 in the evening my time, but when it's only one o'clock in the afternoon in New York. So at 5.00 in the afternoon New York

time, I'll be feeling tired and ready for bed because it's my bed time. But I can't go to sleep because I'm probably still working or having dinner with my American colleagues. Then when I do finally get to bed at say midnight, I find that I wake up in the middle of the night because my body thinks that it's morning because it's still working on UK time.

**Interviewer** And can you get back to sleep when you wake up?

**Steph** No, that's the problem. I can't get back to sleep. And then the next day when I have meetings I feel really sleepy. It's very hard to stay awake all day. And just when I'm finally used to being on New York time, then it's time to fly back to the UK. And flying west to east is even worse.

**Interviewer** Oh! Why's that?

**Steph** Because when I get off the plane it's early morning in the UK. But for me, on New York time, it's the middle of the night. It takes me four or five days to recover from one of those trips.

**Interviewer** Gosh, that must be really difficult for you.

**Steph** Yeah, it is.

 6.9

I know a lot about sleep. I've been involved in sleep research for over 36 years. I call myself a sleep expert, and I think that if you are going to give advice about sleep, you should follow your own rules. So here are some things you should know about my sleep habits.

1 I sleep in a different bedroom from my partner. Everyone should sleep alone. It's much better, if you can, to have your own room. You can wake refreshed, rather than be cross because your partner snored all night. My partner wasn't offended when I suggested we had separate rooms. In fact, she found she slept much better. Apparently, I make funny noises in my sleep.

2 I sleep under natural materials. I wouldn't dream of getting into a bed made with hot, sweaty, man-made fibres. If you're really hot, it's hard to fall asleep or stay asleep. This is why we turn over at night – not just to relieve pressure, but to find a cool spot. To sleep well, we need to lose one degree of body temperature, and cotton is excellent at keeping us cool.

3 I'm obsessive about pillows. Pillows are really necessary for good sleep. It's essential that your body is in the right position, and a pillow should fill the gap between your shoulder and neck, to keep the neck and spine aligned when you lie on your side. I have two pillows because I'm tall and that works for me, but if one pillow holds you in the correct position, that's fine too. I wash my pillows every six months and dry them outside.

4 I sleep with the window open. Fresh air is good for sleep, and a build-up of carbon dioxide disturbs it. It's the warmth under the duvet that's important, not the warmth of the room. So keep your bedroom door open and open the window at least a centimetre every night, all year round. Even if it's minus 5 degrees, I keep the window open, and curl up with a hot water bottle.

5 I don't have dinner late. I prefer to eat before 7.00 p.m. If you have a large meal too close to bedtime, your body will still be working to

digest it, and not resting. Eating your main meal three or four hours before bed is ideal.

6 I drink coffee in the evenings. After dinner in a restaurant I will happily order an espresso. Many people are insensitive to caffeine. Unless you know that you're sensitive to caffeine, it's actually the worrying that you've drunk caffeine that keeps you awake, not the caffeine itself.

7 I need 9½ hours' sleep. It's a myth that you need an average of eight hours' sleep. Sleep need is genetic – some people might need four hours, others eleven. The right amount of sleep for you is something you can work out based on how many hours you need to feel alert during the day. That figure stays the same for you throughout your life. I always wake up at the same time early every morning, so to get the amount of sleep I need, I know I need to be in bed by 9.30 p.m.

8 I read a book before going to sleep. Everyone should have a way to relax before going to sleep. I read a non-thrilling book, often short stories, or a book with short chapters. You don't want something where every chapter ends on a cliffhanger, because that makes you want to read on.

 6.10

**Part 1**

I think it's very interesting that human beings are the only animals which listen to music for pleasure. A lot of research has been done to find out why we listen to music, and there seem to be three main reasons. Firstly, we listen to music to make us remember important moments in the past, for example, when we met someone for the first time. Think of Humphrey Bogart in the film *Casablanca*, saying, 'Darling, they're playing our song'. When we hear a certain piece of music, we remember hearing it for the first time in some very special circumstances. Obviously, this music varies from person to person.

Secondly, we listen to music to help us change activities. If we want to go from one activity to another, we often use music to help us make the change. For example, we might play a certain kind of music to prepare us to go out in the evening, or we might play another kind of music to relax us when we get home from work. That's mainly why people listen to music in cars, and they often listen to one kind of music when they're going to work and another kind when they're coming home. The same is true of people on buses and trains.

The third reason why we listen to music is to intensify the emotion that we're feeling. For example, if we're feeling sad, sometimes we want to get even sadder, so we play sad music. Or we're feeling angry and we want to intensify the anger then we play angry music. Or when we're planning a romantic dinner, we lay the table, we light candles, and then we think, 'What music would make this even more romantic?'

 6.12

**Part 2**

Let's take three important human emotions: happiness, sadness, and anger. When people are happy, they speak faster, and their voice is higher. When they are sad, they speak more slowly and their voice is lower, and when people are angry, they raise their voices or shout. Babies can tell whether their mother is happy or not simply by the sound of her voice, not by her words. What music does is, it copies this, and it produces the same emotions. So, faster, higher-pitched music will sound happy. Slow music with lots of falling pitches will sound sad. Loud music with irregular rhythms will sound angry. It doesn't matter how good or bad the music is, if it has these characteristics, it will make you experience this emotion.

Let me give you some examples. For 'happy', for example, the first movement of Beethoven's *Seventh Symphony*. For 'angry', say, *Mars*, from *The Planets*, by Holst. And for 'sad', something like *Albinoni's Adagio for Strings*.

Of course, the people who exploit this most are the people who write film soundtracks. They can take a scene which visually has no emotion and they can make the scene either scary or calm or happy, just by the music they write to go with it. Think of the music in the shower scene in Hitchcock's film *Psycho*. All you can see is a woman having a shower, but the music makes it absolutely terrifying.

🔊 7.1

F1 = female student 1, M1 = male student 1,
F2 = female student 2, F3 = female student 3,
M2 = male student 2

**F1** Where's my milk? It's not here.

**M1** I haven't seen it. You must have finished it.

**F1** I definitely didn't finish it. I was keeping a bit for my cereal this morning. One of you must have used it.

**F2** It can't have been me. I only drink my soya milk. Could you have drunk it last night and then forgotten? Did you have something before going to bed?

**F1** No I didn't. I just drank a glass of water.

**M1** Someone might have given it to the cat.

**F1** Oh come on. We all know she drinks water, not milk. I'm telling you, last night I know there was some milk in the fridge. MY milk.

**M1** Well, I don't know what's happened to it. In any case, you should have put your name on it.

**F1** I did put my name on it! In capital letters!

**F3** And it wasn't me, because I stayed at Mike's last night and I had breakfast there before getting back here.

**F1** What are you drinking Jack?

**M2** Just coffee.

**F1** Yes, white coffee. That's where my milk went. You didn't have any milk of your own in the fridge.

**F2** Ooh, Jack, you naughty boy!

**F1** Well, you can go to the supermarket and get me some more.

**M2** OK, OK, calm down. I'll go and get you some milk…

🔊 7.7

In life, we sometimes have disagreements with people. It could be with your partner, with your boss, with your parents, or with a friend. When this happens, the important thing is to try not to let a difference of opinion turn into a heated argument. But, of course, it's easier said than done.

The first thing I would say is that the way you begin the conversation is very important. Imagine you live with your partner, and you're feeling annoyed because you feel that you always do most of the housework. If you say, 'Look, you're not doing your share of the housework,' you're beginning the conversation in a very negative way, and the discussion will very soon turn into an argument. It's much more constructive to say something like, 'I think we should have another look at how we divide up the housework. Maybe there's a better way of doing it.'

My second piece of advice is simple. If you're the person who's in the wrong, just admit it! This is the easiest and best way to avoid an argument. Just apologize – say to your flatmate, your parents, or your husband, 'Sorry, it was my fault',

and move on. The other person will have much more respect for you if you do that.

The next tip is, don't exaggerate. Try not to say things like, 'You always forget our wedding anniversary', when perhaps this has only happened once before, or, 'You never ever remember to turn the lights off.' This will just make the other person get very defensive because what you're saying about them just isn't true.

If you follow these tips, you may often be able to avoid an argument. But if an argument does start, it's important to keep things under control and there are ways to do this.

The most important thing is not to raise your voice. Raising your voice will just make the other person lose their temper, too. If you find yourself raising your voice, stop for a moment and take a deep breath. Say, 'I didn't mean to shout. I'd rather we didn't argue, but this is very important to me.', and continue calmly. If you can talk calmly and quietly, you'll find the other person will be more ready to think about what you're saying.

It's also very important to stick to the point. Try to keep to the topic you're talking about. Don't bring up old arguments, or try to bring in other issues. Just concentrate on solving the one problem you're having, and leave the other things for another time. So, for example, if you're arguing about the housework, don't suddenly say, 'And another thing, I was really disappointed with my birthday present – you didn't make any effort at all.'

And my final tip is that, if necessary, call 'Time out' like in a sports match. If you think that an argument is getting out of control, then you can say to the other person, 'Listen, I'd rather talk about this tomorrow when we've both calmed down.' You can then continue talking about it the next day when perhaps both of you are feeling less tense and angry. That way, there's much more chance that you'll be able to reach an agreement. You'll also probably find that the problem is much easier to solve when you've both had a good night's sleep.

But I want to say one last thing which I think is very important. Some people think that arguing is always bad, but that isn't true. Conflict is a normal part of life, and dealing with conflict is an important part of any relationship, whether it's three people sharing a flat, a married couple, or just two good friends. If you don't learn to argue properly, then when a real problem comes along, you won't be prepared to face it together. Think of all the smaller arguments as training sessions. Learn how to argue cleanly and fairly. It will help your relationships become stronger and last longer.

🔊 7.10

This still is from the film *Atonement*, a period drama set in the 1930s. It shows Keira Knightley, who plays Cecilia Tallis, the elder daughter of a wealthy family, and James McAvoy who plays Robbie, the son of the family's housekeeper. Cecilia is studying at Cambridge University, and, unusually, Robbie is too, his studies being paid for by Cecilia's father. Despite moving in very different circles at university, they have always been close and they are now back at the family home for the holidays. This evening, there's going to be a dinner party, to which Robbie has been invited. In this shot, he is following her in to dinner. She is feeling anxious and indecisive, because she has just realized that she is in love with him, but knows that their relationship would be frowned on given their difference in status. Despite this, soon after they declare their love for each other. The film was one of Knightley's first big starring roles. It won several awards and was nominated for several others, including costume design. This green dress is one of the stunning outfits she appears in.

🔊 7.12

**A** Helen Mirren won a well-deserved Oscar for her performance as Queen Elizabeth II in *The Queen*. The film is about how the Royal Family responds to the tragic death of Diana, Princess of Wales in a car crash in 1997. The Queen had had a troubled

relationship with Diana, who had divorced Prince Charles. When Diana dies, she feels the death is a private affair, and wants to protect her grandchildren, Princes William and Harry, from the paparazzi, so she keeps them at her castle in Scotland. However, there is a massive outpouring of grief from the general public, who surround Buckingham Palace with flowers, and both the Prime Minister and Prince Charles think the Queen should return to London. At first, she refuses, but in the end, she is persuaded to come back, and in this scene, the climax of the film, she inspects the thousands of flowers outside the palace. Her expression shows a mixture of feelings: sadness, perhaps some surprise at the strength of the public's love for Diana, and perhaps relief that she'd made the right decision in the end to come back to London.

**B** This is a scene from the fantasy film *Fantastic Beasts and Where to Find Them*, which is a prequel to the Harry Potter films. Set in 1926, the film stars Eddie Redmayne as the wizard Newt Scamander, who comes to New York with a suitcase containing several magical creatures. When he's at the bank, one of the creatures escapes from the suitcase. In this scene, he's desperately trying to recapture it, and is watching, horrified, as it starts stealing things from people in the bank. J.K. Rowling herself both wrote the script and co-produced the film, and it was the first film set in Harry Potter's wizarding world to win an Oscar.

**C** Frances McDormand, who won an Oscar for best actress in *Three Billboards Outside Ebbing, Missouri*, is without doubt one of the most versatile actresses of her generation. This still is from the Coen brothers' black comedy *Burn after Reading*, which also starred George Clooney and Brad Pitt. McDormand plays the role of Linda Litzke, a personal trainer, who, with her co-worker Chad, tries to steal money from a retired CIA worker. Linda is in desperate need of money, mainly because she's obsessed with expensive cosmetic surgery. In this scene, she's discussing with the doctor the work she wants done. During the discussion, the doctor has suggested that she have an operation to get rid of her crow's feet – the lines and wrinkles around the eyes. Linda protests that they're baby, tiny crow's feet, and as the doctor explains the procedure, she feels more and more unsure and indecisive about what to do. The genius of McDormand's acting is that although the character of Linda is self-centred, superficial and not very bright, McDormand manages to portray her as a true American heroine.

**D** This still shows Daniel Kaluuya in the 2017 American horror movie *Get Out*. Daniel plays the role of Chris, a young black photographer, who goes to meet the parents of his white girlfriend Rose, who live in a large house in the country. Although the parents try to make it clear that they're not at all racist, Chris quickly realizes that there is something very strange about them, and about the black servants they employ. In this scene, Rose's mother, a psychiatrist who practises hypnotherapy, is hypnotizing him. Although in theory it is to help him to stop smoking, here she gets him to relive the horror and the shock of the evening when he was six years old and his mother was killed in a car accident. Kaluuya was nominated for an Oscar for his performance, and the movie won the Oscar for best screenplay.

🔊 7.14

Exercise 2 is called: Stroking an animal.
This exercise is often used in drama classes for beginners, to help them to develop their body language. It should be done in a group.
Each person must think of an animal they really like. It can be a wild or tame animal, big or small.

Then imagine stroking it. Think about where it is, in your hand, in your arms, standing or sitting next to you. Now, one by one, mime the action to the rest of the group. They have to guess which animal it is.

OK, now exercise 3 is called: What were they wearing?

The exercise is aimed at developing attention. Attention is very important for an actor, as you have to be able to observe every detail of other people.

The exercise is done in a group, with one person acting as the host. In a group, sit in a circle and, for three minutes, try to focus on what everyone is wearing. It's important to remember as many details as you can: clothes, accessories, etc. After three minutes, close your eyes unless you're the host of the game, and the host asks questions, for example, 'Anna, tell me, please, what's Helen wearing?', 'John, what colour are Anna's shoes?', etc. At the end, everyone opens their eyes and checks the answers.

The last exercise we're going to do today is exercise 4: The 'magic' image.

Showing emotions on stage or on camera can be very hard for some beginners. One trick, which this exercise helps with, is to develop a way of recalling the desired emotion.

The exercise can be done individually or in groups. Choose one emotion, for example, 'anger', and then on a piece of paper, write down some situations that make you angry, for example, noisy neighbours, or bad drivers. If you're doing this in a group, show each other what you've written down – you may want to choose some ideas from another person's list to add to your own list. Choose no more than five situations in total. When you have your final list, think of an image for each situation, for example, for noisy neighbours, it could be a dog, for bad drivers, a car, and so on. Now the important part – you need to create one new image on the sheet of paper which combines your separate anger images, for example, a car with a dog in the back, etc. This is your 'magic image' of anger. Recalling this image will help you to show anger when you're acting. You can do the same thing with other emotions, such as happiness, sorrow, and so on. So now let's actually do these exercises. We'll start with number two, stroking an animal. So if you get into groups of five or six, we'll get going.

### 🔊 8.1
**Stay safe**

Street crime is often unplanned, so making yourself less of a target, moving with purpose, and being aware of your surroundings will go a long way to keeping you safe when you're out and about. Here are eight important pieces of advice.

1 Be prepared. Always plan your route in advance. Carry a fully charged mobile phone and some cash, and tell someone where you're going.

2 Be assertive. From the moment you step out onto the street in the morning, you need to look assertive, and act and walk with confidence. This will always make you appear in control and you will seem much less vulnerable.

3 Be aware. Using a mobile phone, whether you're calling, messaging, or looking up information, reduces your awareness of your surroundings. So does listening to loud music on headphones, or wearing a hooded jacket or sweatshirt.

4 Hide it. Keep your valuables hidden either in a bag or under your clothes. This includes your phone, other devices such as cameras or tablets, and jewellery. Remember – out of sight, out of mind.

5 Go against the flow. When you're walking on the pavement, always face towards the oncoming traffic. This will make it more difficult for thieves on two-wheels to ride up from

behind and snatch your bag. But, don't forget to still be aware of anyone approaching from ahead of you.

6 Trust your instincts. At night, try to avoid walking alone in places such as parks and quiet side streets, or in fact, in any area you don't know. If you do have to walk, keep to busy places where there is a lot of activity, good lighting, and CCTV. And if you're on public transport, it's much better to travel with people you know or stick to routes that other people are using.

7 Make a plan. Discuss with friends what to do if something were to go wrong on your night out together, for example, if you were to get separated. Agree on a backup plan and keep an eye on each other during the evening. And stick to what you've agreed.

8 Look out for trouble. Alcohol and drugs make it harder for you to assess risks and decide how to deal with them. So, be careful how much you drink, and never let your glass or bottle out of your sight, in case someone puts something into your drink. Stay safe!

### 🔊 8.7
**Newsreader** Police in Stockport are looking for a man who is said to be Britain's most polite armed robber. The robber always says please and thank you when he orders shop staff to give him money from the till. It is believed that he is a tall man in his early forties and that he wears a mask and washing-up gloves during the robberies. It is thought that he has robbed at least four shops in Stockport in recent weeks. DI Anderson from Greater Manchester Police has given a warning to the public.

**Police Officer** He is reported to be polite to his victims, but there's nothing polite about armed robbery. Last week, this man used a knife to threaten shop staff and they were terrified. Saying please and thank you doesn't change that.

### 🔊 8.11
**Story 1**

And now, some news for wine drinkers. It seems that 'red' and 'white' are no longer the only options. France finally has a wine to match all three of the colours on its national flag, as a new blue variety hits the shelves. Vindigo is a chardonnay that gets its distinctive blue colour by being passed through red grape skins. The grape skins contain a natural dye found in blackcurrants, red cabbage, and raspberries. The new wine is the responsibility of French entrepreneur, Rene Le Bail. He persuaded a company in Almeria in Spain, to produce the wine, after he was unable to convince anyone in France to become involved. Around 35,000 bottles of Vindigo are now on sale in the south of France – in the port city of Sete – for about €12 a bottle. In an interview with a French newspaper, Monsieur Le Bail describes the wine as 'ideal for the summer'. He says that it has aromas of cherry, blackberry, and passionfruit, and recommends drinking it on the beach, or around the swimming pool.

**Story 2**

And now for our last story today – a zoo in Egypt has denied painting a donkey with black stripes in order to make it look like a zebra. Egyptian student Mahmoud Sarhan, 18, was visiting the zoo in Cairo, when he noticed the animal, which had strange looking black stripes. Mr Sarhan was suspicious, and took a photo of the animal, which appeared to have strange black marks on its face, and posted it online. He later told the media, 'I knew it was a donkey as soon as I saw it. I'm an artist. I know the different shape of a donkey and a zebra, so it was easy to tell the difference.' After the image was shared on social media, it went viral. Egyptian news site Extranews.tv approached a local vet, who agreed to examine the photo. He pointed

out that zebras usually have a black nose and mouth, whereas the animal in Mr Sarhan's photo appears to be pale in this area. The vet added that authentic zebra stripes are usually straighter and clearer than those on the animal in Mr Sarhan's photo. The local radio station contacted the zoo's director, Mohamed Sultan. However, he refused to admit that the animal was a donkey.

### 🔊 9.1

The first point to bear in mind is that nothing, but nothing, is ever free. How often have you seen adverts saying things like, 'Get a free Bluetooth speaker when you subscribe to our magazine for six months'? There's something about the word 'free' that immediately attracts us – I want it! It makes us feel clever, as if we're going to get something for nothing. But, of course, that Bluetooth speaker (which, incidentally, will probably break the second time you use it) wasn't free at all. In spite of what the advert said, its price was really included in the magazine subscription. So, don't trust any advert which offers something for free.

A second trick which advertisers use is when they tell us, 'There are only a few left! Buy now while stocks last!' What happens to us when we read or hear these words? Even though we don't really need the products, and maybe don't even like them, we immediately want to be among the lucky few who have them. But – let's be clear about this – companies just don't run out of products. Do you really think the manufacturers couldn't produce a few more, if they thought they could sell them? Of course they could.

When it comes to new products, we, the consumers, are like sheep and we follow each other. So, another way advertisers have of getting us to use something is to tell us, 'Everybody's using it'. And of course, we think everybody can't be wrong, so the product must be fantastic. So as to make us believe it, they use expressions like, 'It's a must-have' or 'It's the in thing', and they combine this with a photograph of a large group of people, so that we can't fail to get the message. But don't be fooled. Even if everybody is using it (and they may not be), everybody can be wrong.

Another favourite message is 'You too can look like this', accompanied by a photo of a fabulous-looking man or woman. But the problem is, you can't look like this because actually the woman or man in the photo is a model and also because he or she doesn't really look like that, either. The photo has been airbrushed in order to make the model look even slimmer, with perfect skin, and even more attractive than they are in real life.

Adverts also often mention a particular organization which recommends their product – for example things like, 'Our dog biscuits are recommended by the International Association of Dog Nutritionists' – well, that's probably an organization which the company set up themselves. Or, 'A recent independent study found that our toothpaste cleans your teeth better than any other brand'. What study was it? Who commissioned the study? It was probably produced for the company itself, and paid for by them, too.

Finally, what most annoys me is, 'Trust me, I'm a doctor' or 'Trust me, I'm a celebrity'. The idea is that if a celebrity is using the product, it must be fantastic, or if a doctor recommends it, it must really work. But be careful. Although the actress is holding the product in the photo, do you really think she colours her hair with it at home? And the doctor in the advert, is he really a doctor or just an actor wearing a white coat?

### 🔊 9.11

1 I think I'd have to say Venice in Italy. In spite of all the tourists, all the clichés, I still think it's the most beautiful city I know. I always remember

the first time I went – I arrived by train – and we stepped out of the station and suddenly it was all there, the canals, the wonderful old buildings. What makes it beautiful for me is the light, the combination of the reflections of the churches and palaces in the water, the wonderful winding streets alongside canals, which are all different but also all similar – it's an incredibly easy city to get lost in. And of course, the fact that there are no cars, no traffic. I fell totally in love with it that first time, and I've been back since then and loved it just as much. It's difficult to think of just one thing to see, I mean, Piazza San Marco is beautiful, the Rialto bridge, but I wouldn't say they were the things I remember most. I would actually say just wander, without a map or a goal and get lost. Everything is beautiful. The one thing I'd say to do is go on a *vaporetto* – a water bus – down the Grand Canal. I don't think gondolas are worth it – they're ridiculously expensive – and you can enjoy everything just as much on a *vaporetto*.

2 The most beautiful city I've been to recently is probably Curitiba, which is in southern Brazil. I think one of the things I liked about it most was, it's described as the greenest city on earth, and they've really focused on creating a quality public transportation system, there's a huge number of parks in Curitiba, in fact, there's so much grass that the local authority use sheep to cut the grass, not lawnmowers. And I just think that what I like about it is their commitment to trying to make the city, er, an environmentally-friendly place to live. One place you need to see there is the Wire Opera House which, it's built in the middle of an artificial lake in the middle of a park, and it's built out of steel tubes, it's really extraordinary, and beautiful I think. And if I had to recommend one thing to do I'd say go for a walk in the Bosque Alemão, it's one of the wonderful parks in Curitiba, and visit the free environmental university which is built up in the trees just nearby. Its mission is to educate people about the environment, and I just think that's a wonderful goal to have.

3 The most beautiful city I've ever been to is Bruges in Belgium – well, I'm not absolutely sure if it's a city or a town – but anyway it's my all-time favourite place. What makes it beautiful for me is the fact that it just looks as if it came out of a fairy tale, it's, er, there are very old buildings that aren't too tall and it's very traditional and the whole place is like that, there's nothing super modern like skyscrapers that breaks that illusion of being somewhere magical. There are lots of things to see – there are two really beautiful churches, but I think that the whole of the old city is just amazing to look at and also there are hardly any cars so you can just cycle or walk round. There are lots of canals with swans, I just sat there staring at everything and feeding the swans – it was so peaceful and beautiful. Something everyone who visits Bruges needs to do is go to the market, which is like a square with lots of shops and most of the shops sell chocolate, which is one of the main things they sell in Bruges and it's absolutely delicious, so I think you need to sit down and have a tea or a coffee and a couple of chocolates just looking out on this really beautiful square.

4 I know lots of beautiful cities and, er, I wouldn't choose one above all the others, but one I always love going back to is Edinburgh in Scotland, and something I really love about Edinburgh is that because it's quite compact, more or less wherever you are in the city you can see outside the city, so you can see the sea, you can see the hills around, so you always have a sense of the city and the landscape and I really like that. And one place, one thing I would recommend people to see in Edinburgh

is something called the Scotsman's Steps which is a staircase that goes from the wall that joins the old town to the new town and it's actually an art work, it's called work number 1059 by an artist called Martin Creed and it's basically a staircase made of marble steps, each one is a different colour marble, so you really have a feel of going somewhere, you're going from one colour to the next, and I love that place. And something I would do in Edinburgh would be to walk along the river Leith either way, either from the port of Leith up into the city or the other way, because it's like a secret bit of Edinburgh and you see Edinburgh from a different perspective.

5 The most beautiful city I've been to is Kyoto in Japan. It's a really lovely place because it's a mix of, well, like many Japanese cities, very, very modern buildings and a lot of traditional, er, temple areas as well and you can walk down any Japanese shopping street and find a big supermarket or a modern office block next to a little temple where you step back in time many centuries. The one place that I would recommend you see is the Kinkaku-ji temple which is a very, very famous tourist site, it has a golden pavilion in the middle and it's the most wonderful place. It gets very, very busy but I was lucky enough to visit it when I lived in Japan and I was able to stay with a friend and go there very early in the morning to avoid the crowds. One thing you need to do if you go to Kyoto is to try to stay not in a modern hotel but in a ryokan which is a traditional Japanese guest house where you can sleep on tatami matting and have, er, Japanese breakfast which is rice, eggs, fish, and seaweed.

🔊 10.1

1
**Child** Why is the sky blue?
**Scientist** To understand why the sky is blue, we first need to understand a little about light. Although light from the Sun looks white, it is really made up of many different colours, as we see when they are spread out in a rainbow. Light is like a wave of energy, and each colour has a different wavelength. Red is the longest, and blue and violet are the shortest. When the Sun's light reaches the Earth's atmosphere, it's scattered by tiny molecules of gas in the air. Shorter wavelengths (violet and blue) are scattered the most widely, and our eyes are much more sensitive to blue than violet, so we see more of the blue light than the other colours. So that's why we see the sky as blue.

2
**Child** Why is the sea salty?
**Scientist** Most of our planet's surface is covered in salt water. But where does the salt come from? Well, some of it comes from rocks on the bottom of the sea, but most of it actually comes from the land around us. Every time it rains, tiny amounts of mineral salts dissolve into rivers, and these eventually get to the sea. Rivers aren't very salty, because they flow continually, but the Sun's heat causes the seawater to evaporate, so the salt in the sea becomes more concentrated.

3
**Child** Why can we sometimes see the moon during the day?
**Scientist** We all know that the Sun produces a lot of strong light. So when it's in the sky, we can't see the stars, or the other planets. The moon doesn't produce light – it reflects the light of the Sun. The moon is visible for about 12 out of every 24 hours because of the way it rotates around the Earth. This means it's visible for some time during daylight nearly every day.

4
**Child** Why do we have a leap year?
**Scientist** A year is the amount of time it takes the

Earth to go around the Sun, and we've divided our calendar year into 365 days. However, it actually takes the Earth 365 days, 5 hours, 48 minutes and 45 seconds to go round the Sun. To deal with this difference, we add one day (24 hours) to our calendar every four years. This adjustment is not exactly correct, because it effectively adds 6 hours per year rather than the exact amount of the difference.

5
**Child** Why do we blink?
**Scientist** A 'blink of an eye' lasts only a tenth of a second. Every time you blink, your eyelids spread fluid across the surface of your eyes, to keep them moist, and also to stop them getting dirty. Blinking also keeps eyes safe from things that might damage them, such as bright light and sometimes, bigger objects coming into our eyes like a small stone. Blinking stops the activity in your brain that detects changes, so you never notice that you actually stop seeing for a very short time when you blink.

6
**Child** Why does cutting onions make us cry?
**Scientist** For a vegetable, onions have very complicated chemistry. When you cut them, a chemical reaction changes molecules in the onion into a gas. When this gas reaches the cornea, the transparent layer that covers and protects the outer part of your eye, the cornea senses it as an irritant. It acts to protect your eyes by making you cry, and the tears clean your eyes.

7
**Child** What is a cloud?
**Scientist** We all enjoy looking at clouds and seeing their different shapes but what's the science behind them? Well, the sky is full of drops of water. But most of the time you can't see them, because they are too small; the drops have turned into water vapour. As the water vapour goes higher in the sky, the air gets cooler. The cooler air causes the drops to start to stick to things, like bits of dust, ice, or sea salt, which make them visible. So that's what we see when we see clouds.

8
**Child** What is a black hole?
**Scientist** This is another physics question. A black hole is caused by gravity. There are places in space where gravity pulls so hard that even light cannot get out. The reason that gravity is so strong in a black hole is that a lot of matter – that's physical 'stuff'– has been compressed into a tiny space. A lot of matter has a high mass and this creates a strong gravitational pull. Inside a black hole, space is falling faster than light, which is why light can't escape.

🔊 10.11

**Presenter** When Neil Armstrong became the first man to walk on the Moon on July 20th 1969, a global audience of 500 million people were watching and listening. As he climbed down the steps from the spacecraft and stepped onto the moon they heard him say, 'That's one small step for man, one giant leap for mankind'. It seemed like the perfect quote for such a momentous occasion. But from the moment he said it, people have argued about whether Armstrong got his lines wrong and made a mistake. James, tell us about it.

**James** Well, Armstrong always said that he wrote those words himself, which became some of the most famous and memorable words in history, during the time between landing on the moon and actually stepping out of the capsule onto the moon. That was nearly seven hours.

**Presenter** And so what is the controversy about what Armstrong said when he stepped down the ladder onto the moon?

**James** The question is, did he say, 'one small step for man' or 'one small step for a man'. That's to say did he use the indefinite article or not? It's just a little word, but there's a big difference in meaning. Armstrong always insisted that he wrote 'one small step for a man, one giant leap for mankind'. Of course, this would have been a meaningful sentence. If you say 'a man' then it clearly means that this was one small step for an individual man, i.e. himself, but one giant leap for mankind, that's to say, men and women in general. But what everybody actually heard was, 'One small step for man, one giant leap for mankind', with no indefinite article, and that sentence means, 'One small step for people in general, one giant leap for people in general.' And that doesn't really make sense.

**Presenter** So, did he just get the line wrong when he said it?

**James** Well, Armstrong himself was never sure if he actually said what he wrote. In his biography *First Man*, he told the author James Hansen, 'I must admit that it doesn't sound like the word "a" is there. On the other hand, certainly the "a" was intended, because that's the only way it makes sense.' He always regretted that there'd been so much confusion about it. But, almost four decades later, Armstrong was proved to be right. Peter Shann Ford, an Australian computer expert, used very hi-tech sound techniques to analyse his sentence and he discovered that the 'a' was said by Armstrong. It's just that he said it so quickly that you couldn't hear it on the recording which was broadcast to the world on 20th July 1969.

**Presenter** Was Armstrong relieved to hear this?

**James** Yes, he was. I think it meant a lot to him to know that he didn't make a mistake.

🔊 10.15

**Elizabeth I A** I know I have the body of a weak and feeble woman, but I have the heart and stomach of a king, and a king of England too.

**Abraham Lincoln B** It is rather for us to be here dedicated to the great task remaining before us - that from these honored dead we take increased devotion to that cause for which they gave the last full measure of devotion – that we here highly resolve that these dead shall not have died in vain – that this nation, under God, shall have a new birth of freedom – and that government of the people, by the people, for the people, shall not perish from the earth.

**Emmeline Pankhurst C** The title of my speech today is 'The laws that men have made'. Men politicians are in the habit of talking to women as if there were no laws that affect women. 'The fact is', they say, 'the home is the place for women. Their interests are the rearing and training of children. These are the things that interest women. Politics have nothing to do with these things, and therefore politics do not concern women.'

**Winston Churchill D** We shall fight on the beaches, we shall fight on the landing grounds, we shall fight in the fields and in the streets, we shall fight in the hills; we shall never surrender.

**John F Kennedy E** And so, my fellow Americans, ask not what your country can do for you; ask what you can do for your country. My fellow citizens of the world, ask not what America will do for you, but what together we can do for the freedom of man.

**Martin Luther King F** I have a dream that my four little children will one day live in a nation where they will not be judged by the color of their skin but by the content of their character. I have a dream today!

**Nelson Mandela G** I have cherished the ideal of a democratic and free society in which all persons live together in harmony, and with equal opportunities. It is an ideal which I hope to live for and to achieve. But, if needs be, it is an ideal for which I am prepared to die.

**Barack Obama H** For when we have faced down impossible odds, when we've been told we're not ready, or that we shouldn't try, or that we can't, generations of Americans have responded with a simple creed that sums up the spirit of a people. Yes we can! Yes we can! Yes we can!

🔊 10.16

**Presenter** Welcome to today's programme. Our topic today is public speaking. Public speaking is right up there at the top of what most people say they're most afraid of. There is even a name for it – glossophobia. But hopefully after this programme you will feel a lot more confident if you do have to make a speech or give a presentation.
First we have Lynne Parker, an expert in the art of public speaking, who's going to tell us some of her do's and don'ts. Then after that, we're going to talk to Anya Edwards from Chile. Anya was a finalist in last year's English Speaking Union International public speaking competition. Welcome to you both.

**Lynne** Hello.

**Anya** Hello.

**Presenter** Lynne, I believe you have six key tips for us, is that right?

**Lynne** Yes that's right. My first tip, and maybe the most important one, is be yourself. This applies both to how you speak, and to what you actually do on the stage, whether that's standing up, sitting down, or moving about. Do what you feel comfortable with. The only don't as regards how you are on stage I'd say is, try not to continually walk up and down, because this tends to distract people from what you're saying.

**Presenter** Yes, I do find that distracting.

**Lynne** Secondly, if you're using PowerPoint, don't just type out your talk. You want people to listen to what you're saying, not to read ahead. Slides are best for illustrating your talk or for drawing attention to a point. Pictures are often better than words, but if you use words, do keep it short. And do remember the 10-20-30 rule. Do you know what that is?

**Presenter** Er, no, do tell us.

**Lynne** The 10-20-30 rule is that the ideal presentation should have 10 slides, last 20 minutes, and never have a font size on the slides that's less than 30 points.

**Presenter** Ah, great, that's an easy one to remember. And tip number 3?

**Lynne** Maintain eye contact with your audience, whether it's to 500 people in a room or 20 people in a classroom or round a table. Don't spend the whole talk looking at your notes or slides.

**Presenter** How can you maintain eye contact with 500 people?

**Lynne** Well, you can't with all of them, of course, but a good technique is to scan the audience occasionally from side to side and front to back, to give the impression you're talking to everyone.

**Presenter** Number 4?

**Lynne** Rehearse, rehearse, rehearse. In front of a mirror, or even better video yourself. It'll make you aware of how you use your hands and body, and even what clothes look right.

**Presenter** Number 5?

**Lynne** Include a couple of good sound bites. Whenever you hear something good, write it down, as you might be able to use it later.

**Presenter** So sound bites, rather than stories or examples?

**Lynne** Well, no, not instead of – a good story or example can also help to illustrate a situation, or help people to remember the point you were making. Just don't make it too long, and if you're telling a little story, remember, good

stories have a beginning, a middle and an end.

**Presenter** And your last point?

**Lynne** Listen to other speakers. There are lots of good resources online, such as TED talks and The Moth, which is a great storytelling website. Also, listen to people talking when you're out and about, for example travelling on public transport or queuing up in the supermarket. You never know what witty remarks or good stories you might pick up along the way.

**Presenter** Thank you very much Lynne.

🔊 10.17

**Presenter** And now, moving on to Anya. Anya, you took part in the competition last year, is that right?

**Anya** Yes.

**Presenter** Can you tell us a bit about it?

**Anya** Well, it's open to people from any country between the ages of 16 and 18. First you compete at home, so for me, in Chile, and then the international finals take place in London.

**Presenter** What exactly did you have to do there?

**Anya** So you have to give two speeches. The first one is a prepared speech which is a maximum of five minutes on a subject that they give you – that year for me it was on the role of education. And then after your speech you have to answer questions for three to four minutes. And then the second speech, and this was definitely the scariest, was the impromptu speech. You are given three subjects to choose from which you've never seen before, and then 15 minutes to choose one and prepare a speech of 3 minutes.

**Presenter** What did you choose?

**Anya** I chose the title 'to be grown up is a state of mind'.

**Presenter** Were you nervous?

**Anya** I was nervous, very nervous. But then I've never not been nervous before speaking in front of an audience. I've done a lot of drama, of acting, and that's taught me that nerves are good because you can learn to channel them into a better performance.

**Presenter** How is public speaking different from acting?

**Anya** Well in many ways they're similar because you need many of the same qualities: to be able to stand in front of an audience confidently and speak clearly, to be convincing. But I'd say that public speaking is harder because you can't rely on anyone else. If you miss a line, there won't be someone next to you to give you your cue, and you're the main focus of attention 100% of the time.

**Presenter** And what did you learn from the experience?

**Anya** I think it was one of the most useful skills I've ever learnt, and that any person can have. If you've learnt to do it well, and practised, it means that you'll never ever have to worry about standing up and speaking in front of other people.

**Presenter** What tips would you give to someone about writing a speech?

**Anya** Well for writing a speech, I'd say, to start by talking about the topic out loud and record whatever comes into your head on your phone. Then listen back to it, and start by ordering your ideas on paper. And if you think the subject you have to talk about is a bit dry, try to come up with some anecdotes to illustrate it. Also, use plain simple language. Vocabulary that's too complicated puts people off.

**Presenter** And to deliver it?

**Anya** I agree entirely with Lynne about being authentic, being yourself. If you want your speech to be effective, people need to believe what you say, and in order to convince them, you need to be convinced yourself.

 **Go online** to listen to the audio and see all the Listening scripts

## used to, be used to, get used to

### used to / didn't use to + infinitive

> 1 I **used to sleep** for eight hours every night, but now ◀)) 6.3
> I only sleep for six.
> I hardly recognized Alan. He **didn't use to have** a beard.
> 2 When I lived in France as a child, we **used to have** croissants
> for breakfast. We **would buy** them every morning from the
> local baker.

1 We use *used to / didn't use to* + infinitive to talk about past
habits or repeated actions or situations / states which have
changed.

* *used to* doesn't exist in the present tense. For present
habits, use *usually* + the present simple, e.g. *I usually walk to
work.* **NOT** ~~I use to walk to work.~~

2 We can also use *would* (instead of *used to*) to refer to
repeated actions in the past with action verbs (e.g. *run,
listen, study, cook,* etc.). However, we can only use *used to*,
not *would*, for non-action verbs (e.g. *be, need, know, like,*
etc.). *Alan didn't use to be so thin.* **NOT** ~~Alan wouldn't be
so thin.~~

* With *would*, you must use a past time expression, or it must
be already clear that you are talking about the past.

* We can use the past simple, often with an adverb of
frequency, in the same way as *used to* and *would* to talk
about repeated past actions, e.g. *I often got up / used to
get up / would get up early when I lived in Africa, to watch
the sun rise.*

### be used to / get used to + gerund

> 1 I'm **used to sleeping** with the curtains open. I've ◀)) 6.4
> never slept with them closed.
> Carlos has just moved to London. He **isn't used to driving** on
> the left.
> 2 A I can't **get used to working** at night. I feel tired all the
> time.
> B Don't worry, you'll soon **get used to it**.

1 Use *be used to* + gerund to talk about things you are
accustomed to doing, or a new situation which is **now**
familiar or less strange.

2 Use *get used to* + gerund to talk about a new situation
which is **becoming** familiar or less strange.

> The difference between *be used to* and *get used to* is
> exactly the same as the difference between *be* and *get* +
> adjective, e.g. *It's dark* and *It's getting dark.*

---

a Right (✓) or wrong (✗)? Correct the mistakes in the
highlighted phrases.

> I can't get used to getting up so early. ✓
> She isn't used to have a big dinner in the evening. ✗
> *She isn't used to having*

1 When we were children, we didn't used to like having
our hair washed.
2 When we visited our British friends in London,
we couldn't get used to have lunch and dinner so early.
3 Have you got used to living in the country, or do you
still miss the city?
4 I'm really sleepy this morning. I'm not used to going
to bed so late.
5 There used to be a cinema in our village, but it closed
down three years ago.
6 Paul would have very long hair when he was younger.
7 I don't start work until 9.30, so I use to get up at
about 8.00.
8 Did you use to wear a uniform to school?
9 It's taking me a long time to be used to living on my
own.
10 When I had exams at university, I would stay up all
night revising.

b Complete the sentence with *used to, be used to,*
or *get used to* (positive or negative) and the verb
in brackets.

> My boyfriend is Spanish, so he *isn't used to having*
> lunch early. (have)

1 When Nathan started his first job, he couldn't
_____ at 6.00 a.m. (get up)
2 I didn't recognize you! You _____ blonde
hair, didn't you? (have)
3 Isabelle _____ a flat when she was at
university, but now she has a house of her own. (rent)
4 When we were children, we _____ all day
playing football in the park. (spend)
5 Jasmine has been a nurse all her life, so she
_____ nights. (work)
6 I've never worn glasses before, but now I'll have to
_____ them. (wear)
7 Amelia is an only child. She _____ her
things. (share)
8 Although I've lived in Spain for years, I've never
_____ dinner at nine or ten o'clock at
night. (have)
9 I _____ spinach, but now I love it. (like)
10 If you want to get fit, then you'll have to
_____ more. (exercise)

➜ p.56

## gerunds and infinitives

### verbs followed by the gerund and verbs followed by the infinitive

> 1 I **enjoy listening** to music.   We **couldn't help laughing**.   ◀))6.14
> 2 I'm really **looking forward to seeing** you.
>    I think you should **give up drinking** coffee after dinner.
> 3 I **want to speak** to you.   They **can't afford to buy** a new car.
> 4 I'd **rather eat in** than go out tonight.   She **let** him **borrow** her car.
> 5 It **started to rain**.   It **started raining**.

- When one verb follows another, the first verb determines the form of the second. This can be the gerund (verb + -ing) or the infinitive.

1 Use the **gerund** after certain verbs and expressions, e.g. *enjoy*, *can't help*, *feel like*.

2 When a phrasal verb is followed by another verb, the second verb is in the **gerund**.

3 Use the **infinitive (with to)** after certain verbs, e.g. *want*, *afford*.

4 Use the **infinitive (without to)** after modal verbs and some expressions, e.g. *might*, *would rather*, and after the verbs *make* and *let*.

5 Some verbs, e.g. *start*, *begin* and *continue* can be followed by the gerund or infinitive (with *to*) **with no difference in meaning**.

➡ **p.164 Appendix Verb patterns:** verbs followed by the gerund or the infinitive

> 🔍 *like, love, hate, and prefer*
> *like*, *love*, *hate*, and *prefer* are usually used with the gerund in British English, but they can also be used with the infinitive.
> We tend to use the gerund when we talk generally and the infinitive when we talk specifically, e.g.
> *I like swimming.* (general)   *I like to swim first thing in the morning.* (specific)
> When *like*, *love*, *hate*, and *prefer* are used with *would*, they are always followed by *to* + infinitive, e.g. *I'd prefer to stay at home tonight.*

### verbs that can be followed by the gerund or infinitive with a change in meaning

> 1 **Remember to lock** the door.   ◀))6.15
>    I **remember going** to Venice as a child.
> 2 Sorry, I **forgot to do** it.
>    I'll never **forget seeing** the Taj Mahal.
> 3 I **tried to open** the window.
>    **Try calling** Miriam on her mobile.
> 4 You **need to clean** the car.
>    The car **needs cleaning**.

1 *remember + to infinitive* = not forget to do sth, to do what you have to do
   *remember + gerund* = (remember doing sth) have or keep an image in your memory of sth you did or that happened in the past

2 *forget + to infinitive* = not remember to do sth that you have to do
   *forget + gerund* = be unable to remember sth that you did or that happened in the past

3 *try + to infinitive* = make an attempt or effort to do sth difficult
   *try + gerund* = use, do, or test sth in order to see if it is good, suitable, etc.

4 *need + gerund* is a passive construction, e.g. *the car needs cleaning* = needs to be cleaned **NOT** ~~needs to clean~~

---

**a** Complete the sentence with a gerund or infinitive verb (with or without *to*) from the list.

call   carry   come   do   drive   eat out   ~~go out~~
take   tidy   wait   work

I'm exhausted! I don't fancy *going out* tonight.

1 I suggest _____ a taxi to the airport tomorrow.
2 Even though the snow was really deep, we managed _____ to the local shop and back.
3 We'd better _____ some shopping – there isn't much food for the weekend.
4 I'm very impatient. I can't stand _____ in queues.
5 A young man kindly offered _____ my bags.
6 My parents used to make me _____ my room.
7 We threatened _____ the police if the boys didn't stop throwing stones.
8 Do you feel like _____ to the gym with me?
9 I'd prefer _____ instead of getting a takeaway.
10 I don't mind _____ late tonight if you want me to.

**b** Circle the correct form.

Your hair needs (cutting) / to cut. It's really long!

1 I'll never forget *to see* / *seeing* the Grand Canyon for the first time.
2 I need *to call* / *calling* the helpline. My computer has crashed.
3 Have you tried *to take* / *taking* a tablet to help you sleep?
4 I must have my keys somewhere. I can remember *to lock* / *locking* the door this morning.
5 I had to run home because I had forgotten *to turn* / *turning* the oven off.
6 Our house needs *to paint* / *painting*. Do you know any good house painters?
7 Did you remember *to send* / *sending* your sister a card? It's her birthday today.
8 We tried *to reach* / *reaching* the top of the mountain, but we had to turn back because of the bad weather.

↩ p.61

## past modals

**must, may / might / could, can't / couldn't + have + past participle**

1  I **must have left** my phone at Anna's. I definitely remember having it there.  🔊 7.3

You **must have seen** something. You were there when the accident happened.

2  Somebody **might have stolen** your wallet when you were getting off the train.

I wonder why she's not here. I suppose she **could have forgotten** about the meeting.

He still hasn't arrived. I **may not have given** him the right directions.

3  She **can't have gone** to work. Her car's still there.

You **couldn't have seen** their faces very clearly. It was too dark.

- We use *must, may / might / could*, or *can't / couldn't + have + past participle* to make deductions or speculate about past actions.

1  We use *must have* when we are almost sure that something happened or was true.

The opposite of *must have* is *can't have* **NOT** ~~mustn't have~~ – see 3.

2  We use *might / may / could + have* when we think it's possible that something happened or was true.

- We can also use *may / might not have* (but **NOT** ~~couldn't have~~) to talk about the possibility that something didn't happen. **NOT** ~~I couldn't have given him the right directions.~~

3  We use *can't have* and *couldn't have* when we are almost sure something didn't happen or that it is impossible. We only use *couldn't have* when the speculation is about the distant past, e.g. *They couldn't have been married. They both died young.*

**should have / ought to have + past participle**

We've gone the wrong way. We **should have turned** left at the traffic lights.  🔊 7.4

It's my fault. I **ought to have told** you earlier that my party was on Saturday.

- We use *should / shouldn't + have + past participle* to say that somebody didn't do the right thing, or to express regret or criticism.

- We can use *ought / oughtn't to have* as an alternative to *should / shouldn't have*, e.g. *I ought to have told you earlier.*

- *must have* and *should have* have completely different meanings. Compare:
*She should have phoned me.* = I told her to phone me but she didn't.
and
*She must have phoned me.* = I'm sure she phoned me. I think that missed call was her number.

---

a  Rewrite the **bold** sentences using *must / might (not) / can't + have + verb*.

> **I'm certain I left my umbrella at home.**
> *I must have left my umbrella at home.*

1  Holly's crying. **Perhaps she's had an argument with her boyfriend.** *She…*

2  **I'm sure Ben has read my email.** I sent it first thing this morning. *Ben…*

3  **I'm sure Sam and Ginny haven't got lost.** They have satnav in their car. *They…*

4  **You saw Ellie yesterday? That's impossible.** She was in bed with flu. *You…*

5  **Perhaps John didn't see you.** That's why he didn't say hello. *John…*

6  **I'm sure Lucy has bought a new car.** I saw her driving a blue VW Golf! *Lucy…*

7  **I'm sure Alex wasn't very ill.** He was only off work for one day. *Alex…*

8  They didn't go to Tom's wedding. **Maybe they weren't invited.** *They…*

9  This tastes very sweet. **I'm sure you used too much sugar.** *You…*

10 **It definitely wasn't my phone** that rang in the cinema. Mine was on silent. *It…*

b  Respond to the first sentence using *should / shouldn't have* or *ought / oughtn't to have* + a verb from the list.

| buy | drive | go | invite | ~~learn~~ | sit | take | write |
|-----|-------|-----|--------|-----------|-----|------|-------|

> **A** We couldn't understand anybody in Paris.
> **B** You <u>should have learned</u> some French before going.

1  **A** Tom told me the date of his party, but I've forgotten it.
   **B** You _____ it down.

2  **A** Sorry I'm late! The traffic was terrible.
   **B** You _____ here. The metro is faster.

3  **A** Amanda was rude to everyone at my party.
   **B** You _____ her. You know what she's like.

4  **A** I don't have any money left after going shopping.
   **B** You _____ so many shoes.

5  **A** You look really tired.
   **B** I know. I _____ to bed earlier last night.

6  **A** The chicken's still frozen solid.
   **B** I know. You _____ it out of the freezer earlier.

7  **A** I think I've burned my face.
   **B** I'm not surprised. You _____ in the sun all afternoon without any sunscreen.  ⟵ p.66

## verbs of the senses

*look / feel / smell / sound / taste*

> 1 You **look tired**.
>   That cake **smells good**!
>   These jeans don't **feel comfortable**.    🔊 7.11
> 2 Tim **looks like his father**.
>   Are you sure this is coffee? It **tastes like tea**.
>   This material **feels like silk** – is it?
> 3 She **looks as if she's been crying**.
>   It **smells as if something's burning**.
>   It **sounds as if it's raining**.
> 4 I saw Jane this morning. She **looked** sad.
>   I spoke to Jane this morning. She **seemed** sad.

1 We use *look*, *feel*, etc. + adjective.

2 We use *look*, *feel*, etc. + *like* + noun (phrase).

3 We use *look*, *feel*, etc. + *as if* + clause.

- You can use *…like* or *…as though* instead of *…as if*, e.g. *It sounds like / as though it's raining.*

4 We use *look* to describe the specific impression we get from someone's appearance. We use *seem* to describe a general impression we get (not necessarily appearance).

- *seem* can be followed by the same structures as *look*, e.g. *Mark seems like a nice man.*

🔍 **feel like**

*feel like* can also be used as a verb meaning *want / would like*. It is followed by a noun or a verb in the gerund, e.g. *I **feel like pasta** for lunch today.* (= I'd like pasta for lunch today). *I **don't feel like going** to bed.* (= I don't want to go to bed).

**as**

*as* is often used before *if* to talk about how something appears, sounds, feels, etc.: *It looks as if it's going to snow.* However, it is also used:

- to describe somebody or something's job or function: *She works as a nurse. You can use that box as a chair.*
- to compare people or things: *She's as tall as me now.*
- to give a reason: *As it was raining, we didn't go out.* (*as = because*)
- to say that something happened while something was happening: *As they were leaving, the postman arrived.* (*as = when / at the same time*)
- after *such* to give an example, e.g. *I like soft fruits, such as strawberries and raspberries.*

**a** Match the sentence halves.

| | | |
|---|---|---|
| 1 That group sounds like | F | A her mother. |
| 2 That boy looks | | B a really nice place. |
| 3 Nora looks like | | C very soft. |
| 4 That guitar sounds | | D someone has been smoking in here. |
| 5 Tom looks as if | | E really sweet. |
| 6 Our car sounds as if | | F ~~Coldplay.~~ |
| 7 Your new cashmere sweater feels | | G too young to be drinking beer. |
| 8 This apple tastes | | H it's got coffee in it. |
| 9 It smells as if | | I roses. |
| 10 Your perfume smells like | | J it's going to break down any moment. |
| 11 This cake tastes as if | | K he's just run a marathon. |
| 12 The restaurant seems like | | L awful! You need to tune it. |

**b** Circle the correct form.

Your boyfriend *looks /* (*looks like*) a rugby player. He's huge!

1 You've gone completely white. You *look / look as if* you've seen a ghost!
2 What's for dinner? It *smells / smells like* delicious!
3 I think John and Megan have arrived. That *sounds / sounds like* their car.
4 Have you ever tried frogs' legs? Apparently, they *taste like / taste as if* chicken.
5 Are you OK? You *sound / sound as if* you've got a cold.
6 Can you put the heating on? It *feels / feels like* really cold in here.
7 You *seem / seem like* really happy. Does that mean you got the job?
8 Your new bag *feels / feels like* real leather. Is it?
9 Let's throw this milk away. It *tastes / tastes like* a bit off.
10 Can you close the window? It *smells / smells as if* someone is having a barbecue.

← p.70

🌐 **Go online** to review the grammar for each lesson

## the passive (all forms); *have something done*; *it is said that…, he is thought to…,* etc.

### the passive (all forms)

> 1 The trial **is being held** at the moment.  🔊 8.8
> Jim **was arrested** last month.
> We saw that one of the windows **had been broken**.
> People used **to be imprisoned** for stealing bread.
> He paid a fine to avoid **being sent** to jail.
> 2 People think he **was murdered by** his wife.
> The body **was discovered by** a dog-walker.

1 We use the passive when we talk about an action but are not so interested in who or what does / did the action.

• To make the tense or form, we use the verb *be* + past participle, e.g. *Murderers are usually sentenced to life in prison. The prisoner will be released next month.* The tense changes are shown by the verb *be*, e.g. *are, will be,* etc.

2 To mention the person or thing that did the action (the agent), we use *by*. However, in the majority of passive sentences, the agent is not mentioned.

### *have something done* (causative *have*)

> 1 I**'ve** just **had** my bank account **hacked**.  🔊 8.9
> We **had** our passports **stolen** from our hotel room.
> **Have** you ever **had** your car **vandalized**?
> 2 We**'ve** just **had** a burglar alarm **installed**.
> You ought to **have** your locks **changed**.
> We need to **have** the broken window **repaired**.

1 We can use *have something done* to refer to something (usually bad) that is done to us.

• Remember, *have* is the main verb, so it changes according to the tense. We use auxiliary verbs (*do, did,* etc.) to make questions and negatives.

2 This structure is also used to talk about something that we arrange (and usually pay) for someone to do for us, because we can't or don't want to do it ourselves.

### *is said that…, he is thought to…,* etc.

| active | passive  🔊 8.10 |
|---|---|
| 1 They say that the fire was started deliberately. | **It is said that** the fire was started deliberately. |
| People think that the mayor will resign. | **It is thought that** the mayor will resign. |
| 2 People say the man is in his 40s. | **The man is said to be** in his 40s. |
| The police believe he has left the country. | **He is believed to have left** the country. |

• This formal structure is used especially in news reports with the verbs *know, tell, understand, report, expect, say, believe,* and *think.* It makes the information sound more impersonal.

1 We use *It is said, believed,* etc. + *that* + clause.

2 We use *He, The man,* etc. (i.e. the subject of the clause) + *is said, believed,* etc. + *to* + infinitive (e.g. *to be*) or perfect infinitive (e.g. *to have been*) when talking about the past.

---

**a** Rewrite the sentence in the passive.

> The police caught the burglar immediately.
> *The burglar was caught immediately.*

1 Somebody has stolen my phone.
   My phone…
2 They are painting my house.
   My house…
3 They'll hold a meeting to discuss the problem.
   A meeting…
4 If they hadn't found the bomb, it would have exploded.
   If the bomb…
5 Miranda thinks someone was following her last night.
   Miranda thinks she…
6 I hate somebody waking me up when I'm fast asleep.
   I hate…
7 They're going to close the local police station.
   The local police station…

**b** Complete the second sentence using *have something done.*

> I was mugged and my iPhone was stolen.
> *I was mugged and I had my iPhone stolen.*

1 Tim's social media account was hacked.
   Tim…

2 Has someone ever snatched your bag?
   Have you ever…
3 They need to get someone to check the CCTV to make sure that it's working.
   They…
4 Someone took our photo in front of the Colosseum.
   We…
5 As a result of the burglary, they're going to pay someone to put in a safe.
   As a result of the burglary, they…

**c** Rephrase the sentence to make it more formal.

> People think the murderer is a woman.
> It *is thought that the murderer is a woman.*
> The murderer *is thought to be a woman.*

1 Police believe the burglar is a local man.
   The burglar…
2 People say the muggers are very dangerous.
   It…
3 Police think the robbers entered through an open window.
   The robbers…
4 Police say the murderer has disappeared.
   It…
5 Lawyers expect that the trial will last three weeks.
   The trial…  ◀ p.78

## reporting verbs

### structures after reporting verbs

1 Jack **offered to drive** me to the airport. 🔊 **8.12**
   I **promise not to tell** anybody.
2 Doctors **advise us to do** more exercise.
   I **persuaded my sister not to go out** with George.
3 I **apologized for being** so late.
   The police **accused Karl of stealing** the car.

- To report what other people have said, we can use *say* or a specific verb, e.g.
  *'I'll drive you to the airport.'*
  Jack **said** he would drive me to the airport. **OR**
  Jack **offered** to drive me to the airport.
- After specific reporting verbs, there are three different grammatical patterns (1–3 in the chart).
- In negative sentences, we use the negative infinitive (*not to do*) or the negative gerund (*not doing*), e.g. *He reminded me not to be late. She regretted not going to the party.*
- In group 3, we can use a perfect gerund with very little difference in meaning, e.g. *He admitted stealing the money. He admitted having stolen the money.*

| Grammatical patterns after reporting verbs | | |
|---|---|---|
| 1 + *to* + infinitive | agree  offer  refuse  promise   threaten | (not) to do sth |
| 2 + person + *to* + infinitive | advise  persuade  ask  remind  convince  tell  encourage  warn  invite | sb (not) to do sth |
| 3 + *-ing* form | apologize (to sb) for  insist on   accuse sb of  recommend   admit  regret   blame sb for  suggest   deny | (not) doing sth |

🔎 **Verbs that use a *that* clause**
With *agree, admit, deny, promise,* and *regret*, you can also use *that* + clause.
*Leo admitted stealing the watch.*
*Leo admitted that he had stolen the watch.*

**a** Complete the sentence with the gerund or infinitive (with *to*) of the verb in brackets.

> The garage advised me *to buy* a new car. (buy)

1 Jamie insisted on _____ for the meal. (pay)
2 Lauren has agreed _____ late next week. (work)
3 I warned Jane _____ those shoes to the park. (not wear)
4 The man admitted _____ the woman's handbag. (steal)
5 The doctor advised Lily _____ drinking coffee. (give up)
6 The boss persuaded Megan _____ the company. (not leave)
7 Freya accused me of _____ to steal her phone. (try)
8 I apologized to Evie for _____ her birthday. (not remember)
9 Did you manage to convince your parents _____ tonight instead of tomorrow? (come)
10 My neighbour denies _____ my car, but I'm sure it was him. (damage)

**b** Complete the sentence using a reporting verb from the list and the correct form of the verb in brackets. Use an object where necessary.

accuse   invite   ~~offer~~   promise   recommend
refuse   remind   suggest   threaten

> Diana said to me, 'I'll take you to the station.'
> Diana *offered to take* me to the station. (take)

1 Ryan said, 'Let's go for a walk. It's a beautiful day.'
   Ryan _____ for a walk. (go)
2 'You copied Anna's exam!' the teacher said to Simon.
   The teacher _____ Anna's exam. (copy)
3 Sam's neighbour told him, 'I'll call the police if you have any more parties.'
   Sam's neighbour _____ the police if he had any more parties. (call)
4 The children said, 'We aren't going to bed. It's much too early.'
   The children _____ to bed. (go)
5 Peter said to me, 'Would you like to have dinner with me?'
   Peter _____ dinner with him. (have)
6 Molly said to Jack, 'Don't forget to phone the electrician.'
   Molly _____ the electrician. (phone)
7 Ricky said, 'I'll never do it again.'
   Ricky _____ it again. (do)
8 Sarah said, 'You really must try Giacobazzi's. It's a fantastic restaurant.'
   Sarah _____ Giacobazzi's. She said it was fantastic. (try)

⬅ p.81

## clauses of contrast and purpose

### clauses of contrast

1 **Although / Though** the advert said it would last  🔊 9.3
for years, my dishwasher broke down after two months.

My dishwasher broke down after two months, **although /
though** the advert said it would last for years.

My dishwasher broke down again, **even though** I'd had it
repaired the week before.

My dishwasher has never broken down. I hardly ever use it,
**though**.

2 **In spite of / Despite**…
her age, my mother is still very active.
being 85, my mother is still very active.
the fact that she's 85, my mother is still very active.

• We use *although, though, even though,* and *in spite of* or
*despite* to express a contrast.

1 *although, though* and *even though* are usually used at the
beginning or in the middle of a sentence.

• *though* is more informal than *although*.

• *even though* is stronger than *although / though* and is used
to express a big or surprising contrast.

• *though* can also be used as an adverb, usually at the end of a
sentence, after a comma. In this case, it means *however*.

2 After *in spite of* or *despite*, we can use a noun, a verb in the
*-ing* form, or *the fact that* + subject + verb.

• Remember <u>not</u> to use *of* after *despite*. **NOT** ~~*Despite of the
rain,…*~~

### clauses of purpose

| 1 | I went to the bank | to | ask for a loan. | 🔊 9.4 |
|---|---|---|---|---|
| | | in order to | | |
| | | so as to | | |

2 I went to the bank **for** a meeting with my bank manager.

3 I went to the bank **so that** I could talk to the manager in
person.

| 4 | I wrote down what he said | so as not to | forget it. |
|---|---|---|---|
| | | in order not to | |

• Use *to, in order to, so as to, for,* and *so that* to express
purpose.

1 After *to, in order to,* and *so as to,* use an infinitive.

• *in order to* and *so as to* are more formal than *to.*

2 Use *for* + a noun, e.g. *for a meeting.*

• You can also use *for* + gerund to describe the exact purpose
of a thing, e.g. *This liquid is for cleaning metal.*

3 After *so that,* use a subject + modal verb (*can, could, would,*
etc.).

• When there is a change of subject in a clause of purpose, we
use *so that,* e.g. *We bought a new car so that the children
would have more space.* **NOT** ~~*to / in order to / so as to the
children…*~~ This is the only way of expressing purpose when
there is a change of subject.

4 To express a negative purpose, use *so as not to* or *in order
not to,* e.g. *I wrote down what he said in order not to forget
it.* **NOT** ~~*…to not forget it.*~~

---

**a** Complete the sentences with **one** word.

We're very happy in our new house, *though* there's a
lot to do.

1 We loved the film, _____ the fact that it was
nearly three hours long!

2 Carl doesn't like spending money, _____ though
he's very well off.

3 They went down to the harbour _____ see if they
had fresh fish.

4 I'll make a list, so _____ not to forget anything.

5 My mother called the doctor's in _____ to make
an appointment.

6 The cake tasted good, in _____ of not looking
like the photo in the recipe book.

7 I've put the heating on quite high, so _____ the
house will warm up quickly.

8 I must say that, _____ the service was poor, the
meal was delicious.

9 I stopped at a motorway café _____ a quick meal
before continuing on my journey.

10 He really isn't very fit. He sometimes manages to
cycle to work, _____.

**b** Rewrite the sentences.

Despite not getting very good reviews, the book sold
really well.

Even though *the book didn't get very good reviews,
it sold really well.*

1 We stayed at a bed and breakfast so as not to spend
too much money on accommodation.

We stayed at a bed and breakfast so that…

2 Despite earning a fortune, she drives a very old car.

Although…

3 Everyone enjoyed the film, even though the ending
was sad.

Everyone enjoyed the film, in spite of…

4 The plane managed to land despite the terrible
weather conditions.

The plane managed to land, even though…

5 I told her I enjoyed the meal she had cooked me, so
that I wouldn't offend her.

I told her I enjoyed the meal she had cooked me, so
as…

6 The police closed the roads so as to allow the
president's car through safely.

The police closed the roads in order… ⟵ p.87

## uncountable and plural nouns

### uncountable nouns

> 1 The **weather** is fantastic there and there's very little **traffic**, so you can walk everywhere. 🔊 9.12
> The **scenery** is beautiful here, but it's spoiled by all the **rubbish** people leave.
> 2 Could you give me **some advice** about where to stay?
> One useful **piece of advice** is to get a travel card.
> 3 The new opera house is made mainly of **glass**.
> Can I have **a glass** of tap water, please?

1 The following nouns are always uncountable: *accommodation, behaviour, health, politics* (and other words ending in *-ics*, e.g. *athletics, economics*), *progress, rubbish, scenery, traffic, weather, work.*
- Uncountable nouns don't have a plural form, and they use a singular verb. **NOT** ~~The sceneries are beautiful here.~~
- Don't use *a / an* with uncountable nouns. **NOT** ~~There's a terrible traffic this evening.~~
2 These nouns are also uncountable: *advice, bread, equipment, furniture, homework, information, luck, luggage, news, research, toast.* With these, you can use *a piece of* to talk about an individual item.
3 Some nouns can be either countable (C) or uncountable (U), but the meaning changes, e.g. *a glass* (C) = the thing you drink out of; *glass* (U) = the material used to make windows. Other examples: *business, iron, light, paper, space, time.*

### plural and collective nouns

> 1 One of the best museums is on **the outskirts** of the city. 🔊 9.13
> My **clothes are** filthy. I'll put on **some clean trousers** / I'll put on **a pair of clean trousers**.
> 2 The hotel **staff are** very efficient.
> The **cabin crew are coming round** with the drinks trolley in just a few minutes.

1 *arms* (= guns, etc.), *belongings, clothes, manners, outskirts, scissors,* and *trousers / shorts* are plural nouns with no singular. They need a plural verb, and they can't be used with *a / an*.
- If the word refers to something with two parts, e.g. *scissors, shorts, trousers,* etc., it can be used with *a pair of* or *some.*
2 *crew, family, government, police, staff, team,* etc. are collective nouns and refer to a group of people. We use them with a singular verb when we are referring to the group, e.g. *My family is very big,* but they can also be used with a plural verb when we are thinking of the people as individuals, e.g. *My family are all very talkative.*
- *police* is always used with a plural verb.

---

a Circle the correct form. Tick (✓) if both are correct.

> The traffic *is* / *are* awful during the rush hour.

1 Athletics *is* / *are* my favourite sport.
2 I bought *a pair of* / *some* new jeans.
3 Harvey's clothes *look* / *looks* really expensive.
4 The flight crew *work* / *works* hard to make passengers comfortable.
5 I found out *some* / *a piece of* interesting information at the meeting.
6 Could I have *a paper* / *a piece of paper* to write down the new words?
7 I think I'll have *a* / *some* time after lunch to help you with that report.
8 I've got *a* / *some* good news for you about your job application.
9 We've made a lot of *progress* / *progresses* this term.
10 Hello, Reception? Do you have *an* / *some* iron I could use?

b Right (✓) or wrong (✗)? Correct the mistakes in the highlighted phrases.

> Our accommodation isn't satisfactory. ✓
> The news are good. ✗ *The news is*

1 We had a beautiful weather when we were on holiday.
2 They have some lovely furnitures in their house.
3 My brother gave me a useful piece of advice.
4 Do you have a scissors? I need to wrap this present.
5 The hotel staff are real professionals.
6 I need to buy a new trousers for my interview tomorrow.
7 Your glasses are really dirty. Can you see anything?
8 The homeworks were very difficult last night.
9 There isn't any more space in my suitcase. Can I put this jacket in yours?
10 The police is sure that they know who was responsible for the vandalism.

⟲ p.91

---

 **Go online** to review the grammar for each lesson

## quantifiers: *all, every, both,* etc.

### *all, every, most*

1 **All** animals need food.  🔊 10.6
  **All** fruit contains sugar.
  **All (of) the** scientists at the conference agree with the theory.
  The animals **all** look sad.   The animals are **all** healthy.
2 **Everybody** is here.   **Everything** is very expensive.
3 **Most people** live in cities.
  **Most of the people** in this class are women.
4 **All of us** work hard and **most of us** come to class every week.
5 **Every** room has a bathroom.
  I work **every** Saturday.

1 We use *all* or *all (of) the* + a plural or uncountable noun.
  • *all* = in general, *all (of) the* = specific
  • *all* can be used before a main verb (and after *be*).
2 We use *everybody / everything* (= all people, all things) + singular verb, e.g. *Everything is very expensive.* **NOT** ~~All is very expensive.~~
  • We sometimes use *not* before *everybody / everything,* etc., e.g. *Not everybody likes sunbathing.*
3 We use *most* to say *the majority; most* = general, *most of* = more specific.
4 We often use *all / most of* + an object pronoun, e.g. *all of us, most of them, all of you, most of it.*
5 Use *every* + singular countable noun to mean 'all of a group'.

> 🔍 **every and all + time expressions**
> Note the difference between *every* and *all* + time expressions.
> *every day* = Monday to Sunday
> *all day* = from morning to night

### *no, none, any*

1 Is there **any** milk? Sorry, there's **no** milk. There **isn't any** (milk). 🔊 10.7
2 A Is there **any** food?
  B No, **none**. / There's **none**. But **none of us** are hungry.
3 Come **any** weekend! **Anyone** can come.

1 We use *no* + a noun after a ⊞ verb, or *any* + noun after a ⊟ verb, to refer to zero quantity.
2 We use *none* in short answers, or with a ⊞ verb to refer to zero quantity. We can also use *none* + *of* + pronoun / noun.
3 We use *any* (and *anything, anyone,* etc.) and a ⊞ verb to mean it doesn't matter what, who, etc.

### *both, neither, either*

1 **Both** Pierre **and** Marie Curie were scientists. **Neither** Pierre 🔊 10.8 **nor** Marie Curie was (were) aware of the dangers of radiation. Marie Curie wanted to study **either** physics **or** mathematics. In the end, she studied the two subjects.
2 She and her husband **both** won Nobel Prizes.
  Pierre and Marie were **both** interested in radium.
3 **Both of them** won the Nobel Prize.
  **Neither of them** realized how dangerous radium was.

1 We can use *both…and…, neither…nor…,* and *either…or…* to join two nouns, verbs, or other kinds of expressions.
  • Use *both…and…* + nouns to talk about two people / things, etc., when they are the same. The verb is always plural.
  • Use *neither…nor* + nouns to refer to two people / things, etc., when you mean not the one and not the other. You can use either a singular or plural verb. *Neither John nor his brother live / lives at home.*
  • Use *either…or…* to talk about a choice between two alternatives.
2 When *both* refers to the subject of a clause, it can also be used before a main verb but after *be.*
3 We often use *both / either / neither* + *of* + object pronoun, e.g. *us, them,* etc., or + *of the* + noun.

---

**a** Circle the correct word or phrase.

  We've eaten ~~all the~~ / all cake.
  1 *Most of / Most* my family live near me.
  2 *All / Everything* is ready for the party. We're just waiting for the guests to arrive.
  3 *Most / Most of* people enjoy the summer here, but for some it's too hot.
  4 Gina goes dancing *all / every* Friday night.
  5 We haven't got *any / no* onions for the soup.
  6 *Any / None* of us want to go out tonight. We're all exhausted.
  7 *Nobody / Anybody* can go to the festival. It's free.
  8 I've got two very close friends, but unfortunately *either / neither* of them lives near me.
  9 I'd like to have a bigger table, but there's *no / none* room in my kitchen.

**b** Right (✓) or wrong (✗)? Correct the wrong sentences.

  Both Mike and Alan passed the exam. ✓
  He neither watches the news or reads a newspaper. ✗
  *He neither watches the news nor reads a newspaper.*
  1 Both the kitchen and the bathroom needs cleaning.
  2 The food wasn't cheap nor tasty.
  3 I have two children, but neither of them look like me.
  4 My sister and I both were late for school.
  5 It's or Jane's or Karen's birthday today.
  6 Neither the food nor the service in this restaurant is good enough for what they charge.
  7 Neither my best friends called to see how I was.
  8 We can walk either or take the bus.
  9 My parents love horses, and both of them ride every day.
  10 We can go on holiday either in July or in August.

← p.99

## articles

### basic rules: *a* / *an* / *the*, no article

> 1  My neighbour has just got **a** dog and **a** cat.  🔊 10.12
> **The** dog is **an** Alsatian and **the** cat is **a** Siamese.
> Jack got into **the** car and drove to **the** town hall.
> 2  **Children** are often better than **adults** at new technology.
> I don't like **sport** or **classical music**.
> 3  **Last night** I **came home** late and went straight **to bed**.

1  Use *a* or *an* when you mention somebody or something for the first time or say who or what somebody or something is. Use *the* when it's clear who or what somebody or something is (e.g. it has been mentioned before, or it's unique, i.e. the only one that exists or that you own).

2  Don't use an article to speak in general with plural and uncountable nouns.

3  Don't use an article in phrases like *at home / work*, *go / come home / to bed*, *next / last* (*week*), etc.

### institutions

> My father's **in hospital**.  🔊 10.13
> They're building **a new hospital** in my town.
> He was sent **to prison** for two years.
> My grandmother used to work in **the prison** as a cleaner.

• With words like *prison*, *church*, *school*, *hospital*, and *university*, don't use an article when you are thinking about the institution and the normal purpose it is used for. If you are just thinking about the building, use *a* or *the*.

### more rules: geographical names

> 1  **Tunisia** is in **North Africa**.  🔊 10.14
> 2  **Selfridges**, one of London's biggest department stores, is in **Oxford Street**.
> 3  **Lake Victoria** and **Mount Kilimanjaro** are both in Africa.
> 4  **The River Danube** flows into **the Black Sea**.
> 5  **The National Gallery** and **the British Museum** are London tourist attractions.

• We **don't normally use** *the* with the names of:

1  most countries, continents, and regions ending with the name of a country / continent (e.g. *North America*, *South East Asia*), islands, states, provinces, towns, and cities (exceptions: *the USA*, *the UK / United Kingdom*, *the Netherlands*, *the Czech Republic*).

2  roads, streets, parks, bridges, shops, and restaurants (exceptions: motorways and numbered roads: *the M6*, *the A25*).

3  individual mountains and lakes.

• We **normally use** *the* with the names of:

4  mountain ranges, rivers, seas, canals, deserts, and island groups.

5  the names of theatres, cinemas, hotels, galleries, and museums.

---

**a**  Circle the correct article.

James bought **a** / *the* / (–) new suit at the weekend.

1  The weather was awful, so we stayed at *a* / *the* / (–) home.
2  *A* / *The* / (–) washing machine we bought last week has stopped working already.
3  I love reading *a* / *the* / (–) historical novels.
4  Sarah had had an exhausting day, so she went to *a* / *the* / (–) bed early.
5  I saw a man walking with a woman in the park. *A* / *The* / (–) woman was crying.
6  The teachers are on strike, so the children aren't going to *a* / *the* / (–) school.
7  Turn left immediately after *a* / *the* / (–) church and go up the hill.
8  My neighbour's in *a* / *the* / (–) prison because he didn't pay his taxes.
9  People are complaining because the council have refused to build *a* / *the* / (–) new school.
10  Visitors are not allowed to enter *a* / *the* / (–) hospital after 7 p.m.

**b**  Complete the sentence with *the* or (–).

They're going to *the* USA to visit family.

1  _____ Sicily is the largest island in _____ Mediterranean.
2  Cairo is on _____ River Nile.
3  We didn't have time to visit _____ Louvre when we were in Paris.
4  _____ south-west England is famous for its beautiful countryside and beaches.
5  _____ Mount Everest is in _____ Himalayas.
6  The largest inland lake is _____ Caspian Sea.
7  We stayed at _____ Palace Hotel while we were in Madrid.
8  *Romeo and Juliet* is on at _____ Globe Theatre.
9  Pico d'Aneto is the highest mountain in _____ Pyrenees.
10  I've always wanted to visit _____ India.

↩ p.100

# Verbs often confused

**a** Complete the **verbs** column with the correct verb in the right form.

| | verbs |
|---|---|
| **argue / discuss**<br>1 I need to ___ the problem with my boss.<br>2 I often ___ with my parents about doing housework. | _____ (= talk about sth)<br>_____ (= speak angrily to sb) |
| **notice / realize**<br>3 I didn't ___ you were so unhappy.<br>4 I didn't ___ that Karen had changed her hair colour. | _____ (= understand fully, become aware of sth)<br>_____ (= see, observe) |
| **avoid / prevent**<br>5 Jack always tries to ___ arguing with me.<br>6 My dad can't ___ me from seeing my friends. | _____ (= try not to do something)<br>_____ (= stop) |
| **lend / borrow**<br>7 When are you going to pay me back the £50 that I ___ you?<br>8 Could I ___ your car tonight? I know you're not using it. | _____ (= give sth to sb that you want them to give back)<br>_____ (= ask for sth that you intend to give back) |
| **mind / matter**<br>9 My parents don't ___ if I stay out late.<br>10 It doesn't ___ if we're five minutes late. | _____ (= have a problem / feel strongly)<br>_____ (= be a problem) |
| **remember / remind**<br>11 Can you ___ me to call my mum later?<br>12 ___ to turn off the lights before you go. | _____ (= help sb to remember)<br>_____ (= not forget) |
| **expect / wait**<br>13 I ___ that Daniel will forget our anniversary. He always does.<br>14 We'll have to ___ half an hour for the next train. | _____ (= think that sth will happen)<br>_____ (= stay where you are until something happens) |
| **wish / hope**<br>15 I ___ I was a bit taller!<br>16 I ___ that you can come on Friday. I haven't seen you for ages. | _____ (= want sth to be true, even if it is unlikely or impossible)<br>_____ (= want sth to happen) |
| **beat / win**<br>17 Arsenal ___ the match 5–2.<br>18 Arsenal ___ Manchester United 5–2. | _____ (= be successful in a competition)<br>_____ (= defeat sb) |
| **refuse / deny**<br>19 Tom always ___ to discuss the problem.<br>20 Tom always ___ that he has a problem. | _____ (= say you don't want to do sth)<br>_____ (= say that sth isn't true) |
| **raise / rise**<br>21 The cost of living is going to ___ again this month.<br>22 It's hard not to ___ your voice when you're arguing with someone. | _____ (= go up)<br>_____ (= make sth go up) |
| **lay** (past *laid*, past participle *laid*) **/ lie** (past *lay*, past participle *lain*)<br>23 Go and ___ on the bed if you're tired.<br>24 I usually ___ my baby on the bed to change his nappy. | _____ (= put your body in a horizontal position)<br>_____ (= put sth or sb in a horizontal position) |
| **steal / rob**<br>25 The men had been planning to ___ the bank.<br>26 If you leave your bike unlocked, somebody might ___ it. | _____ (= take sth from a person or place by threat or force)<br>_____ (= take money or property that isn't yours) |
| **advise / warn**<br>27 I think I should ___ you that Liam doesn't always tell the truth.<br>28 My teachers are going to ___ me what subjects to study next year. | _____ (= tell sb that sth unpleasant is likely to happen)<br>_____ (= tell sb what you think they should do) |

**b** 🔊 **7.9** Listen and check.    **ACTIVATION** Cover the verbs column. Say the sentences with the correct verbs.

⟲ p.68

# The body

## 1 PARTS OF THE BODY AND ORGANS

a Match the words and pictures.

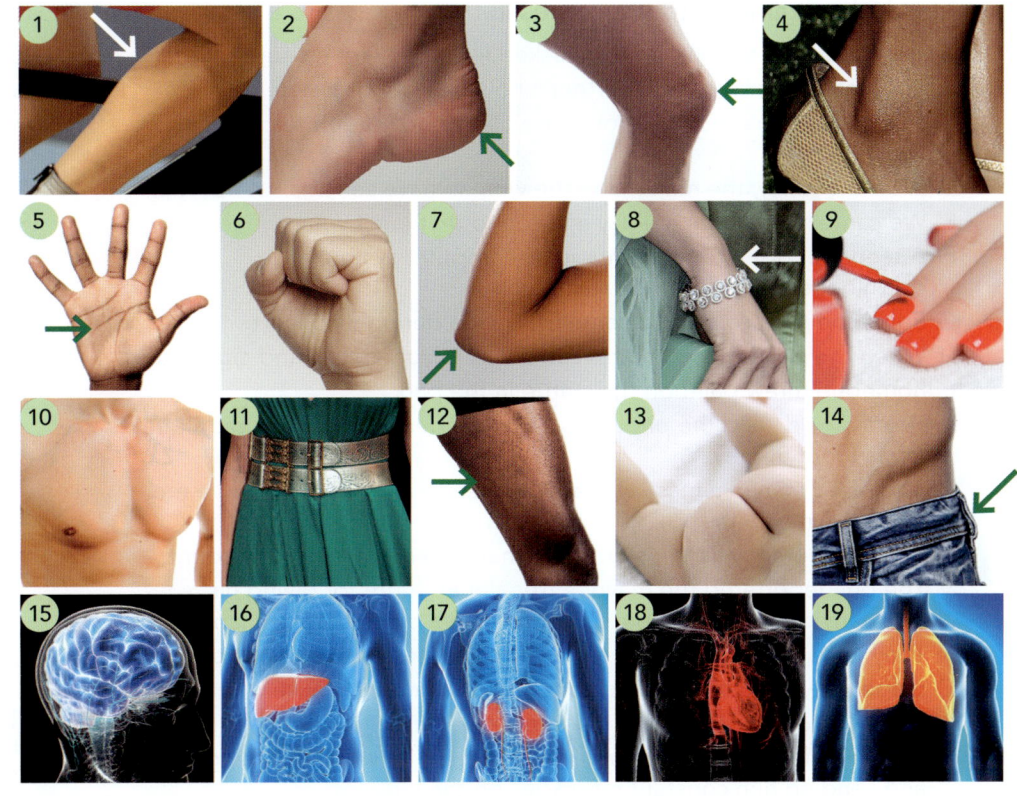

☐ ankle /'æŋkl/
1 calf /kɑːf/ (pl calves)
☐ heel /hiːl/
☐ knee /niː/

☐ elbow /'elbəʊ/
☐ fist /fɪst/
☐ nails /neɪlz/
☐ palm /pɑːm/
☐ wrist /rɪst/

☐ bottom /'bɒtəm/
☐ chest /tʃest/
☐ hip /hɪp/
☐ thigh /θaɪ/
☐ waist /weɪst/

☐ brain /breɪn/
☐ heart /hɑːt/
☐ kidneys /'kɪdniz/
☐ liver /'lɪvə/
☐ lungs /lʌŋz/

b 🔊 7.16 Listen and check.

**ACTIVATION** Cover the words. Look at the pictures and say the words.

## 2 VERBS AND VERB PHRASES

a Complete the verb phrases with the parts of the body.

---
arms  eyebrows  hair (x2)  hand  hands
head  nails  nose  shoulders  teeth
thumb  toes
---

1 **bite** your _nails_ /baɪt/
2 **blow** your _____ /bləʊ/
3 **brush** your _____ / **brush** your _____ /brʌʃ/
4 **comb** your _____ /kəʊm/
5 **fold** your _____ /fəʊld/
6 **hold** somebody's _____ /həʊld/
7 **touch** your _____ /tʌtʃ/
8 **suck** your _____ /sʌk/
9 **shake** _____ / **shake** your _____ /ʃeɪk/
10 **shrug** your _____ /ʃrʌg/
11 **raise** your _____ /reɪz/

b 🔊 7.17 Listen and check.

c Read the sentences. Write the part of the body related to the **bold** verb.

1 He **winked** /wɪŋkt/ at me to show that he was only joking. _eye_
2 The steak was tough and difficult to **chew** /tʃuː/. _____
3 When we met, we were so happy, we **hugged** /hʌgd/ each other. _____
4 Don't **scratch** /skrætʃ/ the mosquito bite. You'll only make it worse. _____
5 She **waved** /weɪvd/ goodbye sadly to her boyfriend as the train left the station. _____
6 These days, men don't always **kneel** /niːl/ down when they propose marriage. _____
7 The teacher **frowned** /fraʊnd/ when she saw all the mistakes I had made. _____
8 The painting was so strange, I **stared** /steəd/ at it for a long time. _____
9 She got out of bed, and **yawned** /jɔːnd/ and **stretched** /stretʃt/. _____ / _____
10 If you don't know the word for something, just **point** /pɔɪnt/ at what you want. _____

d 🔊 7.18 Listen and check.

**ACTIVATION** In pairs, **A** say a verb phrase to **B**. **B** do the action.

 p.72

🔵 **Go online** to review the vocabulary for each lesson

# Crime and punishment

## 1 CRIMES AND CRIMINALS

**a** Match the examples to the crimes in the chart.

A ~~They took a rich man's son and asked for money for his safe return.~~
B She went to her business partner's house and shot her dead.
C Two passengers took control of the plane and made the pilot land in the desert.
D After the party, the man made the woman have sex against her will.
E We came home from holiday and found that our TV had gone.
F A teenager got into the Pentagon's computer system and downloaded some secret data.
G Someone tried to sell me some marijuana during a concert.
H When the police searched his car, it was full of contraband cigarettes.
I Someone threw paint on the statue in the park.
J He said he'd send the photos to a newspaper if the actress didn't pay him a lot of money.
K An armed man in a mask walked into a shop and shouted, 'Give me all the money in the till!'
L The accountant was transferring money into his own bank account.
M The builder offered the mayor a free flat in return for giving his company permission to build new flats on a piece of green land.
N They left a bomb in the supermarket car park, which exploded.
O Somebody stole my car last night from outside my house.
P A man held out a knife and made me give him my wallet.
Q A woman followed a pop singer everywhere he went, watching him and sending him constant messages on the internet.

|    |   | Crime | Criminal | Verb |
|----|---|-------|----------|------|
| 1  |   | blackmail /ˈblækmeɪl/ | blackmailer | blackmail |
| 2  |   | bribery /ˈbraɪbəri/ | – | bribe |
| 3  |   | burglary /ˈbɜːgləri/ | burglar | break in / burgle |
| 4  |   | drug dealing /ˈdrʌg diːlɪŋ/ | drug dealer | sell drugs |
| 5  |   | fraud /frɔːd/ | fraudster | commit fraud |
| 6  |   | hacking /ˈhækɪŋ/ | hacker | hack (into) |
| 7  |   | hijacking /ˈhaɪdʒækɪŋ/ | hijacker | hijack |
| 8  | A | kidnapping /ˈkɪdnæpɪŋ/ | kidnapper | kidnap |
| 9  |   | mugging /ˈmʌgɪŋ/ | mugger | mug |
| 10 |   | murder /ˈmɜːdə/ | murderer | murder |
| 11 |   | rape /reɪp/ | rapist | rape |
| 12 |   | robbery /ˈrɒbəri/ | robber | rob |
| 13 |   | smuggling /ˈsmʌglɪŋ/ | smuggler | smuggle |
| 14 |   | stalking /ˈstɔːkɪŋ/ | stalker | stalk |
| 15 |   | terrorism /ˈterərɪzəm/ | terrorist | set off bombs, etc. |
| 16 |   | theft /θeft/ | thief | steal |
| 17 |   | vandalism /ˈvændəlɪzəm/ | vandal | vandalize |

**b** ◑ **8.3** Listen and check.

**ACTIVATION** Cover the chart and look at situations A–Q. Say the crimes.

## 2 WHAT HAPPENS TO A CRIMINAL

**a** Complete the sentences with the words in the list.

**The crime**

arrested /əˈrestɪd/   caught /kɔːt/
charged /tʃɑːdʒd/   ~~committed~~ /kəˈmɪtɪd/
investigated /ɪnˈvestɪgeɪtɪd/
questioned /ˈkwestʃənd/

1 Carl and Adam *committed* a crime. They robbed a large supermarket.
2 The police _____ the crime.
3 Carl and Adam were _____ driving to the airport in a stolen car.
4 They were _____ and taken to a police station.
5 The police _____ them for ten hours.
6 Finally they were _____ with (= officially accused of) armed robbery.

**The trial**

accused /əˈkjuːzd/   acquitted /əˈkwɪtɪd/
court /kɔːt/   evidence /ˈevɪdəns/
guilty (opposite *innocent*) /ˈgɪlti/
judge /dʒʌdʒ/   jury /ˈdʒʊəri/
proof /pruːf/   punishment /ˈpʌnɪʃmənt/
sentenced /ˈsentənst/   verdict /ˈvɜːdɪkt/
witnesses /ˈwɪtnəsɪz/

7 Two months later, Carl and Adam appeared in _____.
8 They were _____ of **armed robbery** and car theft.
9 _____ told the court what they had seen or knew.
10 The _____ (of 12 people) looked at and heard all the _____.
11 After two days, the jury reached their _____.
12 There was no _____ that Adam had committed the crime.
13 He was _____ and allowed to go free.
14 Carl was found _____. His **fingerprints** were on the gun used in the robbery.
15 The _____ decided what Carl's _____ should be.
16 He _____ him to ten years in **prison (jail).**

**b** ◑ **8.4** Listen and check.   ← p.77

# The media

## 1 THE LANGUAGE OF HEADLINES

> 🔍 **The language of headlines**
> Newspaper headlines, especially in tabloids*, often use short snappy words. These words use up less space and are more emotive, which helps to sell newspapers.
>
> *newspapers with smaller pages that print short articles with lots of photos, often about famous people

**a** Match the highlighted 'headline verbs' with their meaning.

1. ☐ **Prime minister backs his Chancellor in latest scandal**

2. ☐ **Thousands of jobs axed by UK firms**

3. ☐ **Stock market hit by oil fears**

4. ☐ **Astronaut bids to be first man on Mars**

5. ☐ **MINISTERS CLASH OVER NEW CAR TAX PROPOSAL**

6. ☐ **Bayern Munich boss vows to avenge defeat**

7. ☐ **Police quiz witness in murder trial**

8. ☐ **Actress rows with co-star over unfair pay**

A have been cut
B question, interrogate
C is going to attempt
D supports
E disagree
F has been badly affected
G argues
H promises

**b** 🔊 8.16 Listen and check.

**ACTIVATION** Cover A–H. Look at 1–8 and say the meanings.

## 2 JOURNALISTS AND PEOPLE IN THE MEDIA

**a** Match the words and definitions.

agony aunt /ˈæɡəni ɑːnt/   commentator /ˈkɒmənteɪtə/   critic /ˈkrɪtɪk/   editor /ˈedɪtə/   freelance journalist /ˌfriːlɑːns ˈdʒɜːnəlɪst/   newsreader /ˈnjuːzriːdə/   paparazzi (pl) /ˌpæpəˈrætsi/   presenter /prɪˈzentə/   reporter /rɪˈpɔːtə/

1. *critic* — a person who writes (a review) about the good / bad qualities of books, concerts, theatre, films, etc.
2. _____ a person who describes a sports event while it's happening on TV or radio
3. _____ a person who collects and reports news for newspapers, radio, or TV
4. _____ a person who is in charge of a newspaper or magazine, or part of one, and who decides what should be in it
5. _____ a person who introduces the different sections of a radio or TV programme
6. _____ a person who writes articles for different papers and is not employed by any one paper
7. _____ a person who reads the news on TV or radio
8. _____ photographers who follow famous people around to get photos of them to sell to newspapers and magazines
9. _____ a person who writes in a newspaper or magazine giving advice to people in reply to their letters

**b** 🔊 8.17 Listen and check.

**ACTIVATION** Are there any people in the media in your country that you really like or really dislike?

## 3 ADJECTIVES TO DESCRIBE THE MEDIA

**a** Match the sentences.
1. ☐ The reporting in the paper was very **sensational**. /senˈseɪʃənl/
2. ☐ The news on Channel 12 is really **biased**. /ˈbaɪəst/
3. ☐ I think *The Observer* is the most **objective** of the Sunday papers. /əbˈdʒektɪv/
4. ☐ The film review was quite **accurate**. /ˈækjərət/
5. ☐ I think the report was **censored**. /ˈsensəd/

A It said the plot was poor but the acting good, which was true.
B It bases its stories just on facts, not on feelings or beliefs.
C The newspaper wasn't allowed to publish all the details.
D It made the story seem more shocking than it really was.
E You can't believe anything you hear on it. It's obvious what political party they favour!

**b** 🔊 8.18 Listen and check.

**ACTIVATION** Name publications you know that are sensational, biased, or objective.

◀ p.82

🔵 **Go online** to review the vocabulary for each lesson

# Business

## 1 VERBS AND EXPRESSIONS

**a** Complete the sentences with a verb from the list in the correct form (present simple, past simple, or past participle).

---

become   close down   drop   grow   expand   export   import
launch   manufacture   market   merge   produce   set up   take over

---

1 Apple products are easy to _market_ because people are immediately attracted to the stylish designs.
2 In 1989, Pepsi-Cola _____ **a new product** called *Pepsi A.M.*, which was aimed at the 'breakfast cola drinker'. It was an immediate **flop**.
3 The Spanish airline Iberia _____ with British Airways in 2011 and became one of the world's biggest airline groups.
4 Although GAP stands for Genuine American Product, most of its clothes are _____ in Asia.
5 Prosciutto is a kind of Italian ham. Two of the best-known kinds are San Daniele and Parma, which are _____ in the Friuli and Emilia regions of Italy, and are _____ all over the world.
6 When BMW _____ Mini, the smaller company became part of the larger organization.
7 The supermarket chain Tesco _____ **the market leader** in 1995, and is still the UK's biggest-selling **chain**.
8 The first Zara store was opened in La Coruña in Spain in 1975, where its **head office** still is today. The company started to _____ into new markets in 1988, and it now has **branches** in 96 countries.
9 Many banks are now offering loans to people who want to _____ a new **small business**.
10 The cost of living in Iceland is so high because so many food products have to be _____.
11 During **a boom** period, the economy _____ quickly and living standards improve.
12 During **a recession**, many companies _____ and living standards _____.

**b** 🔊**9.5** Listen and check. What do the bold words mean?

**c** *Do* or *make*? Put the phrases in the correct column.

---

business (with)   a deal (= business agreement)   a decision
a job   a loss (opposite *profit*)   market research   money
somebody redundant   well / badly

---

| do | make |
|---|---|
| business (with) | |

**d** 🔊**9.6** Listen and check.

**ACTIVATION** Cover the columns in **c**. Say the phrases in the list with *do* or *make*.

## 2 IDIOMS WITH *BUSINESS*

> 🔍 **business**
> business is an uncountable noun when it means trade, work, etc., e.g. *do business* **NOT** ~~do a business~~. It is only countable when it means a company, shop, or factory, e.g. *I'm going to set up a business*, or an event or situation, e.g. *It was a terrible business*.

**a** Match the idioms with *business* to their meanings A–H.

1 ☐ I think we've been through everything on today's agenda. Now, is there any other business?
2 ☐ Now that so many people book their holidays and travel online, many travel agencies have gone out of business.
3 ☐ Let's get down to business right away – we'll have a break after an hour or so.
4 ☐ She looks very determined – like a woman who means business.
5 ☐ **A** What are you doing?
   **B** I'm sorry, but it's none of your business.
6 ☐ **A** Is he your new boyfriend?'
   **B** Mind your own business!
7 ☐ He arranged to meet his ex-girlfriend because they had some unfinished business.
8 ☐ Why are you taking your tennis racket on a work trip? It's never a good idea to mix business with pleasure.

A important things that still need to be discussed or dealt with
B (informal) it's not something that concerns you
C start dealing with the matter that needs to be dealt with, or doing the work that needs to be done
D closed down because there is no more money or work
E (informal) have serious intentions
F things that are discussed at the end of an official meeting
G try to do something enjoyable when you also need to work
H (informal) think about your own affairs and don't get involved in other people's lives

**b** 🔊**9.7** Listen and check.

**ACTIVATION** Cover the idioms and look at the definitions. Say the idioms. 🔶 p.89

# Word building

## 1 PREFIXES AND SUFFIXES WHICH ADD MEANING

**a** Match the **bold** prefixes in sentences 1–11 to their meanings A–K.

1 [G] Mumbai is a very **over**crowded city.
2 ▢ Tokyo was one of the first **mega**cities.
3 ▢ This part of the city is very poor and **under**developed.
4 ▢ London is a very **multi**cultural city, with many different races and religions.
5 ▢ The quickest way to get around New York is on the **sub**way.
6 ▢ Many people in Montreal, Canada, are **bi**lingual – they speak English and French.
7 ▢ If you want to avoid the traffic jams in Bangkok, get the **mono**rail.
8 ▢ The **auto**pilot was switched on after the plane had taken off.
9 ▢ Vandalism, especially breaking public property, is very **anti**social behaviour.
10 ▢ I **mis**understood the directions that man gave me, and now I'm completely lost.
11 ▢ He's doing a **post**graduate degree in aeronautical engineering.

| | |
|---|---|
| A against | G ~~too much~~ |
| B many | H two |
| C enormous | I after |
| D not enough | J under |
| E one | K wrongly |
| F by (it)self | |

**b** 🔊 **9.14** Listen and check.

**c** Match the **bold** suffixes to their meaning.

1 ▢ There are a lot of home**less** people in this city. The situation is hope**less**.
2 ▢ Be care**ful** how you drive! The instructions were very use**ful**.
3 ▢ The police usually wear bullet**proof** vests. My watch is water**proof**.
4 ▢ Their new laptops are completely unbreak**able**. I don't think the tap water here is drink**able**.

| | |
|---|---|
| A with | C resistant to |
| B can be done | D without |

**d** 🔊 **9.15** Listen and check.

**ACTIVATION** Cover sentences 1–11 in **a**. Look at meanings A–K and say the prefixes.

## 2 NOUNS FORMED WITH SUFFIXES

> 🔍 **Common noun suffixes**
> For nouns made from verbs:
> *-ion / -(a)tion*   po<u>llute</u> – pollution; ex<u>pect</u> – expec<u>ta</u>tion
> *-ment*        deve<u>lop</u> – deve<u>lop</u>ment
> For nouns made from adjectives:
> *-ness*        cold – <u>coldness</u>
> *-ence / -ance*   con<u>venient</u> – con<u>venience</u>; a<u>bundant</u> – a<u>bundance</u>
> For abstract nouns made from nouns or adjectives:
> *-hood*        <u>neighbour</u> – <u>neighbourhood</u>
> *-ism*        <u>modern</u> – <u>modernism</u>

**a** Complete the chart with nouns from the words in the list.

absent   accommodate   alcohol   brother   child   distant
employ   entertain   excite   friendly   govern   ignorant   improve
intend   lonely   race   reduce   ugly   vandal   violent   weak

| -ion / -(a)tion | -ment | -ness | -ence / -ance | -ism | -hood |
|---|---|---|---|---|---|
| | | | | | |

**b** 🔊 **9.16** Listen and check.

**ACTIVATION** Cover the chart and look at the words in the list. Say them with the correct suffix.

## 3 NOUNS WHICH ARE DIFFERENT WORDS

> 🔍 **Noun formation with spelling or word change**
> Some nouns made from verbs or adjectives are completely different words, e.g. *choose – choice, poor – <u>poverty</u>*.

**a** Write the verb or adjective for the following **nouns**.

| | | Noun |
|---|---|---|
| 1 | _____ (verb) | loss /lɒs/ |
| 2 | _____ (verb) | death /deθ/ |
| 3 | _____ (verb) | su<u>ccess</u> /sək'ses/ |
| 4 | _____ (verb) | thought /θɔːt/ |
| 5 | _____ (verb) | belief /brˈliːf/ |
| 6 | _____ (adj.) | heat /hiːt/ |
| 7 | _____ (adj.) | strength /streŋkθ/ |
| 8 | _____ (adj.) | <u>hunger</u> /ˈhʌŋgə/ |
| 9 | _____ (adj.) | height /haɪt/ |
| 10 | _____ (adj.) | width /wɪdθ/ |

**b** 🔊 **9.17** Listen and check.

**ACTIVATION** Cover the **noun** column. Look at the verbs and adjectives and say the nouns.

⊙ p.93

 **Go online** to review the vocabulary for each lesson

# Appendix

## VERB PATTERNS: verbs followed by the gerund or infinitive

### Gerund

| | |
|---|---|
| admit | In court the accused admitted (to) stealing the documents. |
| avoid | I always try to avoid driving in the rush hour. |
| be worth | It isn't worth going to the exhibition. It's really boring. |
| can't help | We can't help laughing when my dad tries to speak French. His accent is awful! |
| can't stand | I can't stand talking to people who only talk about themselves. |
| carry on* | We carried on chatting until about 2.00 in the morning. |
| deny | Miriam denied killing her husband but the jury didn't believe her. |
| enjoy | I used to enjoy flying, but now I don't. |
| fancy | Do you fancy seeing a film this evening? |
| feel like | I don't feel like going out tonight. |
| finish | Have you finished writing the report yet? |
| give up* | Karen has given up eating meat, but she still eats fish. |
| imagine | I can't imagine living in the country. I think I would get bored after a week. |
| involve | My boyfriend's job involves travelling at least once a month. |
| keep (on) | I keep (on) telling my husband to lose some weight, but he just won't listen. |
| look forward to | We are really looking forward to seeing you again. |
| mind | I don't mind doing housework. I find it quite relaxing. |
| miss | Does your father miss working now that he has retired? |
| postpone | We'll have to postpone going to the beach until the weather improves. |
| practise | The more you practise speaking English the more fluent you'll get. |
| recommend | I recommend doing a double-decker bus tour as the best way to see London. |
| regret | I regret not travelling more before I got my first job. |
| risk | If I were you, I wouldn't risk walking through the park at night. |
| spend | I spent half an hour looking for my glasses this morning. |
| stop | Once I open a box of chocolates, I can't stop eating them. |
| suggest | A friend of mine suggested visiting London in the autumn. |

\* All phrasal verbs which are followed by another verb, e.g. *carry on*, *give up*, etc. are followed by the gerund.

### Infinitive (with *to*)

| | |
|---|---|
| afford | I can't afford to go on holiday this summer. |
| agree | I have agreed to pay David back the money he lent me next week. |
| appear | The results appear to support the scientist's theory. |
| arrange | I've arranged to meet Sally outside the restaurant. |
| be able | I won't be able to work for two weeks after the operation. |
| can't wait | We can't wait to see your new flat – it sounds fantastic. |
| choose | I chose to study abroad for a year, and it's the best thing I've ever done. |
| decide | They've decided to call off the wedding. |
| deserve | Kim deserves to get the job. She's a very strong candidate. |
| expect | We're expecting to get our exam results on Friday. |
| happen | Tom happened to be at Alan's when I called in, so I invited him to our party as well. |
| help* | The organization I work for helps young people to find work abroad. |
| hesitate | Don't hesitate to ask a member of staff if you need anything. |
| hope | I'm hoping to set up my own company if I can get a bank loan. |
| learn | I wish I had learnt to play the guitar when I was younger. |
| make | When I was at school, we were made to wear a uniform. It was awful. |
| manage | Did you manage to get to the airport in time? |
| offer | Lucy has offered to give me a lift to the station. |
| plan | We're planning to have a big party to celebrate. |
| pretend | I pretended to be enthusiastic, but really I didn't like the idea at all. |
| promise | Sarah always promises to help me in the kitchen, but she never does. |
| refuse | My neighbour refused to turn down the music and I had to call the police. |
| seem | Something seems to be wrong with the washing machine. |
| teach | Jack's father taught him to drive when he was 17. |
| tend | My boss tends to lose her temper when she's feeling stressed. |
| threaten | The teacher threatened to call my parents and tell them what I had done. |
| want | The police want to interview anyone who witnessed the crime. |
| would like | Would you like to try the dress on? The changing rooms are over there. |

\* *help* can be followed by the infinitive with or without *to*.
*The organization I work for helps young people (to) find work abroad.*

### Infinitive (without *to*)

| | |
|---|---|
| can | Can you help me carry these suitcases? |
| had better | You'd better leave now if you want to catch that train. |
| let | Let me pay for coffee – it must be my turn. |
| make | Sue makes her two teenagers do the washing-up every evening after dinner. |
| may | There's a lot of traffic today, so we may be a bit late. |
| might | It might rain tomorrow, so please bring an umbrella or a raincoat. |
| must | I must remember to phone Harry – it's his birthday today. |
| should | Should we book a table for tomorrow night? It's a very popular restaurant. |
| would rather | You look tired. Would you rather stay in this evening and watch a film? |

← p.143

# Irregular verbs

| Infinitive | Past simple | Past participle |
|---|---|---|
| be /biː/ | was/were /wɒz/ /wɜː/ | been /biːn/ |
| beat /biːt/ | beat | beaten /ˈbiːtn/ |
| become /bɪˈkʌm/ | became /bɪˈkeɪm/ | become |
| begin /bɪˈgɪn/ | began /bɪˈgæn/ | begun /bɪˈgʌn/ |
| bite /baɪt/ | bit /bɪt/ | bitten /ˈbɪtn/ |
| break /breɪk/ | broke /brəʊk/ | broken /ˈbrəʊkən/ |
| bring /brɪŋ/ | brought /brɔːt/ | brought |
| build /bɪld/ | built /bɪlt/ | built |
| burn /bɜːn/ | burnt (burned) /bɜːnt/ /bɜːnd/ | burnt (burned) |
| buy /baɪ/ | bought /bɔːt/ | bought |
| can /kæn/ | could /kʊd/ | – |
| catch /kætʃ/ | caught /kɔːt/ | caught |
| choose /tʃuːz/ | chose /tʃəʊz/ | chosen /ˈtʃəʊzn/ |
| come /kʌm/ | came /keɪm/ | come |
| cost /kɒst/ | cost | cost |
| cut /kʌt/ | cut | cut |
| deal /diːl/ | dealt /delt/ | dealt |
| do /duː/ | did /dɪd/ | done /dʌn/ |
| draw /drɔː/ | drew /druː/ | drawn /drɔːn/ |
| dream /driːm/ | dreamt (dreamed) /dremt/ /driːmd/ | dreamt (dreamed) |
| drink /drɪŋk/ | drank /dræŋk/ | drunk /drʌŋk/ |
| drive /draɪv/ | drove /drəʊv/ | driven /ˈdrɪvn/ |
| eat /iːt/ | ate /eɪt/ | eaten /ˈiːtn/ |
| fall /fɔːl/ | fell /fel/ | fallen /ˈfɔːlən/ |
| feel /fiːl/ | felt /felt/ | felt |
| find /faɪnd/ | found /faʊnd/ | found |
| fly /flaɪ/ | flew /fluː/ | flown /fləʊn/ |
| forget /fəˈget/ | forgot /fəˈgɒt/ | forgotten /fəˈgɒtn/ |
| get /get/ | got /gɒt/ | got |
| give /gɪv/ | gave /geɪv/ | given /ˈgɪvn/ |
| go /gəʊ/ | went /went/ | gone /gɒn/ |
| grow /grəʊ/ | grew /gruː/ | grown /grəʊn/ |
| hang /hæŋ/ | hung /hʌŋ/ | hung |
| have /hæv/ | had /hæd/ | had |
| hear /hɪə/ | heard /hɜːd/ | heard |
| hit /hɪt/ | hit | hit |
| hurt /hɜːt/ | hurt | hurt |
| keep /kiːp/ | kept /kept/ | kept |
| kneel /niːl/ | knelt /nelt/ | knelt |
| know /nəʊ/ | knew /njuː/ | known /nəʊn/ |
| lay /leɪ/ | laid /leɪd/ | laid |
| learn /lɜːn/ | learnt (learned) /lɜːnt/ /lɜːnd/ | learnt (learned) |

| Infinitive | Past simple | Past participle |
|---|---|---|
| leave /liːv/ | left /left/ | left |
| lend /lend/ | lent /lent/ | lent |
| let /let/ | let | let |
| lie /laɪ/ | lay /leɪ/ | lain /leɪn/ |
| lose /luːz/ | lost /lɒst/ | lost |
| make /meɪk/ | made /meɪd/ | made |
| mean /miːn/ | meant /ment/ | meant |
| meet /miːt/ | met /met/ | met |
| pay /peɪ/ | paid /peɪd/ | paid |
| put /pʊt/ | put | put |
| read /riːd/ | read /red/ | read /red/ |
| ride /raɪd/ | rode /rəʊd/ | ridden /ˈrɪdn/ |
| ring /rɪŋ/ | rang /ræŋ/ | rung /rʌŋ/ |
| rise /raɪz/ | rose /rəʊz/ | risen /ˈrɪzn/ |
| run /rʌn/ | ran /ræn/ | run |
| say /seɪ/ | said /sed/ | said |
| see /siː/ | saw /sɔː/ | seen /siːn/ |
| sell /sel/ | sold /səʊld/ | sold |
| send /send/ | sent /sent/ | sent |
| set /set/ | set | set |
| shake /ʃeɪk/ | shook /ʃʊk/ | shaken /ˈʃeɪkən/ |
| shine /ʃaɪn/ | shone /ʃɒn/ | shone |
| shut /ʃʌt/ | shut | shut |
| sing /sɪŋ/ | sang /sæŋ/ | sung /sʌŋ/ |
| sit /sɪt/ | sat /sæt/ | sat |
| sleep /sliːp/ | slept /slept/ | slept |
| speak /spiːk/ | spoke /spəʊk/ | spoken /ˈspəʊkən/ |
| spend /spend/ | spent /spent/ | spent |
| stand /stænd/ | stood /stʊd/ | stood |
| steal /stiːl/ | stole /stəʊl/ | stolen /ˈstəʊlən/ |
| swell /swel/ | swelled /sweld/ | swelled swollen /ˈswəʊlen/ |
| swim /swɪm/ | swam /swæm/ | swum /swʌm/ |
| take /teɪk/ | took /tʊk/ | taken /ˈteɪkən/ |
| teach /tiːtʃ/ | taught /tɔːt/ | taught |
| tell /tel/ | told /təʊld/ | told |
| think /θɪŋk/ | thought /θɔːt/ | thought |
| throw /θrəʊ/ | threw /θruː/ | thrown /θrəʊn/ |
| understand /ʌndəˈstænd/ | understood /ʌndəˈstʊd/ | understood |
| wake /weɪk/ | woke /wəʊk/ | woken /ˈwəʊkən/ |
| wear /weə/ | wore /wɔː/ | worn /wɔːn/ |
| win /wɪn/ | won /wʌn/ | won |
| write /raɪt/ | wrote /rəʊt/ | written /ˈrɪtn/ |

# Vowel sounds

| | | usual spelling | ! but also |
|---|---|---|---|
| fish | | i   linen silk<br>    trip fit<br>    fill pick | pretty women<br>guilty decided<br>village physics |
| tree | | ee  bleed sneeze<br>ea  beat steal<br>e   even medium | people thief<br>key relieved<br>receipt |
| cat | | a   pack campus<br>   active cash<br>   packet stand | |
| car | | ar  scarf smart<br>    sharp hardly<br>a   calf branch | aunt laugh<br>heart |
| clock | | o   cotton top<br>   drop cost<br>   off on | watch want<br>because<br>cough |
| horse | | (o)or sore floor<br>al   stalker wall<br>aw  yawn draw | warm warn<br>pouring<br>thought caught<br>exhausted launch |
| bull | | u   full put<br>oo  hooded<br>    woollen<br>    stood good | could should<br>would woman |
| boot | | oo  loose cool<br>u*  argue refuse<br>ew  chew news | suit recruit<br>shoe prove<br>through queue |
| computer | | Many different spellings. /ə/ is always unstressed.<br>collar patterned advise complain<br>information sandals | |
| bird | | er  verdict prefer<br>ir   dirty skirt<br>ur  hurt burn | research worker<br>worth worse<br>journey |
| egg | | e   denim dress<br>   trendy belt<br>   ever yet | friendly leather<br>deaf threaten<br>anybody said |

| | | usual spelling | ! but also |
|---|---|---|---|
| up | | u   cut scruffy<br>   lungs stunned<br>   upset discuss | money<br>someone<br>enough<br>touch flood<br>blood |
| train | | a*  ache lace<br>ai  faint plain<br>ay  may lay | break steak<br>great<br>weight suede<br>obey grey |
| phone | | o*  choke chose<br>   froze fold<br>oa  toast approach | throw elbow<br>below<br>although<br>shoulders |
| bike | | i*  striped ice<br>y   lycra stylish<br>igh  tight flight | buy eyes<br>height aisle |
| owl | | ou  hour mouth<br>    proud around<br>ow  showers frown | drought |
| boy | | oi  boiling avoid<br>   point noise<br>oy  enjoy employer | |
| ear | | eer career<br>volunteer<br>ere  here we're<br>ear  nearly clear | realize ideally<br>seriously zero |
| chair | | air  airport stairs<br>    fair hair<br>are  scared stare | their there<br>wear<br>area |
| tourist | | A very unusual sound.<br>euro jury sure plural | |
| /i/ | | A sound between /ɪ/ and /iː/. Consonant + y at the end of words is pronounced /i/.<br>windy sunny foggy | |
| /u/ | | An unusual sound between /ʊ/ and /uː/.<br>education usually situation | |

\* especially before consonant + *e*

short vowels    long vowels    diphthongs

# Consonant sounds

| | | usual spelling | | ! but also |
|---|---|---|---|---|
| | parrot | p | postpone polluted hope damp | |
| | | pp | disappointed kidnapping | |
| | bag | b | brain bribe objective biased | |
| | | bb | robbery hobby | |
| | key | c | court critic | choir orchestra stomach-ache question expect accuse |
| | | k | kidneys shake | |
| | | ck | shocked homesick | |
| | girl | g | regret grateful colleague forget | |
| | | gg | hugged mugging | |
| | flower | f | fist theft | enough laugh |
| | | ph | physicist symphony tough | |
| | | ff | offended staff | |
| | vase | v | velvet vandalism nervous prevent evidence review | of |
| | tie | t | taste tend stand chest | produced passed |
| | | tt | matter bottom | |
| | dog | d | deny murder editor redundant | failed bored |
| | | dd | addictive suddenly | |
| | snake | s | stops suck | science scenery fancy |
| | | ss | witness loss | |
| | | ce/ci | notice censored | |
| | zebra | z | breeze freezing | |
| | | zz | dizzy blizzard | |
| | | s | nose raise spends agrees | |
| | shower | sh | shrug brush wish clash | sugar sure chic |
| | | ti (+ vowel) | ambitious sensational | |
| | | ci (+ vowel) | special sociable | |
| | television | An unusual sound. decision conclusion usually genre | | |

| | | usual spelling | | ! but also |
|---|---|---|---|---|
| θ | thumb | th | thunder thick healthy thigh death teeth | |
| ð | mother | th | the that with further rather | |
| tʃ | chess | ch | checked chilly | |
| | | tch | scratch stretch | |
| | | t (+ure) | departure temperature | |
| dʒ | jazz | j | jet-lag hijack | |
| | | g | suggest manager | |
| | | dge | knowledge judge | |
| | leg | l | lie liver heel lonely | |
| | | ll | colleague pillow | |
| | right | r | rise ride risky pretend | written wrong |
| | | rr | terrorism arrested | |
| | witch | w | win waste waist wave | one once |
| | | wh | while wherever | |
| | yacht | y | yet year youth yourself | |
| | | before u | university argue | |
| | monkey | m | mild remind seem remember | comb |
| | | mm | commit commentator | |
| | nose | n | nails honest | kneel knew |
| | | nn | announce beginning | |
| ŋ | singer | ng | length belongings hang bring | |
| | | before g / k | wink sink | |
| | house | h | humid hail behaviour inhabit inherit perhaps | who whose whole |

☐ voiced  ☐ unvoiced

**Go online** to watch the Sound Bank videos

OXFORD
UNIVERSITY PRESS

fourth
edition

# English File

**Upper-intermediate Multipack B**
Workbook B Units 6–10

WITH KEY

Christina Latham-Koenig
Clive Oxenden
Kate Chomacki

with Jane Hudson

Paul Seligson and Clive Oxenden
are the original co-authors of
*English File 1* and *English File 2*

# Contents

# How to use your Workbook and Online Practice

## Student's Book

Use the Student's Book section in class with your teacher.

ACTIVITIES  AUDIO  VIDEO  RESOURCES

Go to **englishfileonline.com** and use the code on your Access Card to log into the Online Practice.

## Workbook

Practise **Grammar**, **Vocabulary**, and **Pronunciation** for every lesson.

Practise the **Practical English** for every episode.

Do the **Can you remember...?** exercises to check that you remember the Grammar, Vocabulary, and Pronunciation every two Files.

## Online Practice

Look again at the Grammar, Vocabulary, and Pronunciation from the Student's Book section before you do the Workbook exercises.

Listen to the audio for the Pronunciation exercises.

Use the Sound Bank videos to practise English sounds.

Watch the Practical English videos before you do the exercises.

Use the interactive video for more Practical English practice.

Look again at the Grammar, Vocabulary and Pronunciation if you have any problems.

Practise Reading, Listening, Speaking and Writing.

**G** *used to, be used to, get used to* **V** sleep **P** /s/ and /z/

## 1 GRAMMAR *used to, be used to, get used to*

**a** Circle the correct word.

1 Before my sister had children, she used to (sleep) / *sleeping* for eight hours every night.

2 When we moved to Britain from Poland, we weren't used to *drive / driving* on the left.

3 Chris got divorced last year, but he soon got used to *live / living* on his own.

4 I *used to / use to* know her quite well, but we lost touch after university.

5 Max *would / used to* have a beard when he was a student.

6 My parents are slowly getting used to *be / being* retired.

7 My new job is exhausting. I'm not used to *work / working* so hard.

8 Did you use to *play / playing* a musical instrument at school?

9 When Lily was a teenager, she *used to / was used to* eat pizza almost every day.

10 When I was a child, my mum *would / was used to* read to me every night before I went to bed.

**b** Complete the sentences with the infinitive or gerund of a verb from the list.

| be   cook   go   have   live   look after |
| ~~play~~   study   talk   use |

1 I used to *play* basketball quite well when I was a teenager.

2 Neil is a chef, so he's used to _____ for a lot of people.

3 My sister has got used to _____ in New York now, though she didn't like it at first.

4 My grandparents didn't use to _____ a phone when they were first married.

5 I don't think I could get used to _____ a total vegetarian.

6 When I was a child, my whole family would _____ for a walk every Sunday afternoon.

7 Emma has never lived on her own before, so she isn't used to _____ herself.

8 Did you use to _____ with music on when you were at university?

9 Ben will have to get used to _____ public transport when he starts his new job.

10 People used to _____ to friends in person, not online.

**c** Complete the second sentence so that it has a similar meaning to the first sentence. Use a form of *used to, be used to,* or *get used to* and a verb.

1 Stephen wasn't so affectionate in the past.
Stephen *didn't use to be* _____ so affectionate.

2 Has working at night become less of a problem now?
Have you _____ at night?

3 Rob couldn't sleep because he doesn't normally sleep on a sofa.
Rob couldn't sleep because he _____ on a sofa.

4 Chloe wore her sister's clothes when she was a child.
Chloe _____ her sister's clothes when she was a child.

5 We have adapted to living in the country very quickly.
We have _____ in the country very quickly.

6 In the past, the high street was full of shops, but now many have closed down.
The high street _____ full of shops, but now many have closed down.

7 They still don't know how to use the new computer system – they keep making mistakes.
They haven't _____ the new computer system yet.

8 I don't normally have breakfast so early.
I'm _____ breakfast so early.

**d** Write about things you *used to / didn't use to* do as a child and things you're *used to / you've got used to* doing these days.

When I was a child...

_____
_____
_____
_____
_____
_____
_____
_____

These days...

_____
_____
_____
_____
_____
_____
_____
_____
_____

## 2 PRONUNCIATION /s/ and /z/

**a** ◀))6.1 Listen and complete the sentences.

1 Terry is *used to working* at night.
2 We've got _____ in a tiny flat.
3 Antibiotics are drugs that are _____ infections.
4 I never _____ problems sleeping.
5 I _____ a room, but now I have my own.
6 A trolley is a small vehicle that is _____ things.

**b** ◀))6.1 Listen again. In which sentences is *used* pronounced /juːzd/ and in which is it pronounced /juːst/?

**c** ◀))6.1 Listen and repeat the sentences. <u>C</u>opy the <u>rhy</u>thm.

**d** Write the words in the correct column.

| bus buzz cause course eyes ice loose lose |
| peace peas place plays price prize race raise |

|  <br>1<br>**s**nake |  <br>2<br>**z**ebra |
| --- | --- |
| bus | buzz |
| | |
| | |
| | |
| | |

**e** ◀))6.2 Listen and check. Then listen again and repeat the words.

⟳ **Go online** for more practice

41

## 3 VOCABULARY sleep

**a** Complete the sentences.

1 I tried not to y*awn*_____, but I was tired and I couldn't help it.

2 We were cold in bed, so we got a bl_____ from the cupboard.

3 She has to wear earplugs at night because her husband sn_____.

4 I was feeling sl_____, so I went to bed.

5 My grandmother takes sl_____ p_____ to help her to sleep.

6 If I get up early, I try to have a n_____ after lunch.

7 It was lovely and warm in the bed because there was a nice thick d_____ on it.

8 I was so tired that I fell asleep as soon as I put my head on the p_____.

9 James has in_____ – he just can't sleep at night.

10 It's very hot in the summer where we live, so we only have a sh_____ on the bed.

**b** Match 1–9 to a–i.

1 Our neighbours often keep ___f___

2 My partner is a light ____

3 I didn't hear last night's storm – I always sleep ____

4 Before I travel, I often have ____

5 On weekdays, I always set ____

6 Our children were ____

7 Apparently, I used to sleepwalk when I was a child; ____

8 I often fall ____

9 If you oversleep, ____

a nightmares about missing my flight.

b fast asleep by the time we got home.

c you'll miss your bus.

d the alarm for seven o'clock.

e sleeper – the slightest noise wakes him up.

f ~~us awake with their loud music.~~

g asleep during long coach journeys.

h like a log.

i one day my mother found me in the garden!

**c** Complete the questions with the correct form of a verb from the list.

be   fall   have   keep   oversleep
set   ~~sleep~~   sleepwalk

1 *Are*_____ you a light sleeper, or do you *sleep*_____ like a log? Why?

2 Do you ever _____ nightmares? What about?

3 Do you wake up on your own, or do you need to _____ an alarm?

4 When was the last time you _____? What time did you wake up?

5 How long does it usually take you to _____ asleep?

6 Do you know anyone who _____? If so, where do they usually go?

7 What sometimes _____ you awake?

8 When was the last time you _____ fast asleep and something or someone woke you up?

**d** Answer the questions in **c** about you.

1 _____

_____

2 _____

_____

3 _____

_____

4 _____

_____

5 _____

_____

6 _____

_____

7 _____

_____

8 _____

_____

**Go online** for more practice

# 6B Music to my ears

> Music expresses that which cannot be put into words and that which cannot remain silent.
> *Victor Hugo, poet, novelist, and dramatist*

**G** gerunds and infinitives  **V** music  **P** words from other languages

## 1 GRAMMAR gerunds and infinitives

**a** Circle a, b, or c.

1 Mia learned _____ the guitar when she was a teenager.
   **a** play   **b** (to play)   **c** playing

2 I don't mind _____ if you tell me which way to go.
   **a** drive   **b** to drive   **c** driving

3 I must _____ to some of their songs before I go to the concert.
   **a** listen   **b** to listen   **c** listening

4 Our teacher makes us _____ a lot of homework.
   **a** do   **b** to do   **c** doing

5 Tom's doctor suggested _____ a specialist about his back.
   **a** see   **b** to see   **c** seeing

6 We'd like _____ our bill now as we're leaving early tomorrow.
   **a** pay   **b** to pay   **c** paying

7 My girlfriend is very possessive. She doesn't let me _____ with my friends any more.
   **a** go out   **b** to go out   **c** going out

8 The man denied _____ the laptop from my bag.
   **a** steal   **b** to steal   **c** stealing

9 Kim expects _____ her exam results on Friday.
   **a** get   **b** to get   **c** getting

10 I've given up _____ to the gym. It was too boring.
   **a** go   **b** to go   **c** going

11 I can't imagine _____ at 5.30 every morning.
   **a** get up   **b** to get up   **c** getting up

12 My son managed _____ his driving test although he was really nervous.
   **a** pass   **b** to pass   **c** passing

**b** Complete the sentences with the infinitive or gerund of the verb in brackets.

1 I remembered *to buy* _____ milk, but I didn't get any bread! (buy)

2 If you can't sleep at night, try _____ for a while. (read)

3 My sister is trying _____ a new job – she doesn't get on with her boss. (find)

4 We need _____ a plumber because the shower's broken. (call)

5 That shirt needs _____ if you want to wear it tonight. (iron)

6 Laura forgot _____ her mother a birthday card. (send)

7 I'll never forget _____ my best friend for the first time. (meet)

8 I remember _____ the apple tree when I was a child. (climb)

**c** Complete the questions with the infinitive or gerund of a verb from the list.

add  ~~download~~  go  learn
listen to  see  take  want

1 What's the first song or album you remember _downloading_?
2 Which song always makes you _____ to dance?
3 Which artist or band would you most like _____ in concert?
4 Have you ever tried _____ an instrument? Which one?
5 Are there any songs you like at the moment that need _____ to your playlist?
6 What kind of music do you avoid _____ if you can?
7 Have you ever forgotten _____ your tickets to a concert? If so, what happened?
8 Would you rather _____ to a small concert or a large music festival? Why?

**d** Answer the questions in **c** about you.

1 _____
2 _____
3 _____
4 _____
5 _____
6 _____
7 _____
8 _____

**2 VOCABULARY & PRONUNCIATION**
music; words from other languages

**a** Complete the crossword.

ACROSS →

DOWN ↓

Go online for more practice

**b** Match the English words borrowed from other languages to the definitions.

ballet  chorus  concerto  encore  genre
mezzo-soprano  rhythm  symphony

1 a style of dancing that tells a story with music but without words _ballet_
2 a long piece of music for a large orchestra, usually in three or four parts _____
3 a short, extra performance at the end of a concert _____
4 a singing voice with a range between soprano and alto

   _____
5 part of a song that is sung after each verse _____
6 a strong, regular, repeated pattern of sounds _____
7 a piece of music for an orchestra and one instrument playing a solo _____
8 a particular type or style of e.g. music _____

**c** Underline the stressed syllable in the words in the list. Then put them in the correct column.

ba|llet  ce|llo  cho|rus  con|cer|to  con|duc|tor  en|core
gen|re  gui|tar  key|board  or|ches|tra  rhy|thm
sax|o|phone  so|pra|no  sym|pho|ny  vi|o|lin

| Stress on first syllable | Stress on second syllable | Stress on third syllable |
|---|---|---|
| ballet | | |
| | | |

**d** 🔊6.3 Listen and check. Then listen again and repeat the words.

**e** Circle the word with a different sound.

| | | | |
|---|---|---|---|
| 1 | 2 | 3 | 4 |
| **k**eys | **ch**ess | **sh**ower | **k**eys |
| **ch**oir | cappu**cc**ino | **ch**auffeur | bou**qu**et |
| ~~**ch**illi~~ (circled) | **c**ello | **ch**ef | en**c**ore |
| or**ch**estra | **c**oncerto | **ch**ic | fian**c**é |
| psy**ch**ology | ma**cch**iato | **ch**orus | hypo**ch**ondriac |

**f** 🔊6.4 Listen and check. Then listen again and repeat the words.

**g** 🔊6.5 Listen and complete the sentences.

1 The _barista_ brought me my _croissant_ .
2 The _____ is ruined by the _____.
3 A lot of _____ took _____ of the film star.
4 The technician gave the _____ a

   _____.
5 The dancers in that _____ had a natural sense of _____.

**h** 🔊6.5 Listen again and repeat the sentences. Copy the rhythm.

Go online for more practice    Go online to check your progress

# 7A Let's not argue

**G** past modals: *must have, etc., would rather*  **V** verbs often confused  **P** weak form of *have*

## 1 GRAMMAR past modals: *must have*, etc.

**a** Match the sentences to the responses.

1 Ryan's phone was switched off.   *c*
2 Stacey can't find her gloves. ____
3 Emma didn't make her bed this morning. ____
4 I was surprised that Tony didn't come to the party. ____
5 Leo has just bought a brand new Porsche. ____
6 Isabel didn't say hello to me this morning. ____
7 I'm not sure where Millie is. ____
8 My dad was made redundant when we were kids. ____

a She can't have seen you.
b She may have left them in her car.
c ~~I think he might have been at the cinema.~~
d He must have paid a fortune for it.
e She could have gone to a friend's house.
f She might not have had time.
g He couldn't have been very happy about that.
h He must have had something else to do.

**b** Complete the sentences with *must have, might have, might not have*, or *can't have* and the verb in brackets.

1 You *must have been*  delighted when you passed your driving test – it was your first time, wasn't it? (be)
2 I'm not sure where Mark is, but he _____ home. He wasn't feeling well this morning. (go)
3 You _____ my parents at the supermarket. They're away on holiday. (see)
4 I don't know why my grandmother didn't open the door, but I suppose she _____ the bell. (hear)
5 The 'For Sale' sign is still up outside their house. They _____ yet. (move)
6 I don't understand how the accident happened, but the driver _____ asleep. (fall)
7 Those boys look really guilty. They _____ something wrong. (do)
8 Ruth hasn't replied to my email. It's possible that she _____ it yet. (read)

**c** Write the next sentence using the words given.

1 My brother isn't talking to me.
I / should / shout at him
*I shouldn't have shouted at him.*
2 We're running out of petrol.
we / should / fill up at the last garage.
_____
3 Someone has taken Ben's smartphone.
he / ought / leave it on his desk
_____
4 You won't be able to walk in those shoes.
you / should / buy such high heels
_____
5 I had a nightmare last night.
I / ought / stay up to watch that horror film
_____
6 Your cousins look really scruffy.
they / ought / dress up for the wedding
_____
7 My alarm clock isn't working.
it / should / go off at 7.30
_____
8 Jessie missed her train.
she / should / take a taxi to the station
_____

**d** Look at the photo. What do you think happened? What do you think the cyclist did wrong? Use *must, might / may / could,* or *can't / couldn't* to make deductions, and *should have / ought to have* to express criticism. Use the words in the list or your own ideas.

| | | |
|---|---|---|
| be / more careful | break / bike | ~~fall off / bike~~ |
| hit / head | hurt / leg | ride / so fast | sprain / ankle |
| wear / protection | | |

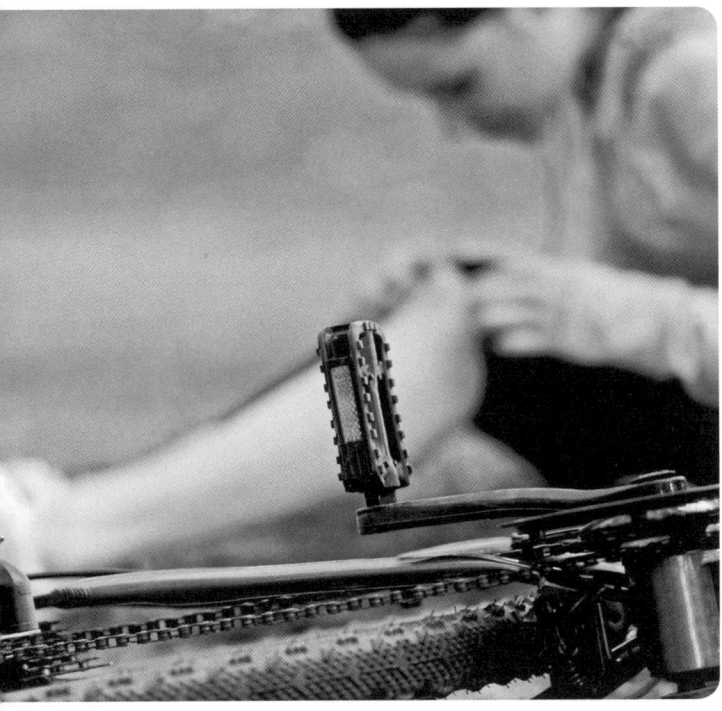

1 *She must have fallen off her bike.*
2 _____
3 _____
4 _____
5 _____
6 _____
7 _____
8 _____

## 2 PRONUNCIATION weak form of *have*

**a** 🔊 7.1 Listen and write the sentences with either *have* or *of*.

1 *I cried at the end of the film*_____.
2 _____.
3 _____?
4 _____.
5 _____?
6 _____.

**b** 🔊 7.1 Listen again and repeat the sentences. Copy the <u>rhy</u>thm.

**c** 🔊 7.2 Listen and complete the sentences.

1 They're taking Steve to hospital. He might have _broken_ a _bone_.
2 Diana isn't here yet. She can't have _____ my _____.
3 It was only a joke. She shouldn't have _____ so _____.
4 This restaurant's packed. We should have _____ a _____.
5 I didn't hear the phone. I must have _____.
6 Becky and Ian haven't come to the party. They may have _____ about it.

**d** 🔊 7.2 Listen again and repeat the second sentences. Copy the <u>rhy</u>thm.

## 3 GRAMMAR IN CONTEXT *would rather*

Rewrite the sentences using *would rather*.

1 I'd prefer it if you didn't post photos of me on Facebook.
  I*'d rather you didn't post photos of me on Facebook*.
2 I don't really want to cook tonight, if you don't mind.
  I _____.
3 What do you want to do: stay in or go out?
  What _____?
4 I'd prefer it if we got a taxi home, if that's OK with you.
  I _____.
5 I'd prefer to see that film at the cinema than on TV.
  I _____.
6 I'd prefer to sit by the window than next to the aisle.
  I _____.

Go online for more practice

## 4 VOCABULARY verbs often confused

**a** Complete the sentences with the correct **bold** verb.

1 **wish / hope**

   I _wish_ we had enough money to buy a bigger flat.

2 **mind / matter**

   I don't _____ where we go. The important thing is to have a holiday.

3 **avoid / prevent**

   My daughter will do anything to _____ doing housework. She's really lazy.

4 **remember / remind**

   _____ me to send my dad a card. It's his birthday next week.

5 **argue / discuss**

   My boyfriend and I often _____ about his friends. I really don't like them.

6 **lend / borrow**

   Could I _____ your phone charger? I've left mine at home.

7 **notice / realize**

   I didn't _____ what the thief was wearing. It was too dark.

8 **beat / win**

   Chelsea managed to _____ the match 1–0.

9 **expect / wait**

   I'll _____ outside while you see the doctor.

10 **raise / rise**

   Please _____ your hand if you have any questions.

11 **advise / warn**

   My uncle asked me to _____ him which laptop he should get.

12 **deny / refuse**

   I _____ to lend Harry any more money. He never pays me back!

13 **lay / lie**

   All I want to do when I'm on holiday is _____ on the beach and sunbathe.

14 **rob / steal**

   Don't leave your phone on the table – somebody might _____ it.

**b** Complete the sentences with the past simple form of a verb from the pairs in the list.

advise / warn   argue / discuss   avoid / prevent
beat / win   deny / refuse   expect / wait   lay / lie
lend / borrow   mind / matter   notice / realize
raise / rise   ~~remember / remind~~   rob / steal   wish / hope

1 When I got to my car, I suddenly _remembered_ that the keys were in my other bag.

2 My parents _____ me the money to buy a new car, but I have to pay them back.

3 Scotland _____ Ireland 3–2.

4 Two men _____ me while I was walking home. They got away with my purse and phone.

5 My colleague _____ taking my scissors, but I saw them later on his desk.

6 Last year we just _____ on the beach all day when we were on holiday.

7 House prices _____ last month for the first time this year.

8 At the meeting we _____ the possibility of working together.

9 The police officer's action _____ anybody from getting hurt.

10 I _____ our team to lose, but in the end they won.

11 At first, she didn't think it _____ that her husband travelled a lot, but eventually she got fed up with it.

12 The moment I heard her voice on the phone, I _____ something was wrong.

13 The tour guide _____ us that the area was dangerous at night.

14 We _____ the weather would be good for the picnic, but unfortunately it rained.

**Go online** for more practice

# It's all an act

**G** verbs of the senses  **V** the body  **P** silent consonants

## 1 GRAMMAR verbs of the senses

**a** Circle the correct form.

1 Your skin *feels* / *feels like* dry. You need to use some cream.

2 Ken is sweating. He *looks* / *looks as if* he's been running.

3 We need to take out the rubbish. The kitchen *smells* / *smells like* terrible.

4 I'm not sure what's in this curry, but it *tastes like* / *tastes as if* chicken.

5 It *sounds* / *sounds as though* Becky has finally got up. I can hear her moving around.

6 Come in and sit by the fire. Your hands *feel like* / *feel as if* ice!

7 This soup *tastes* / *tastes as if* you put a lot of garlic in it.

8 You *seem* / *seem like* happy today. Have you had some good news?

9 I don't feel like *go* / *going out* tonight. Let's stay in and watch a film.

10 You *sound* / *sound like* your mother when you talk like that.

**b** Complete the sentences with *look* / *feel* / *smell* / *sound* / *taste* / *seem* + *like* or *as if* where necessary.

1 My skin *feels*_____ much softer since I've been using a new face cream.

2 What's that noise? It _____ thunder.

3 Ellen's boyfriend _____ a model – he's tall and incredibly good-looking.

4 Have you turned off the cooker? It _____ something's burning.

5 This salad _____ horrible – it's really salty.

6 This swimming pool _____ it's heated. The water is lovely and warm!

7 Your voice _____ strange. Do you have a sore throat?

8 Is anything the matter? You _____ a bit distant today.

9 That aftershave _____ petrol – I'm not sure if I like it.

10 Martha's hair is in a mess. She _____ she's just got out of bed.

**c** Complete the description of the thing in photo 1 with *looks*, *smells*, *feels*, or *tastes*. Then write descriptions of the things in photos 2–4 using verbs of the senses.

**1** a cake  **2** garlic

**3** blue cheese  **4** a Siamese cat

1 It's a kind of food. It *looks*_____ a bit like bread. It _____ hot and quite soft at first, but it goes harder on the outside when it's cold. It _____ delicious when it comes out of the oven, and it _____ even better when you eat it.

2 _____
_____
_____
_____
_____

3 _____
_____
_____
_____

4 _____
_____
_____
_____

## 2 VOCABULARY the body

a   Complete the crossword.

**DOWN ↓**

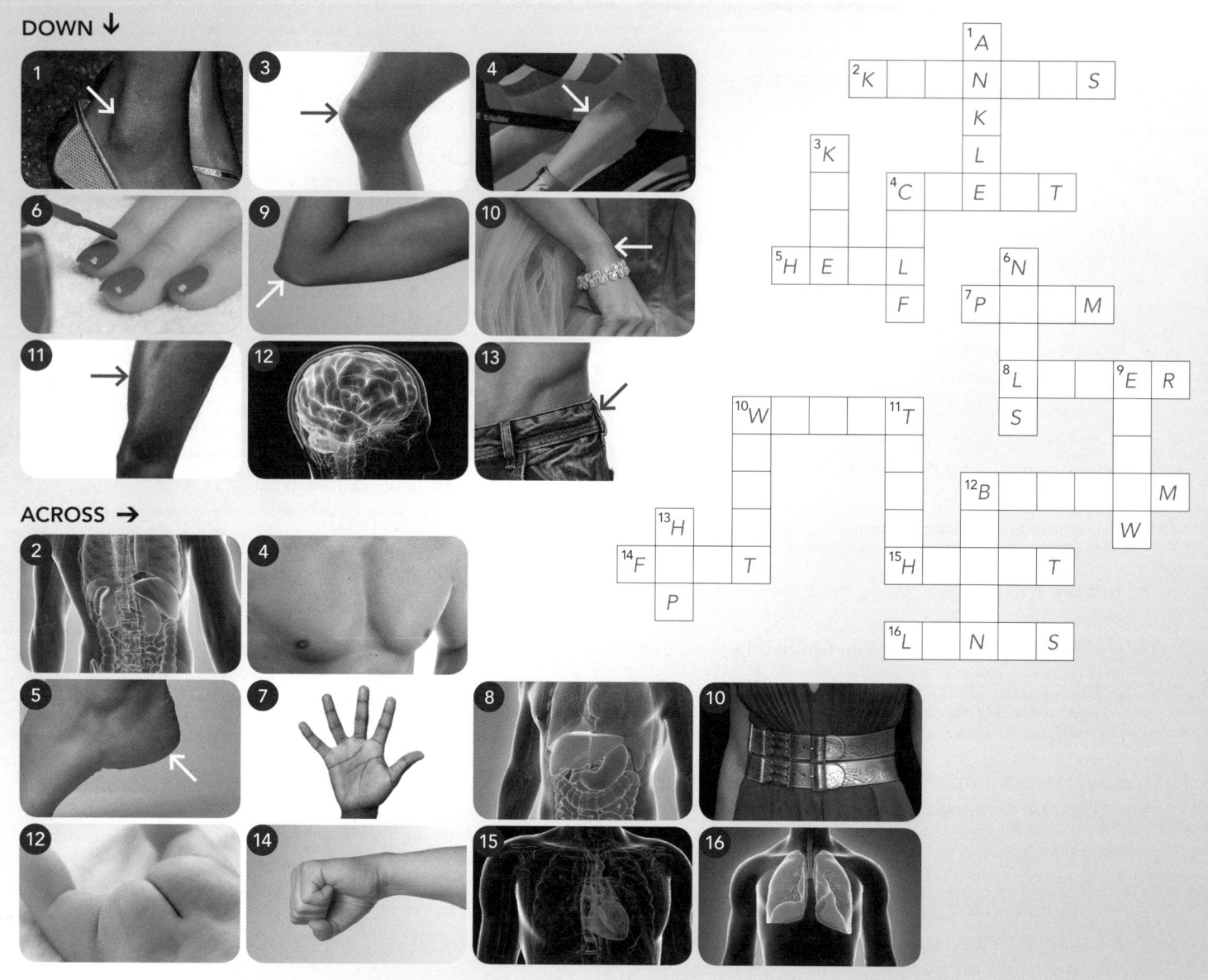

**ACROSS →**

b   Match 1–13 to a–m.

| | | | |
|---|---|---|---|
| 1 | Can you touch | _h_ | a  your nose. |
| 2 | When I asked if she'd passed, she shook | ___ | b  my hand as we walked down the road. |
| 3 | I always brush | ___ | c  her head sadly. |
| 4 | Adam shrugged | ___ | d  his arms and stood watching me. |
| 5 | Here's a tissue so you can blow | ___ | e  my thumb when I was a baby. |
| 6 | I used to suck | ___ | f  his nails when he's nervous. |
| 7 | Jessie combed | ___ | g  her hair and put on her jacket to go out. |
| 8 | She went into the room and shook | ___ | h  your toes? |
| 9 | Remember to brush | ___ | i  his shoulders and said he didn't know. |
| 10 | When I told my boss, she raised | ___ | j  your hair once you've washed it. |
| 11 | My boyfriend bites | ___ | k  hands with the interviewer. |
| 12 | He folded | ___ | l  her eyebrows in surprise. |
| 13 | My niece held | ___ | m  my teeth after every meal. |

🔵 **Go online** for more practice

**c** Complete the sentences with the past simple form of a verb from the list.

chew   frown   hug   kneel   point   scratch
~~stare~~   stretch   wave   wink   yawn

1 The children *stared*_____ at the ice cream in the shop window.
2 Anna _____ her children and gave them each a kiss before she left the house.
3 He _____ as he read the letter – it can't have been good news.
4 We _____ each mouthful to make it last because we didn't know when we'd be eating again.
5 He got up and _____ to try and wake himself up.
6 The police officer _____ on the ground to examine the footprints.
7 I don't speak French, so I just _____ at the cake I wanted.
8 My friend _____ at me when he saw me getting off the train.
9 My dad _____ at my daughter to show he wasn't being serious.
10 The baby _____ twice and then fell asleep.
11 Robin _____ the insect bites on his legs and made them bleed.

## 3 VOCABULARY FROM READING

Complete the sentences.

1 It's a con*tradiction*___ to say that you're friends with somebody but you don't trust them.
2 Don't l_____ to me – I need to know the truth.
3 The best way to de_____ a lie is by watching a person's body language.
4 I'm not a very good l_____, so I generally tell the truth.
5 The present was supposed to be a secret, but his wife g_____ it a_____.
6 People often use de_____ to make money or get something they want.

## 4 PRONUNCIATION
silent consonants

**a** ~~Cross out~~ the silent consonants in the words. Use the phonetics to help you.

1 ~~w~~rist      /rɪst/
2 thumb      /θʌm/
3 kneel      /niːl/
4 palm      /pɑːm/
5 muscle      /ˈmʌsl/
6 whistle      /ˈwɪsl/
7 honest      /ˈɒnɪst/
8 fasten      /ˈfɑːsn/
9 aisle      /aɪl/
10 design      /dɪˈzaɪn/
11 whole      /həʊl/

**b** ◕ 7.3 Listen and check. Then listen again and repeat the words.

**c** Look at the phonetics. Write the word.

1 /ˈkɑːsl/      *castle*_____
2 /huːz/      _____
3 /ˈkʌbəd/      _____
4 /ˈfɒrən/      _____
5 /rɒŋ/      _____
6 /kɑːm/      _____
7 /naɪf/      _____
8 /ˈsɪzəz/      _____
9 /ˈɔːtəm/      _____
10 /ˈaɪlənd/      _____
11 /wɒt/      _____
12 /ˈplʌmə(r)/      _____

**d** ◕ 7.4 Listen and check. Then listen again and repeat the words.

**e** ◕ 7.5 Listen and complete the sentences.

1 They spent the *whole*_____ meeting discussing the new project.
2 I wish I had been more _____ about how I felt.
3 I don't know anyone who likes the _____ of the new shopping centre.
4 It seems to have been much colder than usual this _____.
5 I've found a key, but I don't know _____ it is.
6 She looked surprisingly _____ after the accident.

◉ Go online for more practice      ✓ Go online to check your progress

## 1 LOOKING AT LANGUAGE

**Complete the modifiers in the sentences.**

1 The actors were utt*erly* exhausted when the play was over.
2 The plot left the audience feeling com_____ bewildered.
3 As far as I'm concerned, the film was tre_____ overrated.
4 So far, reviews of the play have been over_____ positive.
5 Mozart was an extra_____ talented musician.
6 The director was ab_____ delighted to receive the award.
7 All of the characters were wearing fan_____ original costumes.

## 2 VOCABULARY FROM THE INTERVIEW

**Match the words from the interview to the definitions.**

1 box office _c_
2 rehearsal ____
3 character ____
4 auditorium ____
5 scene ____

a the place where an incident in real life or fiction occurs or occurred
b a practice or trial performance of a play or other work for later public performance
c a place at a theatre, cinema, etc., where tickets are bought or reserved
d a person in a novel, play, or film
e the part of a theatre, concert hall, or other public building in which the audience sits

## 3 THE CONVERSATION

**Match the beginnings 1–6 to endings a–f.**

1 That's a difficult question. _d_
2 I think it's difficult to say ____
3 But if you go to a live event, you participate, don't you, ____
4 If you're sitting, let's say, ____
5 I've been to plenty of live music events – concerts and festivals and things, you know, ____
6 That's intriguing, isn't it, ____

a high up or with a slightly obstructed view…
b because you're part of it.
c the difference between the two…
d I love going to the cinema…
e if it's better or worse…
f around the country, and I love them.

## 4 VOCABULARY FROM THE CONVERSATION

**Complete the sentences and phrases with a word from the list.**

| | | | | |
|---|---|---|---|---|
| bouncing | certain | factors | flashy | soft |

1 watching a big *flashy* superhero film
2 a big _____ spot for the theatre
3 It has a _____ magic to it.
4 You're part of it because they're _____ off you.
5 It depends on other _____.

## GRAMMAR & VOCABULARY

**a** Complete the sentences with the correct form of the **bold** word.

1 My sister-in-law is rather _____-_____; she has a very high opinion of herself. **HEAD**

2 The boys were wearing _____ tops, so you couldn't see their faces. **HOOD**

3 _____, there's nothing we can do about the current situation; it's up to the politicians. **BASIC**

4 They've said the weather will be _____, so take an umbrella in case it rains later. **CHANGE**

5 Toby's moving house at the moment, which is a bit _____. **STRESS**

6 The town hall is an _____ building in the main square. **IMPRESS**

7 I _____ this morning, so I was late for work. **SLEEP**

8 The sound of the rain on the roof kept me _____ last night. **WAKE**

9 I _____ in bed for hours last night trying to get to sleep. **LIE**

10 Mirga is a famous _____ who has worked with orchestras all over the world. **CONDUCT**

**b** Read the article. Circle a, b, or c.

# So you want to be an actor?

Many people think that acting ¹____ easy. They believe it's just a question of memorizing lines and delivering them in front of the camera. 'If I could remember words, I ²____ be an actor, too,' they say. Yet none of them would expect to become a professional singer overnight. In general, most people think that becoming a ³____ requires far more training than appearing on-screen.

In fact, it takes just as much training to be a good actor ⁴____ it does to become an opera singer. The difference is that an actor has to learn ⁵____ naturally so that the audience doesn't ⁶____ that he or she is acting. According to the famous teacher Stanford Meisner, 'Acting is doing things truthfully under imaginary circumstances.'

If a person ⁷____ to become a successful actor, they have to learn how to bring a script to life. From the moment he or she receives the pages, an actor will ⁸____ for action in the lines in order to make choices about his or her performance. The words are the writer's, but it's the actor who creates a believable character to express them.

In conclusion, it is impossible to wake up one morning and spontaneously decide to go out and get an acting job. The naturalness of an actor's performance might make you ⁹____ that anyone who can read or speak can be one. However, it's more than likely that it ¹⁰____ them many years of training to get where they are now.

| 1 | **a** looks | **b** looks like | **c** looks as if |
|---|---|---|---|
| 2 | **a** can | **b** could | **c** will be able to |
| 3 | **a** concerto | **b** soprano | **c** symphony |
| 4 | **a** as | **b** like | **c** than |
| 5 | **a** perform | **b** performing | **c** to perform |
| 6 | **a** advise | **b** deny | **c** realize |
| 7 | **a** had wanted | **b** wanted | **c** wants |
| 8 | **a** be looking | **b** have looked | **c** to look |
| 9 | **a** think | **b** thinking | **c** to think |
| 10 | **a** had taken | **b** has been taking | **c** has taken |

✓ **Go online** to check your progress

> No-one truly knows a nation until
> one has been inside its jails.
> *Nelson Mandela*

**G** the passive (all forms); *have something done; it is said that..., he is thought to...,* etc.  **V** crime and punishment  **P** the letter *u*

## 1 VOCABULARY crime and punishment

**a** Complete the text with the words in the list.

be burgled   break into   burglar   burglary   steal

I never thought that my flat would ¹*be burgled*
because I live on the third floor. But one day, I
came home to find the lock on my front door was
broken. When I called the police to report the
² _____, a police officer came to the flat
and had a look round. She said that the ³ _____
had probably climbed over the roofs of the houses
behind to ⁴ _____ the flat through a
window. He had then broken the lock on the front door
to leave. The thief didn't ⁵ _____ much –
just some money and an old camera of mine – but I was
shocked that it had been so easy for him to get into
my flat.

**b** Read the definitions and complete the missing
letters in the crime.

1 entering a building illegally and stealing things from it
   b u r gl a r y

2 killing somebody deliberately
   m __ __ d __ __

3 giving money or valuable items to a person to
   persuade them to help you
   br __ b __ __ __ __

4 following and watching somebody over a long period
   of time in a way that is annoying or frightening
   st __ __ k __ __ __ __

5 destroying or damaging something, especially public
   property, deliberately and for no good reason
   v __ __ d __ l __ __ __ __

6 demanding money from a person by threatening to
   tell somebody else a secret about them
   bl __ __ __ m __ __ __ __

7 using violence or threats to take control of a
   vehicle, often in order to demand something from a
   government
   h __ j __ ck __ __ __

8 selling illegal drugs
   dr __ __ __ d __ __ l __ __ __

9 using violent action in order to achieve political aims
   or force a government to act
   t __ rr __ r __ __ __

10 finding a way to look at or change information on
   somebody else's computer system without permission
   h __ ck __ __ __

11 forcing somebody to have sex with you when they do
   not want to by threatening them or using violence
   r __ __ __

12 stealing something from a person or place
   th __ __ __

13 cheating somebody to get money or goods illegally
   fr __ __ __

14 stealing money from a bank, shop, person, etc.,
   especially using violence or threats
   r __ bb __ __ __ __

15 attacking somebody violently in order to steal their
   money, especially in a public place
   m __ gg __ __ __

16 taking, sending, or bringing goods secretly or illegally
   into or out of a country
   sm __ __ __ l __ __ __

17 taking somebody away illegally and keeping them as
   a prisoner, especially in order to get money
   k __ __ n __ pp __ __ __

**c** Complete the chart.

| criminal | verb |
|---|---|
| ¹*burglar* | burgle |
| 2 | murder |
| ✗ | bribe |
| 3 | stalk |
| 4 | vandalize |
| 5 | blackmail |
| 6 | hijack |
| 7 | sell drugs |
| 8 | set off bombs, etc. |
| 9 | hack |
| 10 | rape |
| 11 | steal |
| 12 | commit fraud |
| 13 | rob |
| 14 | mug |
| 15 | smuggle |
| 16 | kidnap |

**d** Complete the sentences with the past simple form of a verb from **c**.

1 Police are looking for a man who attacked and _raped_ a woman yesterday afternoon as she was walking home.
2 Fortunately, the gang _____ the bank when there were no customers inside.
3 The woman _____ the actor for many years, following him wherever he went.
4 They _____ $1 million worth of electronic goods into the country before they were caught at customs.
5 The construction company _____ the mayor with tens of thousands of pounds for permission to build houses on the land.
6 Two men _____ my friend at knifepoint yesterday. They took all her money.
7 The woman _____ fraud by pretending she was a psychic and charging people.
8 Some teenagers _____ my house while I was away and took all my music equipment.
9 Apparently, she _____ her husband by poisoning him because she was planning to claim the insurance money.
10 Someone _____ my car from outside my house last night.
11 They _____ the businessman by threatening to send the photographs to his wife if he didn't pay them the money.
12 Two armed men _____ the plane and forced the pilot to take them to the nearest airport.
13 The boy _____ drugs because he thought it was an easier way to get money than having a job.
14 The terrorists _____ a bomb inside a crowded shopping centre.
15 A couple _____ the politician as he left his house and later demanded £1 million for his safe return.
16 Youths _____ the park last night and damaged a lot of trees and flowers.
17 Someone _____ my computer last month and stole my personal details.

**e** Complete the text with the words in the lists.

**Nouns**

court  evidence  judge  jury  proof  punishment
verdict  witnesses

**Verbs**

accused  acquitted  arrest  catch  charged
committed  ~~investigate~~  question  sentenced

It is the job of the police to [1] _investigate_ crimes and try to [2] _____ the criminal or criminals who [3] _____ the crime. When the police have a suspect, they can [4] _____ him or her and take them to the police station to [5] _____ them. If the suspect is [6] _____ with the crime, they have to appear in front of a [7] _____ and maybe a [8] _____ (of 12 people) in [9] _____. Here they are [10] _____ of the crime and [11] _____ may be called to give [12] _____. If there is no [13] _____ that they were involved in the crime, they are [14] _____. If not, they have to wait for the [15] _____. If they are found guilty, they are given a [16] _____. In some cases, they may be [17] _____ to spend a period of time in prison.

## 2 VOCABULARY FROM READING

Complete the sentences with a word from the list.

~~con~~  claim  hand over  impression  prey  scam
target  wary

1 Be careful when buying something from an unfamiliar website, because someone might try to _con_ you.
2 Fake gas inspectors _____ on elderly people living alone.
3 We were under the _____ that we had booked an apartment, but in fact it didn't exist.
4 The robbers ordered the bank staff to _____ the money if they didn't want to get hurt.
5 He tried to _____ he had made a mistake, but it was obvious he was lying.
6 I'm _____ of giving someone my email address if I don't know them very well.
7 A common _____ in big cities is for a tourist to be sprayed with a liquid and then have their wallet stolen by a person helping to clean the mess.
8 The gang chose to _____ small jewellery shops in the hope that they would be easier to rob.

🕐 **Go online** for more practice

## 3 PRONUNCIATION the letter u

**a** Circle the word with a different sound.

| | | | |
|---|---|---|---|
| 1 | bird | **bur**glar  **mur**derer  **ver**dict  (**ver**y) |
| 2 | up | comm**u**nity  dr**u**gs  j**u**dge  sm**u**ggle |
| 3 | t**ou**rist | d**u**ring  f**u**ture  j**u**ry  sec**u**re |
| 4 | /juː/ | acc**u**se  n**ew**  p**u**nish  **u**seful |
| 5 | h**or**se | c**ou**rt  g**ui**lty  st**a**lker  fr**au**d |

**b** 🔊 8.1 Listen and check. Then listen again and repeat the words.

## 4 GRAMMAR the passive (all forms); *have something done*; *it is said that…, he is thought to…*, etc.

**a** Complete the text with the correct active or passive form of the verbs in brackets.

Last month my motorbike ¹ *was taken* (take) from outside my house. When I called the police, I ² *found out* (find out) that over 20 motorbikes ³_____ (steal) in my area in the previous six months. The officer I spoke to promised me that the thief would ⁴_____ (catch) and punished as soon as possible.

First, the police ⁵_____ (question) all the victims of the thefts and ⁶_____ (visit) all the motorbike dealers in the area. Their investigations came to an end late last night when they identified the criminal…as my next-door neighbour!

He ⁷_____ (just arrest), and at the moment he ⁸_____ (hold) at the local police station. His case ⁹_____ (hear) in the magistrate's court next week and everyone ¹⁰_____ (expect) him to be found guilty. He might ¹¹_____ (give) a short prison sentence, but the best thing is that no more motorbikes ¹²_____ (steal) in my area in the future.

**b** Rewrite the sentences with *have something done*.

1 Someone is going to change the lock on my front door.
  I'm going to *have the lock on my front door changed*.
2 Someone tests our burglar alarm twice a year.
  We _____ twice a year.
3 A mechanic has repaired my car.
  I _____.
4 Someone broke our windows when we were on holiday.
  We _____ when we were on holiday.
5 Someone will clean my carpets in the spring.
  I _____ in the spring.
6 Someone has hacked my boyfriend's computer.
  My boyfriend _____.
7 Someone cleans Oliver's flat once a week.
  Oliver _____ once a week.
8 A company is redesigning our garden.
  We _____.

**c** Complete the second sentence so that it means the same as the first sentence.

1 It is known that the rapist is a local man.
  The rapist *is known to be a local man*.
2 The blackmailer is understood to be a colleague of the victim.
  It is *understood that the blackmailer is a colleague of the victim*.
3 It is expected that the man will be acquitted.
  The man _____.
4 It is reported that kidnappers have taken the president's wife.
  Kidnappers _____.
5 The terrorists are thought to be in hiding somewhere in France.
  It is _____.
6 The suspect is known to be dangerous.
  It is _____.
7 The police are said to have arrested three men.
  It is _____.
8 It is reported that vandals have damaged several buildings in the area.
  Vandals _____.

**d** Write an anecdote about a crime that you or someone you know was affected by. Use the passive and causative *have*.

🔄 **Go online** for more practice

# 8B Fake news

A newspaper is a device unable to discriminate between a bicycle accident and the collapse of civilization.
*George Bernard Shaw, Irish author and playwright*

**G** reporting verbs  **V** the media  **P** word stress

## 1 GRAMMAR reporting verbs

**a** Circle the correct form.

1 I agreed (to meet) / meeting my old school friend under the clock in the station.
2 My husband denied to eat / eating the last cream cake.
3 Jane promised to give back / giving back my book the next day.
4 The tour guide recommended to visit / visiting the Picasso museum.
5 The girl refused to dance / dancing with my friend.
6 The police accused him to commit / of committing fraud.
7 My boyfriend asked me to take / taking him to the airport.
8 The teacher threatened to give / giving them extra homework if they didn't stop talking.
9 Nina's parents told her not to be / not being late.
10 The woman admitted to steal / stealing the man's watch.

**b** Complete the sentences reporting the direct speech using a reporting verb from the list.

~~advise~~  apologize  insist  invite  offer  remind  suggest  warn

1 'I really don't think you should leave your job,' Jack's friend told him.
Jack's friend *advised him not to leave* his job.
2 'I'm going with you to the doctor's, whether you like it or not,' Alice said to me.
Alice _____ to the doctor's with me, whether I liked it or not.
3 'Why don't we go for a walk?' said Katie.
Katie _____ for a walk.
4 'Shall I make the lunch?' her husband said.
Her husband _____ the lunch.
5 'Don't park there,' the man said to us. 'You'll get a fine.'
The man _____ there or we'd get a fine.
6 'I'm sorry I was so rude,' I said.
I _____ so rude.
7 'Would you like to have dinner with me?' Andy asked Sarah.
Andy _____ with him.
8 'Don't forget to sign the documents,' my boss told me.
My boss _____ the documents.

**c** Write about six things that people have said to you today. Use the reporting verbs from **a** and **b**.

1 _____
2 _____
3 _____
4 _____
5 _____
6 _____

## 2 PRONUNCIATION word stress

a Underline the stressed syllable in the reporting verbs in the list. Then put them in the correct column.

a|ccuse  ad|mit  ad|vise  a|gree  con|vince  de|ny  in|sist  in|vite  o|ffer  or|der  per|suade  pro|mise  re|fuse  re|gret  re|mind  su|ggest  threa|ten

| Stress on first syllable | Stress on second syllable |
|---|---|
|  | accuse |
|  |  |

b 🔊 8.2 Listen and check. Then listen and repeat the reporting verbs.

c 🔊 8.3 Listen and complete the sentences.

1 She _offered to_____ make the lunch.
2 He _____ tidy his room.
3 They _____ call the police.
4 She _____ come home early.
5 They _____ give me more time.
6 He _____ her for his behaviour.

d 🔊 8.3 Listen again and repeat the sentences. Try to link the verbs and *to* where appropriate.

## 3 VOCABULARY the media

a Complete the headlines with a verb from the list that means the same as the verb in brackets.

~~axed~~  back  bids  clash  hit  quit  quiz  rows  split  tipped  vows  wed

1  **TV series _axed_____ after drop in audience figures (cut)**

2  **Singer to _____ Brazilian model (marry)**

3  **Minister to _____ after revelations about personal life (resign)**

4  **Police _____ wife after man disappears (question)**

5  **Hollywood stars _____ presidential candidate (support)**

6  **US stock market _____ by new company scandal (badly affected)**

7  **Ex-footballer _____ to win reality show (predicted)**

8  **Government _____ to invest more money in rural areas (promises)**

9  **Prince _____ with brother over treatment of staff (argues)**

10  **Celebrity couple _____ after five years (separate)**

11  **Former lawyer _____ to become country's new President (attempts)**

12  **Players _____ over referee's decision (disagree)**

🔄 **Go online** for more practice

**b** Complete the sentences with a media job from the list.

agony aunt   commentator   critics
editor   freelance journalist   newsreader
~~paparazzi~~   presenter   reporter

1 The _paparazzi_____ were waiting outside the restaurant to photograph the princess.
2 Have you ever written an email to an _____, asking for advice?
3 I'm surprised none of the _____ liked the film; I thought it was great!
4 The _____ got very excited when the first goal was scored.
5 A _____ at the scene of the crime gave more details about the murder.
6 The newspaper _____ decided not to print the reporter's story because it was too politically sensitive.
7 I've stopped watching that chat show because I can't stand the _____.
8 Laura writes articles for different newspapers as a _____.
9 The _____ looked very serious when he announced that the president had been shot.

**c** Complete the sentences.

1 The newspaper my father reads is bi_ased_____ towards the government.
2 It's impossible for a journalist to be ob_____ about a subject on which he holds a strong opinion.
3 The article was cen_____ because it was too critical of the President.
4 Online papers use sen_____ headlines to make people click on an article and read it.
5 The reporter gave an acc_____ description of events; that's exactly how I remember them.

## 4 VOCABULARY FROM READING

Complete the chart with the words in the list according to their meaning.

~~dubious~~   exaggerated   fake   false
legitimate   made-up   questionable
reliable   reputable   untrustworthy

| can be trusted | can't be trusted |
|---|---|
| | _dubious_ |

| made more dramatic | not true |
|---|---|
| | |

🔘 **Go online** for more practice      ✅ **Go online** to check your progress

There is only one boss. The customer. And he can fire everybody in the company from the chairman on down, simply by spending his money elsewhere.
*Sam Walton, founder of Walmart*

**G** clauses of contrast and purpose   **V** advertising, business   **P** changing stress on nouns and verbs

**1 GRAMMAR** clauses of contrast and purpose

**a** Circle the correct word.

1 The restaurant staff seem happy *despite* / *although* the fact that they work long hours every day.
2 The account manager called his client *for* / *to* arrange a meeting.
3 The company is expanding *even though* / *in spite of* there is a recession.
4 The firm made several people redundant *in order to* / *so that* cut costs.
5 *Although* / *Despite* she's the head of the department, she often goes out with her colleagues after work.
6 I stayed at my desk *to not* / *so as not to* miss an important phone call.
7 Everybody seemed to enjoy Mike's speech at the wedding, *in spite of* / *even though* his terrible jokes.
8 She closed the door of her office *so as to* / *so that* nobody could hear her conversation.
9 I still buy that chocolate bar, *in spite of* / *though* it's much smaller than it used to be.
10 Yuri has to learn English *to* / *for* his job.

**b** Complete the second sentence so that it has a similar meaning to the first sentence. Use the **bold** word or phrase.

1 Is that a machine to make juice?
   **for**
   Is that a machine *for making juice* ?
2 The shop closed down even though it was in an ideal location.
   **in spite of**
   The shop closed down _____ .
3 They reduced their prices so as to sell more products.
   **so that**
   They reduced their prices _____ .
4 I have to leave work by six o'clock so that I don't miss my train.
   **in order not to**
   I have to leave work by six o'clock _____ .
5 Despite the fact that I was very late, my boss wasn't angry.
   **although**
   My boss wasn't angry _____ .
6 Although she's the managing director, she doesn't have her own office
   **despite**
   She doesn't have her own office _____ .

## 2 VOCABULARY advertising, business

**a** Complete the sentences with a word from the list.

advertisement  advertising campaign
be sued  brand  claim  consumer
misleading  publicity  slogan

1 There are lots of websites where you can put an ___advertisement___ if you want to sell your car.
2 As a _____, I want to have as much information about the food I buy as possible.
3 I always buy the same _____ of toothpaste because it's the one I'm used to.
4 They've used young adults in their new _____ because it's aimed specifically at people in their early 20s.
5 It's _____ to suggest that this product is healthier than any others of its kind – it isn't.
6 Their company _____ only has three words: *Just do it.*
7 There has been a lot of _____ about the company owner's recent donation to charity.
8 A company can _____ if it doesn't fulfil the promises it makes about its products.
9 A representative denied the _____ that the company was in financial difficulties.

**b** Read the definitions and complete the missing letters in the word.

1 the main office of a company
  h _e_ _a_ d  o _f_ _f_ _i_ _c_ e
2 a group of shops / stores or hotels owned by the same company
  ch __ __ n
3 stop trading or doing business
  cl __ __ __ __  d __ w __
4 an office or a shop / store belonging to a large company or organization
  br __ n __ __
5 a difficult time for the economy of a country
  a r __ c __ __ __ i __ __
6 a period of sudden economic growth
  a b __ o __
7 a product that is not successful
  a fl __ __
8 fall; become lower or less
  d __ o __
9 make goods in large quantities, using machinery
  m __ n __ __ __ __ t __ __ __
10 combine to form a single thing
  m __ __ g __

**c** Complete the text with the correct form of the verbs and verb phrases in the list.

become the market leader  expand  export  grow
import  launch a new product  market  produce
set up a new business  take over

A friend of mine, Anne, was lucky enough to inherit a farm when she left university, so she decided to ¹ _set up a new business_: an organic food company. The company ² _____ its products under the name Bioplus, and among other things, it ³ _____ muesli. Anne ⁴ _____ nuts and dried fruit from South America and mixes these with cereal from crops on the farm to make the muesli. Her muesli sells well nationally, and recently she ⁵ _____ into new markets abroad. Today, she also ⁶ _____ to northern European countries, like Norway and Sweden.

The company is ⁷ _____ rapidly, and Anne is always looking for new employees. Right now, she's preparing to ⁸ _____: a cereal bar the company has been testing. Anne is very realistic, as she knows she will never ⁹ _____ in the field. However, neither does she want one of the big cereal giants, like Kelloggs or Nestlé, to ¹⁰ _____ her small family company.

**d** Complete the sentences with the correct form of *make* or *do*.

1 A company always _does_ extensive market research before it launches a new product.
2 If a company _____ a loss, the staff often face job cuts.
3 Many countries started _____ business with China when the trade sanctions were lifted.
4 The managing director _____ the decision to close the factory yesterday.
5 The factory is going to _____ 30 people redundant after Christmas.
6 My company _____ really badly last year; if the situation doesn't improve, it may close.
7 Management and unions have _____ a deal that should prevent a strike.
8 If we _____ a profit again next year, the manager may think of opening another office.
9 There's no need to thank me. I'm only _____ my job.
10 She doesn't _____ much money from acting, so she's also got a part-time job as a waitress.

Go online for more practice

**e** Match 1–8 to responses a–h.

1 Where have you been? __c__
2 Shall we start the meeting? ____
3 I'm going out with my boss for a drink tonight. ____
4 Let's go to that lovely old café on the corner. ____
5 Shall we finish now? ____
6 Who are you messaging? ____
7 Your boss is heading in this direction. ____
8 Why do you need to talk to your ex? ____

a Yes, let's get down to business.
b I'm afraid it's gone out of business.
c ~~Mind your own business!~~
d Are you sure you want to mix business with pleasure?
e OK, but first, is there any other business?
f I'm sorry, but it's none of your business.
g Because we have some unfinished business.
h Yes, and it looks as if she means business.

**f** Answer the questions about yourself and your home.

1 How far from your home is the nearest branch of your bank?

_____

2 Name a chain that you can find in your nearest shopping centre.

_____

3 Which products are manufactured in your country?

_____

4 Which companies from your country are market leaders?

_____

5 Which products does your country export and where to?

_____

6 Which industries are growing in your country?

_____

7 Which products does your country import and where from?

_____

8 Would you like to set up your own company? Why / Why not?

_____

**3 PRONUNCIATION** changing stress on nouns and verbs

**a** Underline the stressed syllable in the highlighted words.

1 China exports more goods than any other country.
2 They transport most of their products by lorry.
3 There's been a huge increase in petrol prices recently.
4 The price of wheat has decreased by 5%.
5 Scientists are making progress in finding a cure for AIDS.
6 The visa permits you to stay for three months.
7 Brazil produces about a third of the world's coffee.
8 We do not give refunds without a valid receipt.
9 The government is hoping to reduce foreign imports.
10 Vinyl records are becoming popular again.

**b** 🔊 9.1 Listen and check. Then listen again and repeat the sentences.

🔄 **Go online** for more practice

A city is a large community where
people are lonely together.
*Herbert Prochnow, US banking executive*

| **G** uncountable and plural nouns | **V** word building: prefixes and suffixes | **P** word stress with prefixes and suffixes |
|---|---|---|

## 1 GRAMMAR uncountable and plural nouns

**a** Circle the correct answers. Tick (✓) if both answers are possible.

1 Can I have *a piece of bread / some bread*, please? ✓
2 My grandmother suffers from *bad health / a bad health*.
3 I've bought *a new piece of furniture / some new furniture* for my living room.
4 Did we bring *a pair of scissors / a scissors*? I want to cut my nails.
5 I'm looking for *a cheap accommodation / some cheap accommodation*.
6 Jackie is upset because she's had *a bad news / some bad news*.
7 Be careful with that vase – it's made of *glass / a glass*.
8 My girlfriend gave me *a pair of pyjamas / some pyjamas* for my birthday.
9 The teacher gave the boy extra marks for *a good behaviour / good behaviour*.
10 Can you lend me *a paper / some paper*? I've left my notebook at home.

**b** Complete the sentences with *is* or *are*.

1 My clothes *are* really wet. I got caught in a thunderstorm.
2 Police _____ investigating the murder of an elderly woman in her home.
3 The hotel staff _____ always really polite and helpful.
4 The new research into sleep patterns _____ fascinating.
5 The outskirts of the town _____ quite run down and a bit depressing.
6 The good news _____ that we're getting married in the spring!
7 The flight crew on this plane _____ very young.
8 Politics _____ really fascinating – particularly for politicians!
9 Do you think my belongings _____ safe in the hotel room?
10 The traffic _____ terrible in the rush hour in the city centre.

**c** Complete the sentences with information that is true for you.

1 The scenery in this area _____
_____
_____.

2 The traffic in my area _____
_____
_____.

3 My clothes _____
_____
_____.

4 The furniture in my home _____
_____
_____.

5 The news today _____
_____
_____.

6 Politics in my country _____
_____
_____.

7 The weather today _____
_____
_____.

8 My family _____
_____
_____.

## 2 VOCABULARY word building: prefixes and suffixes

**a** Complete the sentences with a prefix from the list.

anti   auto   bi   mega   mis   mono
multi   over   post   ~~sub~~   under

1 Some of the residents of megacities live in _sub_____standard housing of very poor quality.

2 There was a food shortage in many countries during the _____-war period between 1946 and 1960.

3 Hundreds of fans were waiting for the singer, hoping to get an _____graph.

4 My English teacher recommends us to use a _____lingual dictionary – one that is only in English.

5 My colleagues are always complaining that they are _____worked and _____paid. They say they work long hours and are badly paid.

6 The leader of the protest used a _____phone to make himself heard.

7 You couldn't miss Sandra – she was the one in the _____coloured coat. It was green, purple, yellow, and orange, I think.

8 The town has just celebrated its _____centenary – it was founded 200 years ago.

9 The doctor prescribed _____biotics for my brother's chest infection.

10 It's a popular _____conception that cold weather can give you a cold. This is simply not true.

**b** Complete the sentences. Add -able, -ful, -less, or -proof to a word from the list.

~~break~~   bullet   care   drink   home   hope   use   water

1 Is there anything _breakable____ in this box?

2 Be _____ crossing that road – there's always a lot of traffic.

3 Don't forget to take a _____ jacket with you when you go walking in Scotland.

4 This _____ gadget opens jars for people who have no strength in their hands.

5 Harry became _____ when he was made redundant and could no longer pay his rent.

6 The police officer wasn't injured because he was wearing a _____ vest.

7 Is the tap water _____ in this area?

8 It's _____ asking the boss for a pay rise – the company is losing money.

**c** Complete the sentences with the noun form of the word in brackets.

1 I borrowed the money with the _intention____ of giving it back to you. (intend)

2 His greatest _____ is his inability to express his feelings. (weak)

3 I was away for six months, and there were many changes in my _____. (absent)

4 If you witness an act of _____, you are advised to call the police. (vandal)

5 _____ is one of the greatest problems the elderly have to face. (lonely)

6 Teachers are trying to fight _____ in schools throughout the country. (race)

7 Most of her problems are the result of a very unhappy _____. (child)

8 The best thing about our hotel was that it provided _____ in the evenings. (entertain)

9 There's been a great _____ in public transport recently. (improve)

10 There's a shortage of rented _____ where I live. (accommodate)

11 What's the _____ between Rome and Venice? (distant)

12 Gandhi was a humanist who believed in the _____ of man. (brother)

Go online for more practice

**d** Complete the second sentence with the noun form of the **bold** word in the first sentence.

1 I **believe** that house prices are going to rise.
   It's my *belief* that house prices are going to rise.

2 The staff were shocked when their boss **died**.
   The staff were shocked at the _____ of their boss.

3 You shouldn't go out when it's **hot** in the day.
   You shouldn't go out during the _____ of the day.

4 You need to measure how **wide** the windows are.
   You need to measure the _____ of your windows.

5 I can't believe you're still **hungry** after that huge meal.
   I can't believe that huge meal didn't satisfy your _____.

6 The company may **lose** financially on this deal.
   The company might make a financial _____ on this deal.

7 Do you know how **high** Mount Everest is?
   Do you know the _____ of Mount Everest?

8 I don't like to **think** of you walking home alone.
   I don't like the _____ of you walking home alone.

9 After his illness, they gave him soup to make him **strong** again.
   After his illness, they gave him soup to build up his _____ again.

10 The dinner party was very **successful**.
   The dinner party was a great _____.

## 3 VOCABULARY FROM READING

Complete the sentences with a word or phrase from the list.

a lack of   delivers   echoes   head home   perks
~~sparsely populated~~   sprawling   state-of-the-art

1 Mongolia is one of the most *sparsely populated* countries in the world - there are only one or two people per square kilometre.

2 I have a long commute, so I always _____ straight after work.

3 One of the _____ of city life is the numerous entertainment options.

4 In many big cities there's _____ green spaces to walk or just sit and relax.

5 The design of the town hall _____ that of a palace.

6 Our new home _____ on comfort but looks out on an industrial estate.

7 Los Angeles is recognized as the most _____ city in the US because it covers such a large area of land.

8 The company has just launched a new line of _____ computers.

## 4 PRONUNCIATION word stress with prefixes and suffixes

**a** Underline the main stressed syllable in the words in the list. Then put them in the correct column.

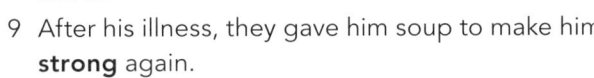

~~an|ti|so|cial~~   bi|lin|gual   con|ve|ni|ence   en|ter|tain|ment
ex|cite|ment   friend|li|ness   go|vern|ment   ig|no|rance
o|ver|crow|ded   po|ver|ty   re|duc|tion   un|em|ploy|ment

| Stress on first syllable | Stress on second syllable | Stress on third syllable |
|---|---|---|
| | | *antisocial* |
| | | |
| | | |

**b**  9.2 Listen and check. Then listen and repeat the words.

Go online for more practice   Go online to check your progress

## 1   LOOKING AT LANGUAGE

Complete the sentences with a phrase from the list.

---
~~an ear worm~~    a captive audience    get into your head
had their day    hit a false note    their ears perk up
word for word

---

1 The best way to get rid of _an ear worm_ is to replace it with another tune.
2 Some people say that libraries have _____ and they will soon disappear.
3 The song has a catchy chorus which can easily _____ and you find yourself singing it all day.
4 I repeated her instructions _____ to avoid any confusion.
5 My dogs love biscuits – _____ as soon as they hear me open the packet.
6 Musicians often play on trains and ask for money because they know they have _____.
7 The mayor _____ with her speech and caused a lot of controversy.

## 2   VOCABULARY FROM THE INTERVIEW

Complete the sentences from the interview with a word from the list.

---
~~baton~~    bet    fan    gold    short    tapped

---

1 I took the _baton_ from him.
2 I _____ you most people would remember these commercials.
3 Using a celebrity is a _____ cut.
4 I'm not a big _____ of it.
5 They _____ into a mind-set.
6 They became the _____ standard.

## 3   THE CONVERSATION

Match beginnings 1–6 to endings a–f.

1 Just by going outside you're seeing these advertisements and you're being influenced, so, for example we, _d_
2 You know, we barely, ____
3 So, there's definitely, ____
4 They see pictures in magazines and they're starting to be, ____
5 Yeah, especially for children, I mean I, I have, ____
6 So, I think, um, I think, ____

a we don't really watch TV and we have a TV, we just don't watch very much.
b definitely I think that the answer to the question is yes, we are all influenced in different ways by advertising, I suppose.
c I have younger siblings and it's kind of like 'Ooh, all of my friends have this toy, I must have it as well'…
d ~~we all know certain brands just because they're everywhere around us.~~
e you're definitely being influenced.
f my 11-year-old is starting to be a little bit more cynical about what he sees.

## 4   VOCABULARY FROM THE CONVERSATION

---
~~blatant~~    point    subtle    rush    subliminally

---

1 So that sort of advertising is _blatant_.
2 And that's super-_____ advertising.
3 You might buy this if you're in a _____.
4 _____, I think, if we recognize something.
5 The _____ of advertisements is that you recognize the products.

# Can you remember...? 1–9

## GRAMMAR & VOCABULARY

**a** Complete the second sentence so that it means the same as the first sentence. Write 2–5 words. Use the word in brackets.

1 Owen started studying at 9.00 a.m. and he's still studying now, at 6.00 p.m. (has)
Owen _____ all day.

2 We aren't very keen on climbing, so we didn't go to the mountains. (much)
We didn't go to the mountains because we don't like _____.

3 I don't have Harry's number, so I can't call him. (his)
I'd call Harry if I _____.

4 Freya still finds it strange to live on her own. She really doesn't like it. (get)
Freya can't _____ on her own. She really doesn't like it.

5 I can't wait to see you next week. (looking)
I'm _____ next week.

6 I'll always remember the first time I visited Florence. I fell in love with the city. (forget)
I'll _____ for the first time. I fell in love with the city.

7 I'm sure you left your jacket in the car. You weren't wearing it when you came in. (have)
You _____ in the car. You weren't wearing it when you came in.

8 I get the impression that Emily has been crying. (as)
It _____ has been crying.

9 We asked a local plumber to fit our shower. (had)
We _____ by a local plumber.

10 His teacher said he should enter the writing competition. (encouraged)
His teacher _____ the writing competition.

11 I arrived on time, although I had left home late. (despite)
_____, I arrived on time

12 Laura bought some new shorts in the sale. (a)
Laura bought _____ in the sale.

**b** Complete the text. Write one word in each gap.

## WORLD NEWS

Home | News | Sport | Weather

### India set to break world records

It would seem that Tokyo is about to lose its position [1]_____ the largest city in the world. According to the UN, Delhi, the capital of India, is set to take the top spot in 2028. The organization predicts that Delhi's population will [2]_____ grown from 29 million to 39 million [3]_____ 2030. Meanwhile, it [4]_____ thought that Tokyo's population will remain at its current level of 37 million.

In [5]_____, it is not only India's capital city that is likely to break records soon, but the country itself. The population of India is expected [6]_____ reach 1.438 billion in 2024, exceeding China's 1.436 billion. This increase would make India the most populous country in the world.

Delhi is not the only city in India where significant population growth is predicted to [7]_____ place. The population of Mumbai is set to rise from 19 million to 25 million. In [8]_____ of this growth, the city will maintain its position as the world's sixth-largest city. [9]_____ though the population of Kolkata will increase from 14 million to 18 million, the city will move down the list, from 13th to 16th position. Bengaluru, which is ranked 29th [10]_____ the moment, will move up to the 21st spot as its population grows from 10 million to 16 million.

Go online to check your progress

In science the credit goes to the man who convinces the world, not to the man to whom the idea first occurs.
*Francis Darwin, botanist and son of Charles Darwin*

**G** quantifiers: *all, every, both, etc.* **V** science **P** stress in word families

## 1 VOCABULARY & PRONUNCIATION
science; stress in word families

**a** Circle a, b, or c.

1 He's working as a biology teacher although he's a qualified ____ .
   a zoology   b (zoologist)   c zoological

2 There are thousands of human ____ diseases.
   a genetics   b geneticist   c genetic

3 My partner has a degree in ____ .
   a physics   b physicist   c physical

4 The results of ____ research have increased the range of medicines available to treat many illnesses.
   a botany   b botanist   c botanical

5 I'm the only ____ in my family.
   a science   b scientist   c scientific

6 I wasn't very good at ____ when I was at school.
   a chemistry   b chemist   c chemical

7 It is thought that there is a ____ reason for his aggressive behaviour.
   a biology   b biologist   c biological

8 My sister is fascinated by space; she's hoping to become an ____ .
   a astronomy   b astronomer   c astronomical

**b** Underline the stressed syllable in the words. Is the stress on the same syllable? Tick (✓) the correct column.

|   | same syllable | different syllable |
|---|---|---|
| 1 a\|stro\|no\|my / a\|stro\|no\|mer | ✓ | |
| 2 bi\|o\|lo\|gy / bi\|o\|lo\|gi\|cal | | |
| 3 bo\|ta\|ny / bo\|ta\|ni\|cal | | |
| 4 che\|mist / che\|mi\|stry | | |
| 5 ge\|ne\|tic / ge\|ne\|ti\|cist | | |
| 6 phy\|sics / phy\|si\|cist | | |
| 7 sci\|en\|tist / sci\|en\|ti\|fic | | |
| 8 zo\|o\|lo\|gist / zo\|o\|lo\|gic\|al | | |

**c** 🔊 **10.1 Listen and check. Then listen again and repeat the words.**

**d** Complete the text with the nouns and verbs in the lists.

**Verbs**

carry out   clone   ~~do~~   prove   volunteer

**Nouns**

clinical trials   discovery   drugs   guinea pigs   ~~pharmaceutical companies~~

Thousands of scientists are employed in [1] *pharmaceutical companies* to [2] *do* research into new [3] _____ .
These people hope to make an important [4] _____ which will help treat or cure an illness or disease. When a team believes they have developed a new drug, they have to [5] _____ experiments to [6] _____ their theory and make sure the drug is effective. The final stage of this process is to organize [7] _____ so that the drug can be tested on humans. People who [8] _____ to take part in these tests are known as [9] _____ , after the animals that were used in 19th-century medical research. If the tests are successful, the drug is launched onto the market.

One branch of science that is becoming increasingly important in these companies is genetics. Genetic engineers have already managed to [10] _____ a number of different animals, including sheep, rabbits, and monkeys.

## 2 VOCABULARY FROM LISTENING

Match the words in the list to the definitions.

dissolve  gas  gravity  moist  particle
reflect  rotate  scatter  water vapour

1  any substance like air that is neither a solid nor a liquid
   _gas_

2  mix with a liquid and become part of it  _____

3  a very small piece of something  _____

4  make things move very quickly in different directions
   _____

5  water in the form of a gas resulting from heating water
   or ice  _____

6  show the image of somebody / something on the
   surface of, e.g., a mirror  _____

7  slightly wet  _____

8  move or turn around a central fixed point  _____

9  the force that causes objects to fall to the ground when
   they are dropped  _____

## 3 VOCABULARY FROM READING

Complete the highlighted words and phrases that
express degrees of likelihood.

1  The new measures could, in th _e_ _o_ r _y_, reduce
   pollution in the city centre dramatically.

2  It seems pl __ __ s __ b __ __ __ that sea levels may rise
   dramatically in the near future.

3  The idea that we'll ever colonize space seems rather
   f __ __ __ -f __ tch __ __ __ to me.

4  We're still a l __ __ __ g way from finding a source of
   energy to replace fossil fuels completely.

5  Slowing global warming might be ach __ __ v __ b __ __ __
   if every country cooperates.

6  The time when I will be able to afford to stop working is
   quite a w __ __ __ off.

7  The poorest countries still face extreme
   obst __ c __ __ __ s to development; for example,
   corruption.

8  The idea that one day cars will fly is
   not totally impl __ __ __ s __ b __ __ __.

9  It might be p __ ss __ b __ __ __ to see Mars in the sky
   tonight, if conditions are right.

10  There is a r __ __ __ l possibility that it might snow
   tomorrow.

11  The theory is only sp __ c __ l __ t __ v __ at the
   moment. Much more evidence is needed before it
   can be proved for certain.

## 4 GRAMMAR quantifiers: *all, every, both*, etc.

a  Right (✓) or wrong (✗)? Correct the mistakes in
   the highlighted phrases.

1  I've taken all luggage up to our room, OK?
   ✗ _all the luggage_

2  Everybody were bad-tempered because it was
   getting late and they were hungry.
   _____

3  All went wrong at my last job interview.
   _____

4  I have a lot of cousins, but most of them live
   abroad. _____

5  Every classroom in that school has an interactive
   whiteboard. _____

6  My mum works as a volunteer at the hospital
   every morning. _____

7  The most people are against eating genetically
   modified food. _____

8  All the men seem to love buying new electronic
   gadgets. _____

Go online for more practice

**b** Complete the conversations with *no*, *any*, or *none*.

1 **A** Can I have a biscuit?
  **B** Sorry, we don't have *any*_____.

2 **A** How much homework have you done?
  **B** _____. I don't feel like doing it right now.

3 **A** How are we going to get home?
  **B** By taxi. There aren't _____ buses at this time of night.

4 **A** Did any of your friends pass the exam?
  **B** No, _____ of them. It was too difficult.

5 **A** Shall we have dinner in our hotel room?
  **B** We can't. There's _____ room service after 9 p.m.

6 **A** When can you come?
  **B** _____ day you like. I'm free all week.

**c** Complete the sentences with a word from the list. Use each word twice.

| both   either   neither   nor |
| --- |

1 *Both*_____ my brother and my sister have children.
2 Dave has two sons, but _____ of them looks like him.
3 We'd like to go to _____ Greece or Portugal for our holiday this year.
4 Neither my boyfriend _____ I eat meat.
5 I can't decide between these two shirts. I like _____ of them.
6 _____ of my parents have ever been to South America.
7 My niece is studying _____ chemistry or biology at university – I can't remember which.
8 Her husband neither calls _____ messages me when he's away.

**d** Complete the text. Write one word in each gap.

# Irène and Ève Curie:
## the scientist and the journalist

Nearly [1] *everyone*_____ knows the names of scientists Marie and Pierre Curie because of the Nobel Prizes they won. However, [2] _____ people are unaware that the couple also had two talented daughters, Irène and Ève. [3] _____ sisters received the same education, but they each pursued a completely different career.

Irène followed in the footsteps of her parents. She began assisting her mother during the First World War, when she was only 18. The two women used some of the first X-ray machines to help doctors locate the exact position of soldiers' injuries. At the time, people had [4] _____ idea of the dangers posed by the machines, and nurses who used them didn't wear [5] _____ protection. As a result, Irène and her mother were exposed to large doses of radiation and [6] _____ of them lived to a very old age.

In 1924, Irène was asked to share her research techniques with a chemical engineer named Frédéric Joliot. They started going out together, but Marie was afraid that Joliot was only interested in becoming associated with the Curie name. She used [7] _____ her influence to try to end the relationship, but Irène took [8] _____ of her advice, and the couple later married. Irène and her husband continued working together, and in 1935 they too were awarded a Nobel Prize.

Ève Curie, on the other hand, preferred the arts and spent most of her time [9] _____ writing or playing the piano. She worked as a journalist and wrote her mother's biography *Madame Curie*, which was published in 1937. Her husband, Henry Richardson Labouisse, was Executive Director of UNICEF, and when the organization was awarded the Nobel Peace Prize in 1965, he collected the award. Ève used to joke that [10] _____ member of her family had received a Nobel Prize except for her.

Irène Joliot-Curie died in Paris in 1956 at the age of 58. Ève Curie was 102 when she passed away in New York in 2007.

**Go online** for more practice

There are always three speeches for every one you actually gave: the one you practised, the one you gave, and the one you wish you had given.
*Dale Carnegie, American lecturer*

**G** articles   **V** collocation: word pairs   **P** pausing and sentence stress

## 1 GRAMMAR articles

**a** Complete the sayings with *a*, *an*, *the*, or no article (–).

1 All you need is ___–___ love.
2 He's _____ man of his word.
3 _____ women are from Venus; _____ men are from Mars.
4 _____ time waits for no man.
5 Don't worry! It isn't _____ end of _____ world!
6 That's _____ life!
7 It's _____ small world!
8 _____ actions speak louder than _____ words.

**b** Complete the sentences with *the* where necessary.

1 ___–___ Mount Aconcagua is in *the* ___ Andes in Argentina.
2 There are 50 states in _____ USA.
3 _____ M1 motorway was closed yesterday because of floods.
4 _____ Royal Lancaster Hotel is near _____ Hyde Park in London.
5 _____ Dodecanese are a group of islands situated in _____ Aegean Sea.
6 _____ Lake Victoria is the largest lake in _____ Africa.
7 _____ Panama Canal connects the Atlantic Ocean to _____ Pacific Ocean.
8 The toy industry in _____ China is the biggest in the world.

**c** Right (✓) or wrong (✗)? Correct the mistakes in the highlighted phrases.

1 The church in my village dates back to the 15th century. ✓ _____
2 My grandfather is in the hospital having an operation. ✗ *in hospital* _____
3 The university in my town has a very good reputation. _____
4 Daisy is taking advantage of the time her children are at the school to do an online course. _____
5 The prison is on the outskirts of the city. _____
6 Somebody broke into my parents' house while they were at the church. _____
7 We caught the bus from the stop near the hospital. _____
8 My boyfriend is at the university. He's studying architecture. _____
9 The man has gone to the prison for the crimes he committed when he was younger. _____
10 My brother teaches at the school he went to when he was a child. _____

**d** Read the text. Circle a, b, or c.

# Five words
## that made history

**At the 2018 Golden Globe Awards, actress and TV presenter Oprah Winfrey was awarded the Cecil B. DeMille Award for lifetime achievement. Here is an extract from the memorable speech she made during the award ceremony.**

In 1964, I was ¹_____ little girl sitting on the linoleum floor of my mother's house in ²_____ Milwaukee, watching Anne Bancroft present the Oscar for Best Actor at ³_____ 36th Academy Awards. She opened the envelope and said five words that literally made ⁴_____ history: '⁵_____ winner is Sidney Poitier.' Up to the stage came ⁶_____ most elegant man I had ever seen. I remember his tie was white and, of course, his skin was black. And I'd never seen ⁷_____ black man being celebrated like that. And I have tried many, many, many times to explain what ⁸_____ moment like that means to a little girl, a kid watching from the cheap seats as my mom came through the door, bone tired from cleaning ⁹_____ other people's houses. But all I can do is quote and say that ¹⁰_____ explanation's in Sidney's performance in *Lilies of the Field*, 'Amen, amen. Amen, amen.'

|   |       |       |       |
|---|-------|-------|-------|
| 1 | **a** (a) | **b** the | **c** – |
| 2 | **a** a | **b** the | **c** – |
| 3 | **a** a | **b** the | **c** – |
| 4 | **a** a | **b** the | **c** – |
| 5 | **a** A | **b** The | **c** – |
| 6 | **a** a | **b** the | **c** – |
| 7 | **a** a | **b** the | **c** – |
| 8 | **a** a | **b** the | **c** – |
| 9 | **a** a | **b** the | **c** – |
| 10 | **a** a | **b** the | **c** – |

🔍 **Go online** for more practice

## 2 VOCABULARY collocation: word pairs

**a** Match questions 1–10 to responses a–j.

1  Did you hear the storm last night? _h_
2  Do you think I should accept the job? _____
3  Why are you moving to the country? _____
4  Why has the shop sold out of bread? _____
5  How was your meeting? _____
6  What did you do while you were waiting at the hospital? _____
7  Why does water boil when you heat it? _____
8  What should I do about the argument I had with my sister? _____
9  Why is the playground closed? _____
10  My bike was stolen because I forgot to lock it up. _____

a  I'd forgive and forget if I were you.
b  Oh well, you live and learn, I suppose.
c  I paced backwards and forwards in the corridor.
d  You need to weigh up the pros and cons to help you make a decision.
e  It's the law of cause and effect.
f  I guess it's a question of supply and demand.
g  Short and sweet – it only lasted ten minutes.
h  ~~Yes, the thunder and lightning woke me up.~~
i  We're looking for some peace and quiet.
j  For health and safety reasons.

**b** Find the word pairs in the list and link them with *or*. Then complete the sentences.

~~alive~~   all   ~~dead~~   later   less   more   never
nothing   now   once   rain   right   shine
sooner   twice   wrong

1 The criminal was wanted *dead or alive* and there was a $500 reward for his capture.
2 She goes jogging every morning, _____.
3 I'm not sure if this answer in my maths homework is _____.
4 Patricia is about to leave, so it's _____ – I may not get another chance to ask her out.
5 It's _____ with Sue; either she calls every day or you don't hear from her for weeks.
6 I've been skiing _____, but I'm not very good at it.
7 Nathan has _____ finished his homework – all he has to do now is to print it out.
8 There's no point waiting – I'll have to tell John the truth _____.

**c** Complete the word-pair idioms.

1 We only take a few b*its* and p*ieces* with us when we go on holiday.
2 I'm s_____ and t_____ of having to tidy up after my children.
3 B_____ and l_____, I'd say I had a happy childhood.
4 She's fine now, but it was t_____ and g_____ whether she would survive the operation.
5 The streets were very dangerous because of the lack of l_____ and o_____ in the city.
6 We arrived s_____ and s_____ after a difficult three-day journey through the mountains.
7 I've no idea what we're having for my birthday lunch because my wife told me to w_____ and s_____.
8 We go to the cinema n_____ and a_____, but more often than not, we just watch a film on TV.

## 3 VOCABULARY FROM READING

Complete the missing vowels in the words and phrases.

1 A speaker doesn't have to be a comedian to include a little w*i*t in his or her speech.
2 Salespeople need to have the g __ ft of the g __ b to sell as many products as possible.
3 That politician is very good at making memorable s __ __ ndb __ t __ s when he talks to journalists.
4 Winston Churchill was famous for being a great __ r __ t __ r who made powerful speeches.

## 4 PRONUNCIATION  pausing and sentence stress

**a** ◉10.2 Listen to a talk about an interesting place to visit. Mark the pauses.

Good morning, and thank you for coming. I'm here to talk about an interesting place to visit in my country. I'm going to tell you about the city of Bath in the south-west of England. Bath is on the River Avon, and it has one of the only bridges in the world with shops on either side. The city is famous for its ancient Roman Baths, which can still be visited today. It has many beautiful streets, such as the Royal Crescent and the Circus. Bath is full of museums, independent shops, and wonderful places to eat and drink. The city is easily accessible from London by train, and it is perfect for a day trip or a weekend break.

**b** Practise giving the talk, pausing and trying to get the right rhythm.

**c** Now write your own talk about an interesting place to visit in your country. Mark the pauses.

**d** Read your speech. If you can, record it on your phone and send it to your teacher.

◉ Go online for more practice    ✓ Go online to check your progress

## 6A

### 1 GRAMMAR

**a** 2 driving, 3 living, 4 used to, 5 used to, 6 being, 7 working, 8 play, 9 used to, 10 would

**b** 2 cooking, 3 living, 4 have, 5 being, 6 go, 7 looking after, 8 study, 9 using, 10 talk

**c** 2 got used to working
3 isn't used to sleeping
4 used to wear
5 got used to living
6 used to be
7 got used to using
8 not used to having

**d** Student's own answers

### 2 PRONUNCIATION

**a** 2 used to living
3 used to treat
4 used to have
5 used to share
6 used to carry

**b** /juːzd/: Sentences 3, 6
/juːst/: Sentences 1, 2, 4, 5

**e** /s/: course, ice, loose, peace, place, price, race
/z/: cause, eyes, lose, peas, plays, prize, raise

### 3 VOCABULARY

**a** 2 blanket, 3 snores, 4 sleepy, 5 sleeping pills, 6 nap, 7 duvet, 8 pillow, 9 insomnia, 10 sheet

**b** 2 e, 3 h, 4 a, 5 d, 6 b, 7 i, 8 g, 9 c

**c** 2 have, 3 set, 4 overslept, 5 fall, 6 sleepwalks, 7 keeps, 8 were

**d** Student's own answers

## 6B

### 1 GRAMMAR

**a** 2 c, 3 a, 4 a, 5 c, 6 b, 7 a, 8 c, 9 b, 10 c, 11 c, 12 b

**b** 2 reading, 3 to find, 4 to call, 5 ironing, 6 to send, 7 meeting, 8 climbing

**c** 2 want, 3 to see, 4 to learn, 5 adding, 6 listening to, 7 to take, 8 go

**d** Student's own answers

### 2 VOCABULARY & PRONUNCIATION

**a** **Down:** 3 cello, 5 bass guitar, 6 choir, 9 flute
**Across:** 2 violin, 4 keyboard, 7 saxophone, 8 drums, 10 conductor, 11 orchestra

**b** 2 symphony , 3 encore, 4 mezzo-soprano, 5 chorus, 6 rhythm, 7 concerto, 8 genre

**c** **Stress on first syllable:** cello, chorus, encore, genre, keyboard, orchestra, rhythm, saxophone, symphony
**Stress on second syllable:** concerto, conductor, guitar, soprano
**Stress on third syllable:** violin

**e** 2 macchiato, 3 chorus, 4 fiancé

**g** 1 croissant
2 architecture, graffiti
3 paparazzi, photographs
4 soprano, microphone
5 ballet, rhythm

## 7A

### 1 GRAMMAR

**a** 2 b, 3 f, 4 h, 5 d, 6 a, 7 e, 8 g

**b** 2 might have gone
3 can't have seen
4 might not have heard
5 can't have moved
6 might have fallen
7 must have done
8 might not have read

**c** 2 We should have filled up at the last garage.
3 He oughtn't have left it on his desk.
4 You shouldn't have bought such high heels.
5 I oughtn't have stayed up to watch that horror film.
6 They ought to have dressed up for the wedding.
7 It should have gone off at 7.30.
8 She should have taken a taxi to the station.

**d** Student's own answers

### 2 PRONUNCIATION

**a** 2 He can't have got my message.
3 What do you think of my new flat?
4 The supermarket will have closed by now.
5 How long have you been waiting?
6 We went to see some friends of ours.

**c** 2 got, message
3 got, angry
4 booked, table
5 been, asleep
6 forgotten

### 3 GRAMMAR IN CONTEXT

2 would / 'd rather not cook tonight, if you don't mind
3 would you rather do: stay in or go out
4 would / 'd rather we got a taxi home, if that's OK with you
5 would / 'd rather see that film at the cinema than on TV
6 would / 'd rather sit next to the window than by the aisle

### 4 VOCABULARY

**a** 2 mind, 3 avoid, 4 Remind, 5 argue, 6 borrow, 7 notice, 8 win, 9 wait, 10 raise, 11 advise, 12 refuse, 13 lie, 14 steal

**b** 2 lent, 3 beat, 4 robbed, 5 denied, 6 lay, 7 rose, 8 discussed, 9 prevented, 10 expected, 11 mattered, 12 realized, 13 warned, 14 hoped

## 7B

### 1 GRAMMAR

**a** 2 looks as if
3 smells
4 tastes like
5 sounds as though
6 feel like
7 tastes as if
8 seem
9 going out
10 sound like

**b** 2 sounds like, 3 looks like, 4 smells as if, 5 tastes, 6 feels as if, 7 sounds, 8 seem, 9 smells like, 10 looks as if

**c** 1 feels, smells, tastes

### 2 VOCABULARY

**a** **Down:** 3 knee, 4 calf, 6 nails, 9 elbow, 10 wrist, 11 thigh, 12 brain, 13 hip
**Across:** 2 kidneys, 4 chest, 5 heel, 7 palm, 8 liver, 10 waist, 12 bottom, 14 fist, 15 heart, 16 lungs

**b** 2 c, 3 m, 4 i, 5 a, 6 e, 7 g, 8 k, 9 j, 10 l, 11 f, 12 d, 13 b

**c** 2 hugged, 3 frowned, 4 chewed, 5 stretched, 6 knelt, 7 pointed, 8 waved, 9 winked, 10 yawned, 11 scratched

### 3 VOCABULARY FROM READING

2 lie, 3 detect, 4 liar, 5 gave, away, 6 deception

### 4 PRONUNCIATION

**a** 2 b, 3 k, 4 l, 5 c, 6 h and t, 7 h, 8 t, 9 s, 10 g, 11 w

**d** 2 whose, 3 cupboard, 4 foreign, 5 wrong, 6 calm, 7 knife, 8 scissors, 9 autumn, 10 island, 11 what, 12 plumber

**e** 2 honest, 3 design, 4 autumn, 5 whose, 6 calm

## Colloquial English 6 & 7

### 1 LOOKING AT LANGUAGE

2 completely, 3 tremendously, 4 overwhelmingly, 5 extraordinarily, 6 absolutely, 7 fantastically

### 2 VOCABULARY FROM THE INTERVIEW

2 b, 3 d, 4 e, 5 a

### 3 THE CONVERSATION

2 e, 3 b, 4 a, 5 f, 6 c

### 4 VOCABULARY FROM THE CONVERSATION

2 soft, 3 certain, 4 bouncing, 5 factors

## Can you remember…? 1–7

### GRAMMAR & VOCABULARY

a 1 big-headed, 2 hooded, 3 Basically, 4 changeable, 5 stressful, 6 impressive, 7 overslept, 8 awake, 9 lay, 10 conductor

b 1 a, 2 b, 3 b, 4 a, 5 c, 6 c, 7 c, 8 a, 9 a, 10 c

## 8A

### 1 VOCABULARY

a 2 burglary, 3 burglar, 4 break into, 5 steal

b 2 murder, 3 bribery, 4 stalking, 5 vandalism, 6 blackmail, 7 hijacking, 8 drug dealing, 9 terrorism, 10 hacking, 11 rape, 12 theft, 13 fraud, 14 robbery, 15 mugging, 16 smuggling, 17 kidnapping

c 2 murderer, 3 stalker, 4 vandal, 5 blackmailer, 6 hijacker, 7 drug dealer, 8 terrorist, 9 hacker, 10 rapist, 11 thief, 12 fraudster, 13 robber, 14 mugger, 15 smuggler, 16 kidnapper

d 2 robbed, 3 stalked, 4 smuggled, 5 bribed, 6 mugged, 7 committed, 8 burgled, 9 murdered, 10 stole, 11 blackmailed, 12 hijacked, 13 sold, 14 set off, 15 kidnapped, 16 vandalized, 17 hacked

e 2 catch, 3 committed, 4 arrest, 5 question, 6 charged, 7 judge, 8 jury, 9 court, 10 accused, 11 witnesses, 12 evidence, 13 proof, 14 acquitted, 15 verdict, 16 punishment, 17 sentenced

### 2 VOCABULARY FROM READING

2 prey, 3 impression, 4 hand over, 5 claim, 6 wary, 7 scam, 8 target

### 3 PRONUNCIATION

a 2 community, 3 future, 4 punish, 5 guilty

### 4 GRAMMAR

a 3 had been stolen
4 be caught
5 questioned
6 visited
7 has / 's just been arrested
8 is / 's being held
9 will be heard
10 expects
11 be given
12 will be stolen

b 2 have our burglar alarm tested
3 have / 've had my car repaired by a mechanic
4 had our windows broken
5 will / 'll have my carpets cleaned
6 has / 's had his computer hacked
7 has his flat cleaned
8 are / 're having our garden redesigned

c 3 is expected to be acquitted
4 are reported to have taken the president's wife

5 thought that the terrorists are hiding somewhere in France
6 known that the suspect is dangerous
7 said that the police have arrested three men
8 are reported to have damaged several buildings in the area

## 8B

### 1 GRAMMAR

a 2 eating, 3 to give back, 4 visiting, 5 to dance, 6 of committing, 7 to take, 8 to give, 9 not to be, 10 stealing

b 2 insisted on going
3 suggested going
4 offered to make
5 warned us not to park
6 apologized for being
7 invited Sarah to have dinner
8 reminded me to sign

c Student's own answers

### 2 PRONUNCIATION

a **Stress on first syllable:** offer, order, promise, threaten
**Stress on second syllable:** admit, advise, agree, convince, deny, insist, invite, persuade, refuse, regret, remind, suggest

c 2 refused to
3 threatened to
4 promised to
5 agreed to
6 apologized to

### 3 VOCABULARY

a 2 wed, 3 quit, 4 quiz, 5 back, 6 hit, 7 tipped, 8 vows, 9 rows, 10 split, 11 bids, 12 clash

b 2 agony aunt, 3 critics, 4 commentator, 5 reporter, 6 editor, 7 presenter, 8 freelance journalist, 9 newsreader

c 2 objective, 3 censored, 4 sensational, 5 accurate

### 4 VOCABULARY FROM READING

**Can be trusted:** legitimate, reliable, reputable
**Can't be trusted:** questionable, untrustworthy
**Made more dramatic:** exaggerated
**Not true:** fake, false, made-up

## 9A

### 1 GRAMMAR

a 2 to, 3 even though, 4 in order to, 5 Although, 6 so as not to, 7 in spite of, 8 so that, 9 though, 10 for

b 2 in spite of its ideal location / being in an ideal location / the fact it was in an ideal location
3 could sell more products
4 in order not to miss my train
5 although I was very late
6 despite being the managing director

### 2 VOCABULARY

a 2 consumer, 3 brand, 4 advertising campaign, 5 misleading, 6 slogan, 7 publicity, 8 be sued, 9 claim

b 2 chain, 3 close down, 4 branch, 5 a recession, 6 a boom, 7 flop, 8 drop, 9 manufacture, 10 merge

c 2 markets, 3 produces, 4 imports, 5 has / 's expanded, 6 exports, 7 growing, 8 launch a new product, 9 become the market leader, 10 take over

d 2 makes, 3 doing, 4 made, 5 make, 6 did, 7 made, 8 make, 9 doing, 10 make

e 2 a, 3 d, 4 b, 5 e, 6 f, 7 h, 8 g

f Student's own answers

### 3 PRONUNCIATION

2 tran<u>s</u>port, 3 in<u>c</u>rease, 4 de<u>c</u>reased, 5 pro<u>g</u>ress, 6 per<u>mit</u>s, 7 pro<u>duc</u>es, 8 <u>r</u>efunds, 9 <u>i</u>mports, 10 <u>r</u>ecords

## 9B

### 1 GRAMMAR

a 3 ✓
4 a pair of scissors
5 some cheap accommodation
6 some bad news
7 glass
8 ✓
9 good behaviour
10 some paper

b 2 are, 3 are, 4 is, 5 are, 6 is, 7 are, 8 is, 9 are, 10 is

c Student's own answers

### 2 VOCABULARY

a 2 post, 3 auto, 4 mono, 5 over, under, 6 mega, 7 multi, 8 bi, 9 anti, 10 mis

b 2 careful, 3 waterproof, 4 useful, 5 homeless, 6 bulletproof, 7 drinkable, 8 hopeless

c 2 weakness, 3 absence, 4 vandalism, 5 Loneliness, 6 racism, 7 childhood, 8 entertainment, 9 improvement, 10 accommodation, 11 distance, 12 brotherhood

d 2 death, 3 heat, 4 width, 5 hunger, 6 loss, 7 height, 8 thought, 9 strength, 10 success

### 3 VOCABULARY FROM READING

2 head home
3 perks
4 a lack of
5 echoes
6 delivers
7 sprawling
8 state-of-the-art

### 4 PRONUNCIATION

a **Stress on first syllable:** friendliness, government, ignorance, poverty
**Stress on second syllable:** bilingual, convenience, excitement, reduction
**Stress on third syllable:** entertainment, overcrowded, unemployment

## Colloquial English 8 & 9

### 1 LOOKING AT LANGUAGE

2 had their day, 3 get into your head,
4 word for word, 5 their ears perk up,
6 a captive audience, 7 hit a false note

### 2 VOCABULARY FROM THE INTERVIEW

2 bet, 3 short, 4 fan, 5 tapped, 6 gold

### 3 THE CONVERSATION

2 a, 3 e, 4 f, 5 c, 6 b

### 4 VOCABULARY FROM THE CONVERSATION

2 subtle, 3 rush, 4 subliminally, 5 point

## Can you remember...? 1–9

### GRAMMAR & VOCABULARY

a 1 has been studying
2 climbing (very) much
3 had his number
4 get used to living
5 looking forward to seeing you
6 never forget visiting Florence
7 must have left your jacket
8 looks as if Emily
9 had our shower fitted
10 encouraged him to enter
11 Despite leaving home late
12 a new pair of shorts

b 1 as, 2 have, 3 by, 4 is / 's, 5 fact, 6 to,
7 take, 8 spite, 9 Even, 10 at

## 10A

### 1 VOCABULARY & PRONUNCIATION

a 2 c, 3 a, 4 c, 5 b, 6 a, 7 c, 8 b

c 2 bi<u>o</u>logy / bio<u>lo</u>gical; different syllable
3 <u>bo</u>tany / bo<u>ta</u>nical; different syllable
4 <u>chem</u>ist / <u>chem</u>istry; same syllable
5 ge<u>ne</u>tic / ge<u>ne</u>ticist; same syllable
6 <u>phys</u>ics / <u>phys</u>icist; same syllable
7 <u>sci</u>entist / scien<u>ti</u>fic; different syllable
8 zo<u>o</u>logist / zoo<u>lo</u>gical; different syllable

d 3 drugs, 4 discovery, 5 carry out,
6 prove, 7 clinical trials, 8 volunteer,
9 guinea pigs, 10 clone

### 2 VOCABULARY FROM LISTENING

2 dissolve, 3 particle, 4 scatter, 5 water
vapour, 6 reflect, 7 moist, 8 rotate, 9 gravity

### 3 VOCABULARY FROM READING

2 plausible, 3 far-fetched, 4 long,
5 achievable, 6 theory, 7 obstacles,
8 implausible, 9 possible, 10 real,
11 speculative

### 4 GRAMMAR

a 2 ✗ Everybody was
3 ✗ Everything went wrong
4 ✓
5 ✓
6 ✓
7 ✗ Most people
8 ✗ All men

b 2 None, 3 any, 4 none, 5 no, 6 Any

c 2 neither, 3 either, 4 nor, 5 both,
6 Neither, 7 either, 8 nor

d 2 most, 3 Both, 4 no, 5 any, 6 neither,
7 all, 8 none, 9 either, 10 every

## 10B

### 1 GRAMMAR

a 2 a
3 –, –
4 –
5 the, the
6 –
7 a
8 –, –

b 2 the
3 The
4 The, –
5 The, the
6 –,–
7 The, the
8 –

c 3 ✓
4 ✗ at school
5 ✓
6 ✗ at church
7 ✓
8 ✗ at university
9 ✗ gone to prison
10 ✓

d 2 c, 3 b, 4 c, 5 b, 6 b, 7 a, 8 a, 9 c, 10 b

### 2 VOCABULARY

a 2 d, 3 i, 4 f, 5 g, 6 c, 7 e, 8 a, 9 j, 10 b

b 2 rain or shine
3 right or wrong
4 now or never
5 all or nothing
6 once or twice
7 more or less
8 sooner or later

c 2 sick and tired
3 By and large
4 touch and go
5 law and order
6 safe and sound
7 wait and see
8 now and again

### 3 VOCABULARY FROM READING

2 gift of the gab
3 soundbites
4 orator

### 4 PRONUNCIATION

a Good morning / and thank you for
coming. / I'm here / to talk about / an
interesting place to visit / in my country.
I'm going to tell you / about the city of
Bath / in the south west of England. /
Bath is on the River Avon, / and it has
one of the only bridges in the world
with shops on either side. / The city is
famous / for its ancient Roman Baths, /
which can still be visited today. / It has
many beautiful streets, / such as the
Royal Crescent / and the Circus. / Bath is
full of museums, / independent shops, /
and wonderful places / to eat and drink.
/ The city / is easily accessible from
London / by train, / and it is perfect / for
a day trip / or a weekend break.

c Student's own answers

d Student's own answers